COMMON THREADS

COMMON THREADS

A CULTURAL HISTORY

OF CLOTHING IN

AMERICAN CATHOLICISM

SALLY DWYER-MCNULTY

THE UNIVERSITY OF NORTH CAROLINA PRESS

Chapel Hill

· Portions of Chapter 3 appeared in somewhat different form in
Sara Dwyer-McNulty, "Hems to Hairdos: Cultural Discourse and Philadelphia Catholic
High Schools in the 1920s, a Case Study," *Journal of American Studies* 37, no. 2 (2003):
179–200. © Cambridge University Press, reproduced with permission.

Library of Congress Cataloging-in-Publication Data
Dwyer-McNulty, Sally.
Common threads : a cultural history of clothing in American Catholicism /
Sally Dwyer-McNulty. — 1 [edition].
pages cm
Includes bibliographical references and index.
ISBN 978-1-4696-1409-0 (cloth : alk. paper) — ISBN 978-1-4696-1410-6 (ebook)
1. Catholic Church—United States. 2. Catholics—Religious identity—
United States. 3. Catholics—United States—Clothing. 4. Clothing and dress—
Religious aspects—Catholic Church. I. Title.
BX1406.3.D89 2014
391.0088'28273—dc23
2013041245

18 17 16 15 14   5 4 3 2 1

In loving memory of
Mary Patricia and James Dwyer and
Anna and James McNulty

CONTENTS

ILLUSTRATIONS

ACKNOWLEDGMENTS

Over the last decade I have enjoyed the support and encouragement of a number of wonderful people, and I am delighted to have the opportunity to thank them here. When I attended Temple University, both Margaret Marsh and David H. Watt hired me as a research assistant for their respective projects and modeled the tenacity required to finish writing a book. I will always be grateful for their mentoring.

When my interest in Catholic clothing was just a seed, the faculty and students at Moore College of Art and Design in Philadelphia encouraged my curiosity. My students, all artists, would tell me, "Catholicism is so visual" — they're right. Friends at Moore lent me photography equipment and taught me the rudiments of photography as I began to pay more attention to Catholicism through the lens of a camera. I thank the community at Moore for turning on my visual thinking.

Support for my interests continues at Marist College in Poughkeepsie, New York, where I benefit from an academic community that supports creative thinking and scholarship. Members of the Marist faculty and administration have sustained me in various ways over the years. Funds from the Office of the Vice President for Academic Affairs and the School of Liberal Arts as well as sabbatical release time enabled me to travel and devote months to research. Marist's formal and informal research gatherings offered me several opportunities over the years to present my work. I gained useful feedback on my research at the School of Liberal Arts Research Forum, Catholic Studies Lectures, and the Women in Society Conference.

My colleagues at Marist College have helped my thinking process all along the way as well. Lynn Eckert, Eileen Curley, Rose DeAngelis, Don Anderson, Nick Marshall, Robyn Rosen, Moira Fitzgibbons, Kristin Bayer, John Knight, Henry Pratt, Cathleen Muller, Michael O'Sullivan, Thomas Wermuth, Radley Cramer, Martin Shaffer, Janine Peterson, and Louis Zuccarello read or listened to different segments of this project and posed helpful questions as well as offering moral support. The assistance provided by James Duryea, manager of production and operations at Marist College, was invaluable. James turned my old slides into jpegs, helped me assemble visual presentations, provided photography instruction, cropped pictures, and much more. I can't thank James enough.

I received guidance outside Marist College as well. James O'Toole and Karen Kennelly both graciously read early drafts of individual chapters and pointed out errors and offered valuable recommendations. Kathleen Sprows Cummings invited me to present at the Cushwa Center for the Study of American Catholicism at the University of Notre Dame, where I was able to discuss my research with an exceptional group of scholars. Likewise, attendees at the Conference on the History of Women Religious provided a vibrant forum to present and test my research. My good friends Joan Saverino and Leonard Primiano were always willing to discuss the writing and research process, a topic unto itself. Joan and Leonard are both cherished friends and impressive scholars.

This project would not have been possible without the encouragement and commitment of Elaine Maisner, my editor at the University of North Carolina Press. Elaine saw this project through from proposal to complete manuscript. I couldn't have asked for a better editor. As one might expect from a terrific editor, Elaine assembled a highly professional staff, and I benefited from the attentiveness of her assistants, Caitlin Bell-Butterfield and Alison Shay, and my project editor, Stephanie Ladniak Wenzel. I thank them as well.

I owe an enormous debt to my readers; one was Colleen McDannell, and the other remains anonymous. Their detailed comments and recommendations directed me to new sources and helped me sharpen my argument. They greatly improved my manuscript, and I hope they will see and be pleased with their contributions to my work. Any errors or shortcomings that remain in this book are my own.

Throughout the process of research and writing, I enlisted the assistance of Laura Costello and Elizabeth Baldetti from the College of St. Rose and Marist College, respectively. Laura met me at the College of St. Rose library, where I searched clerical journals for sartorial material, and she tirelessly copied and organized relevant articles. Elizabeth assembled the first draft of the bibliography and, as a knowledgeable film enthusiast, directed me to the film I Confess, which I included in my analysis. I am deeply grateful for their good humor, interest, and attention to detail. Anne Roller, Carolyn Miller, and Kelsea Burch each read the first full draft of the manuscript and lent their fine editing skills to my work. To all of these readers, listeners, and friends I am truly grateful.

This project would have been impossible without the help of several dedicated archivists: Sister Patricia Annas, SSJ, of the Sisters of St. Joseph Archive; Sister Martha Counihan, OSU, of the College of New Rochelle; Sister Mary Ryan, SP, of the Sisters of Providence of St. Mary-of-the-Woods; Patrick McNamara of the Archdiocese of Brooklyn; Mark Theil, William Fliss, and Phillip Runkell of Marquette University; Lorraine Olley, library director of the Feehan Memorial Library and McEssy Theological Resource Center at Mundelein Seminary; Shawn Weldon of the Philadelphia Archdiocesan Historical Research Center; Brenda Galloway-Wright of Temple University's Urban Archive; Sister Rita King, SC, of the Sisters of Charity of St. Vincent de Paul, New York; and John Ainsley at the Marist College Archive. Special thanks to Shawn Weldon, who identified many valuable sources and received my sporadic visits and emails with kindness.

The members of the library staff at Marist College are nothing short of amazing, and they helped me on countless occasions—whether it was with interlibrary loan or interpreting the mood of the microfilm machine, they were there for me. Ellen Skerrett, Mary Henold, and Maggie McGuiness kindly passed me valuable references regarding Catholic clothing. I also enjoyed assistance from Brother Richard Kestler, FSC, president of Philadelphia's West Catholic High School, as well as Mrs. Sandra Young, president of the John W. Hallahan Catholic Girls' High School, Mrs. Reenie Ednie, and Sister Arlene Ronollo, SSJ, all of whom were receptive to my image permission requests.

Finally, I want to thank my family. My father did not live to see this work completed, but he was there for me through much of its development. His faith in my abilities stays with me. My Aunt Mary Rose is my most cheerful and knowledgeable supporter. Her gentle inquiries about how the writing was going were just what I needed. My siblings, sisters-in-law and brothers-in-law, and nieces and nephews also requested just the right number of updates that I did not feel defeated by the long process of writing a book. They fed me, gave me a bed to sleep in, entertained my children, and looked interested every time I drifted off onto a research discovery or Catholic conundrum. I will end here with a most sincere thanks to my husband, Jim, and children, Declan, Fiona, and Sheena. They are the most patient and loving people I know. They have come to many, many libraries with me, observed me read on every driving trip for the last ten years, and sat and watched an inordinate number of movies with Catholic themes and characters. I know it has not been easy living with me and my work, and I can't thank them enough for believing in me and encouraging my passions. This book is dedicated to them with love.

INTRODUCTION

THE ORIGINS AND SIGNIFICANCE OF

CATHOLIC CLOTHING IN AMERICA

America Magazine's Matt Malone offered a perceptive observation about Catholicism; when it comes to clothing, Catholics take it seriously. Talk of clothing is not "so much irrelevant claptrap" because "Catholicism is rooted in a sacramental worldview. In other words, symbols matter . . . they matter a lot."[1] I agree with Malone, but I would add that symbols are naturalized by those in power, and while they hold sacramental meaning, they are also freighted with social and political significance. When power is destabilized in Catholicism, or in any other symbol-ladened community, symbolic meanings are likewise altered. In consideration of these two observations, this study, first, documents the history of Catholic clothing in America. Catholic apparel is something that appears to have always been there—it has undergone naturalization.[2] As a result of this "time-free" phenomenon, Catholic clothing remains under-studied. Second, this examination reveals why clothing is important. I uncover how Catholics came to rely on clothing to negotiate relations between religious authority and laity, men and women, and adults and youth, and how Catholic clothing continues to function as a battleground where Catholics work out issues of power, identity, and sacredness in their everyday lives.

A recent example of Catholic discord highlights the intriguing significance of attire. In 2008 the Vatican, under the leadership of Pope Benedict XVI, announced that it would conduct Apostolic Visitations of active orders of women religious in the United States. The Vatican also initiated a separate inquest to consider the behaviors and statements of the Leadership Conference of Women Religious, an organization whose membership includes roughly 80 percent of all American women religious.[3] The Vatican was concerned that the Leadership Conference held "radical feminist" views and took up positions that dissented from the teachings of the Roman Catholic Church, as determined by the magisterium, or the official teaching authority of the church. Despite the fear that they ascribed to "radical feminist" views, the sisters seemed to have made few pronouncements on issues such as abor-

{1}

tion and homosexuality, topics high on the list of concerns among the most outspoken male Catholic leaders. Curiously, but significantly, the Vatican exempted congregations of male religious and cloistered contemplative orders from the inquest.

One compelling feature of this case for me is what the cast of characters in this "Catholic moment" are wearing. Almost everyone inquiring into the sisters' thoughts and behaviors or who is exempt from the investigation dresses in some type of distinctive (even Baroque) attire that identifies him or her as Catholic and as a member of a religious order or as a priest. Pope Benedict, under whose watch the assessment began, was known for his splendiferous papal attire. Photographers focused on his red loafers and assorted papal accoutrements, such as his short red mozzetta cape or the fleece-lined camouro bonnet. Another noteworthy dresser, Cardinal Raymond L. Burke, former archbishop of St. Louis and prefect of the Supreme Court of the Apostolic Signature, was quoted in the press and interviewed on television about his concern over the sisters' actions. While observers recognized Burke for his sharp critique of the sisters, he was also known for his elaborate clerical attire. As a promoter of the Latin Rite movement, often termed "restorationist," Cardinal Burke adopted clerical and liturgical dress that set him off in a decidedly imperial manner. Finally, the sister charged with overseeing the visitations of women religious is a habited sister. Mother Mary Clare Millea, a member of the Congregation of the Apostles of the Sacred Heart of Jesus, dresses with a veil and habit just like other members of her order. Her congregation is a member of the Council of Major Superiors of Women Religious, an organization canonically approved in 1995. It represents approximately 20 percent of all sisters in the United States, and its goals include "to promote unity among major superiors, thus testifying to their union with the Magisterium and their love for Christ's Vicar on earth, and, to coordinate active cooperation with the USCCB (United States Conference of Catholic Bishops)."[4] These habited sisters are explicit about their acceptance of Vatican directives and their devotion to the pontiff.

On the other side of the inquiry, almost all the woman whom the Vatican investigated wore varied, though clearly noncouture ensembles. Symbols of "company affiliation" were typically small, such as a ring, pendant, or pin. As the investigation enters its second stage—what to do with the information gathered in the visitation—the papacy has been turned over to a new, more simply dressed man, Pope Francis. Although his wardrobe is perhaps less diverse than that of his predecessor, Francis is nevertheless distinctly Catholic and papal. Supporters of the sisters look to Pope Benedict XVI's replacement,

Pope Francis, for signs that he will treat the sisters with sympathy. Perhaps his sartorial simplicity, which includes black rather than red shoes, is some indication that he is more willing to have a dialogue with the sisters. Only time will tell how this episode will be resolved, but clothing seems to be an indication of allegiance and a fundamental means of communication among all of the parties involved.

INSPIRATIONS AND GOALS

My interest in gaining a better understanding of the origins and significance of Catholic clothing in American history draws on the work of thoughtful scholars from several disciplines and subdisciplines. Historians of Catholicism, especially Joseph P. Chinnici, John Tracy Ellis, Mary Ewen, James M. O'Toole, Leslie Woodcock Tentler, and Joseph M. White, among others, have undertaken the Herculean task of detailing several chapters on the history of clerical and religious life over the last three centuries. Complicating these narratives, scholars such as Paula Kane, Maureen Fitzgerald, Karen Kennelly, Mary J. Henold, Robert Anthony Orsi, and Kathleen Sprows Cummings place gender at the forefront of their inquiries and examine how it shaped the lives of American Catholics over time. Finally, scholarship on clothing, material culture, and popular culture, especially the impressive research of Patricia Campbell Warner, Katherine Haas, Nathan Joseph, William J. F. Keenan, Mark Massa, Colleen McDannell, and Anthony Burke Smith, comes closest to my own concerns and provided instructive models of how clothing functions in religious and popular culture.

Despite the vast wealth of research on American Catholicism, religious culture, and clothing, I found that a relatively open field still remained regarding the history and significance of American Catholic clothing. Certainly more had been written about the significance of clothing than the actual history of particular forms of Catholic dress. I noted that while Catholic clothing is often mentioned and even sometimes the central focus of a historical inquiry, there is almost no discussion, except in the case of Keenan and perhaps McDannell, of when and why Catholics put on distinctive attire. Uniformity is treated as a foregone conclusion; Catholic priests wear Roman collars, sisters and brothers are consistently attired in habits, and most Catholic students are specifically outfitted. If Catholics, especially priests and religious, always wore identifiable clothing, then the contemporary decision of sisters to dispense with habits might be understood as bold. But, consistent uniformity is not the case. Photos and records indicate that Catholics were often indistinguishable from ordinary Americans and dressed in varied attire. In fact, the appearance of Catholics in identifiable and uniformish attire has a surprisingly short history in America.

I received my own jolt of realization about the brevity of the phenomenon while exploring a stack of old yearbooks at the first diocesan girls' high school in the United States, Philadelphia's Catholic Girls' High School, or "Hallahan." As I turned the pages, I found myself distracted by the students' clothing—they were not in uniforms.[5] I had attended Catholic school for twelve years, and uniforms were a signature mark of Catholic education, an indisputable Catholic icon. I started to flip through the images of diversely clad students more quickly. Did picture day have different rules? Was it too hot for the dark serge jumper? The years went on: 1917, 1918, and 1919. Uniforms did not appear until 1924. Why "civilian dress" one year and a uniform the next? Then I began to wonder why I had ever thought Catholic schoolgirls *always* wore uniforms.

School uniforms for girls, I had casually accepted, were a sort of "timeless" aspect of Catholic culture. Gary Wills provides an apt turn of phrase for this way of thinking in *Bare Ruined Choirs*. Catholics lived in "an untime capsule" through the early 1960s, and it included "a fibry cocoon of rites and customs" that were easily recognizable to American Catholics.[6] That disconnection between time, Catholic rituals, and materiality had certainly shaped my perspective. The untime capsule lingered in my native Philadelphia well into the 1970s.

If Catholic school uniforms had a past yet to be uncovered, what of other forms of Catholic dress? The conclusion that Catholic clothing was inevitable seemed wholly unsatisfying to me. I was bolstered by Robert Orsi's observation regarding religious idioms. He points out that "people appropriate religious idioms as they need them, in response to particular circumstances. All religious ideas and impulses are of the moment, invented, taken, borrowed, and improvised at the intersections of life."[7] Considering my own association of Catholicism with specific attire, I set out to explore when and why Catholics adopted or expanded distinctive forms of dress in the United States. I wondered what obstacles they might have faced standing out in a nation that (at least rhetorically) prized the separation of church and state? What social, cultural, technological, and political factors influenced Catholic attention to clothing? And finally, how did Catholics' employment of clothing and the reception of that clothing change over time?

Beyond overcoming the untime capsule approach to Catholic clothing that resided in my and others' thoughts, I found that much of the extant work on Catholics and clothing reflected a deceivingly segmented characterization of

Catholicism.[8] Researchers often study priests or religious, but they typically do not venture beyond these discrete categories specifically, and few scholars include children in their examinations.[9] When I thought about clothing and Catholics, however, I saw priests, brothers, nuns, sisters, and a plethora of youth intermingling. To be fair, segmentation often makes a good deal of sense. Rather than jumping from group to group, we might find it easier and perhaps more revealing to delve into the sources of a single group or organization. One could learn almost everything about the Daughters of Charity and then treat them as "representative" for understanding the history of women religious. Likewise, when we consider groups who have committed to the church, the reality is that men and women were both encouraged to and often chose to segregate themselves. Alternatively, however, it was Orsi who suggested another path. He claimed that thinking about and presenting Catholics in this isolated and disconnected way distorts our understanding of the past. After utilizing a variety of sources, including "memory groups" of people who are or who grew up Catholic, Orsi explained, "what comes clear is the extent to which relationships among adults and children — especially adult religious and children — were at the center of American Catholicism in the 20th century."[10] This bears out in the visual culture as well. There appeared to me to be an unexplained relationship, or thread as it were, connecting Catholics. Arguably certain Catholics are "invested" with special attire, such as members of religious orders, while other Catholics buy their Catholic clothing at neighborhood stores, but the fact that special clothing distinguishes adults and youth as Catholics binds the wearers together relationally and visually. Vestmentary visibility was part of the larger religious culture for American Catholics for much of the twentieth century.

The study that follows therefore attends to my dual motivations both structurally and topically. First, to uncover the when and why of discernible "Catholic clothing" in America, I isolated three subgroups of Catholics who in my estimation were and continue to be the most visually distinct: priests, women religious, and Catholic schoolgirls. I devote a chapter to each subgroup. Each of these Catholic populations has a history in America during which they are not fully identifiably Catholic in their dress, yet eventually they become so. Priests in the nineteenth century often wore flat, lay-down ties; nuns and sisters put aside their habits for traveling outside the convent; and Catholic schools did not impose uniforms immediately upon opening. Publicly and consistently displayed Catholic attire developed over time and, in the case of students, slowly. Considering the Protestant origins of the country and the negative Reformation-inspired rhetoric regarding the clergy and religious, the lack of sartorial distinction in America made sense. Catholics did not want to emphasize their European origins and monarchical bent. Eventually, however, Catholics proved themselves to be acceptable neighbors, and clergy, religious, and schoolgirls, by command in some cases and choice in others, ultimately dressed in identifiable garb.

While I initially isolate subgroups of Catholics, I bring them together for the last two chapters of the book. Chapter 4 examines the clothing of priests, sisters, schoolgirls, and after World War II, schoolboys. The period between World War II and the beginning of the Second Vatican Council in 1962 was the visual high point for Catholics, and during this era Catholic clothing became a fixture in the American imagination. In the fifth chapter I explore the centrality of Catholic clothing to the changes brought about by Vatican II. While the new theology is paramount to the Catholic leadership, the clothing changes accompanying the new theology take center stage, especially in print, television, and film. The epilogue takes the study from the mid-1970s through the present and illustrates how liberal and conservative factions within Catholicism grapple with the significance of Catholic clothing in the twenty-first century.

MAKING SENSE OF CLOTHING AND CATHOLICISM

Clothing is a visual lexicon that humans employ daily.[11] Our apparel indicates gender, age, class, and acceptance of or resistance to social and contextual norms.[12] With the use of our sight, we immediately form impressions about people when we encounter them face to face, and indeed, outfitted people want to make an impression on observers. Job applicants dress with intention, so that the interviewer will conclude that the applicant understands the accepted culture of that particular employer. Therefore, when we dress, we exert control over or manipulate our appearance to communicate something about ourselves. We, in fact, drape our bodies with meaning.

Organizations also use clothing to communicate, sometimes by requiring a type of uniform. For an individual, clothing is thought of as a personal expression, but in an organization, uniform clothing displays "an acceptance of a specific obligation of faithful management" in return for holding a position in the organization.[13] In *Uniforms and Nonuniforms*, sociologist Nathan Joseph explains that the "uniform is a symbolic declaration that an individual will adhere to group norms and standardized roles and has mastered the relevant group skills."[14] If the individual fails to uphold the requirements of the organization, the uniform is revoked. In the military, uniform dress mutes individualism and projects allegiance to the nation or leader and often both. For instance, the actions or behaviors of a soldier, beginning with the act of dressing, are designed to achieve goals that lie beyond individual desires. When a member of the military maintains the designated uniform carefully, we assume that the wearer accepts the discipline of the organization. This is the same for followers of a religious tradition. A priest wearing his clerical attire both neatly and according to his bishop's requirements communicates acceptance of the church's authority and his membership among the class that holds a special role as administrators of the faith in the lives of the laity.

Greater control over the body through dress contributed to the continuity and strength of the church's bureaucratic structure and communication of values and particularly gender ideology. Public displays of allegiance through dress concomitantly increased the accountability of its members as the church commissioned the viewing public to be witnesses and judges of the church's behavior based on its representatives. Catholics, therefore, wore the burden of institutional bureaucracy as the church became more firmly established and confident on American soil.[15] Specific clothing made sense as a communicative device because clothing was part of Catholicism's idiomatic repertoire—Catholics had a long history of expressing themselves to those around them through the language of clothing or sacramentals worn on the body.[16] Nevertheless, bureaucracy building is top down, and dressing a specific way to indicate submission to authority suggests successful suppression of the individual. Catholics were and are not automatons simply wearing what they are told all the time. Dressing included expressions of faith, negotiation, and resistance along with conformity—there is a "lived" approach to regulated dress as well. In some cases, I was able to locate that "innovation" and agency in religious practice amidst the discipline.[17]

Historically, Catholic clothing, along with all other "uniform" clothing, was not strictly uniform. Uniformity did not appear until the industrial revolution, when the mechanization of clothing production made more exact replication possible. Nevertheless, certain styles and costumes with identifiable parameters became established through the centuries and therefore grew recognizable.[18] Catholics developed a common understanding of who wore what, and why. For instance, the pope wears white as a symbol of his singular holiness and purity, bishops carry staffs because they shepherd the people, and nuns mostly wear habits of a dark hue to symbolize death to the world and "marriage" to Christ. Catholics recognized status, gender, and sacrality in the clothing of their leaders.

Upon closer examination, however, the common understanding of Catholic attire becomes less tenable. While all Catholics view garments and sacred accessories, these items do not hold consistent meaning across wearers or viewers. Contrary to Anne Hollander's contention that uniforms communicate a sense that everything has been decided, uniforms also become a valuable canvas for improvisation and resistance.[19] Wearing a scapular, for example, may have been typical behavior among devout Catholics in the 1950s and long before. Symbols of devotion, both private and public, were not unusual. If another Catholic caught a glimpse of the scapular worn under a shirt or blouse, it would simply indicate a sincere expression of faith. In the 1990s, however, after decades of debate over how the church should engage with and accommodate the modern world, a scapular might instead indicate pre–Vatican II style devotionalism and perhaps sympathy with a restoration of the Latin Rite or other traditional Catholic practices.[20] Likewise, a priest wearing a cassock outside church or walking in the community would be unusual in the 1850s, required in the 1930s, and curious in the early 1970s. Pope Benedict XVI and Pope Francis agree that the pope holds a position of unique authority, but all the attention to their different styles of dress indicates that these men differ on how that authority should be conveyed through dress.

The meaning of various styles of Catholic dress changes according to the wearer, as well as when and where the attire is displayed. Even within a specific period, assigning meaning to clothing is not a simple undertaking. An onlooker may perceive a sister in a religious habit to be feminine, modest, and devout. Yet, other eyes may read some other significance entirely. The woman in the habit may assume her unique dress communicates a sisterly bond or elite religious status; to a priest, this same woman in habit may be conveying religious devotion or even misplaced vanity; to a patient in a hospital she may seem like a frightening, costumed stranger or an angelic nurse. Meaning is not static, and context is of fundamental significance. In the Catholic clothing lexicon, one can easily determine affiliation, rank, and gender, but the social construction, or what meaning people assign to Catholic dress or the rejection of Catholic dress, is less clear. By exploring instances when Catholic clothing was adopted, altered, or rejected, we can discern the "uncommon" meanings.

My attempts to make sense of Catholic clothing, especially a representationally and chronologically broad sample, directed me toward a variety of theoretical and disciplinary models that aided my thinking about Catholic clothing. While I did not anchor this study in any one model, a few theories resonated with my work more closely and assisted me in making sense of the various primary documents and people I encountered through my research. A Weberian approach lends itself to understanding the church's growing emphasis on "uniformization" and "rationalization," albeit sometimes in "counter-modern" styles from the mid- to late nineteenth century until the 1960s.[21] Weber is the "go to" theorist for understanding religious orders. The founder of an order is an example of Weber's charismatic leader who, unlike a bureaucrat, derives his (in Weber's examples) position of leadership based on the virtues of his mission and shuns economic rationalism.[22] Charismatic leadership and discipline work well together if regimentation advances the mission, but discipline can overwhelm charism. Both Massa and Keenan found charism suffering under routine in the case of the Immaculate Heart of Mary sisters and the Marist brothers, respectively, when each accounted for dramatic clothing reform upon the communities' examinations of their charismatic origins in the 1960s. Weber explained that "charisma, as a creative power, recedes in the face of domination, which hardens into lasting institutions, and becomes efficacious only in short-lived mass emotions of incalculable effects."[23] Both the Immaculate Heart of Mary sisters and the Marist brothers had been more concerned with charitable "actions" rather than regulated behavior originally; the bureaucratic forces of the church, argued Keenan and Massa, stayed that charitable effervescence. Unlike members of religious orders, diocesan priests are not charismatic and fit more with Weber's view on bureaucracy. Diocesan priests are part of a patriarchal bureaucracy that primarily relies on a judicial system, canon law, to make decisions. Weber argues that charismatic leaders and their followers have an "antagonistic appearance," and this is where Weber's theory meets a complex scenario. In America, priests sometimes had the "antagonistic appearances" Weber finds in charismatic leaders and their followers, but other times they did not.[24] Priests dressed as professional men, albeit in black only. If the charismatics' power is legitimated only through action and not decree, then the religious orders gave in to bureaucratization—they became routinized. Sisters gained greater legitimacy, in part, through bureaucratization witnessed in uniform attire.

Cultural sociologist Gordon Lynch likewise contributed to my analysis. Following in the footsteps of his academic forefather Émile Durkheim, Lynch is concerned with understanding the sacred in the modern world. He offers a way to think about "sacred forms" that we might unhesitatingly associate with "religion," such as the religious habit or a sacralized concern such as nationalism or child welfare. For Lynch, modern media plays a central role in the distribution of ideas about sacrality and how historically contingent circumstances set the stage for sacred identification. The work of both Orsi and Lynch is of particular interest to me because they ground their understanding of religious practice and possibility in history, and they both, at times, direct their focus onto childhood and children's bodies in the context of Catholicism. I incorporate students into my study of Catholicism, not as a separate category, but as part of the larger picture of religious practice.[25] Catholic school administrators' widespread employment of Catholic school uniforms after World War II reflects the sacrality of American nationalism and the need to defend it against "godless" communism. This elevation of the uniform is historically contingent, however, on the pro-religion-and-family discourse prominent during the Cold War, the rise of consumer culture, and the reverence toward military symbols. In the decade after World War II, Catholic school uniforms and dress codes took on "the status of absolute, normative realities."[26] Additionally, although the church is the originator of much of the uniformization and utilized modern communication in the form of newspapers, pictures, films, and television to depict and reinforce the goal of an outfitted religious culture, the church nevertheless shared "distribution" of Catholic clothing culture with popular culture outlets. This lack of bureaucratic control allowed for multiple interpretations to evolve regarding the meaning of Catholic clothing.

OVERVIEW

The time span under consideration, roughly the early nineteenth century until the beginning of the twenty-first century, is not evenly explored and, by recent historical standards, is rather long. Nevertheless, I found it necessary to cast my net far. It goes without saying that Catholic traditions are centuries old and have diverse origins. And although this research centers around the development and significance of Catholic clothing in America, Catholicism is a transnational faith, and even a cursory review would require reaching back over many years and across the Atlantic Ocean to discuss the history surrounding certain apparel. Historian William J. F. Keenan suggested the apt term "mezzo-history" for this style of inquiry. It is somewhere between a microstudy and the long durée, and like Keenan, I found this mezzo approach useful for examining clothing in the American Catholic past.[27]

The first chapter considers the secular priest from the missionary days through the 1930s. I contend that as bishops navigated minority status, democracy, and Catholic diversity, they gradually turned to a familiar religious form, identifiable attire, to exert control and authority over both their middle managers and lay Catholics. Clothing also functioned as a visual message to Rome that, regardless of America's Enlightenment origins, papal rule prevailed. More recognizable clerical dress likewise separated the priest from the laity, providing a symbol of authority. Despite the new regulations, the American context provided an opportunity to compromise on priestly appearance, and black clothing with "Roman collar" and trousers rather than cassocks became the public attire for the everyday priest.

Chapter 2 examines the same time span for nuns and sisters. Fearing anti-Catholic sentiment and attention, many women in religious communities traveled without habits. Once settled, the American milieu required a flexible approach to survival, and teaching became one of the most common and reliable means of economic sustainability. Despite the willingness of these devout women to adjust even when it came to laying aside the habit, I argue that sisters saw their distinctive attire as a means to convey intrachurch political allegiance and to gain spiritual superiority. As a perambulatory cloister, the habit also enabled Catholic sisters, as the numerically dominant and distinct subgroup, to become the most identifiable representatives of the church.

Female students are the subject of Chapter 3. School-age girls who came under the supervision of women religious found their clothing choices curtailed by the turn of the twentieth century. Initially, a scarcity of clothing patterns and the lack of women's and children's ready-to-wear clothing hampered uniformity. The advent of the sewing machine facilitated the manufacture of standardized clothing and sizes for menswear, but due to the complexity of women's clothing styles, women's ready-to-wear was still several decades away. Nevertheless, sisters provided sartorial direction for many of their charges in the way of dress codes—a step toward greater uniformity.

Sisters usually operated asylums, free schools, and select schools. Children attending the asylums and free schools, from the sisters' perspective, required strict guidance. In fact, the church often viewed the children's poverty as a testimony to their parents' inability to raise them properly. Therefore, school administrators adopted dress codes to exercise charity and to convey a form of instruction. The teachers of select schools or tuition-funded schools looked more toward curbing excess, a vice commonly associated with female students. The select schools' tuition supported the maintenance of the free schools, and sisters found that dress codes tempered the material excesses of these society girls and likewise encouraged simplicity.

Joining and eventually surpassing the asylums, free schools, and select schools in number were the parish or parochial schools and, later, the diocesan high schools. American bishops had frequently encouraged pastors to establish Catholic parish schools and had urged parents to send their children to Catholic schools since the early nineteenth century, but the bishops *mandated* Catholic education after 1884. Bishops required pastors to prioritize the establishment of a parish school, and parents sometimes ran the risk of being denied sacraments if they resisted sending their children to Catholic school once a reasonably close school was available.[28] The growth of parochial Catholic education paralleled the modernization of women's and children's clothing production. School administrators capitalized on the ready-made options, and uniform clothing became more commonplace in Catholic schools. Unlike the boarding arrangement that free and select schools often used, parochial schools drew children and young women out in public, walking to their parish schools. Ideally, school uniforms on girls conveyed respectability for a minority religious culture and modesty for its young female practitioners. Uniforms also provided new opportunities for asserting a form of religious authority. Although uniforms were not distributed at solemn occasions, blessed, or invested with special power, they were nevertheless uniforms representing the church as an institution. As emissaries of the church, uniformed girls ideally assisted the church in negating its reputation for being antiwoman.[29] As might be expected, however, the ideal and the real often achieved different ends. Catholic girls wielded a certain amount of control over their appearance, regardless of the uniforms, and took part in shaping the messages they wanted their clothing to convey. Worth noting is that for all the good the uniforms may have done, and the meaning girls expressed with the uniforms, there was an underlying Catholic agreement that girls needed uniforms more than boys. As Colleen McDannell points out in *Material Christianity*, certain groups are more commonly associated with the material dimension of Catholicism: "women, children, and illiterates."[30] Restrictive dress for girls elucidated (and continues to illustrate) the Catholic Church's view both that girls needed to be guided more due to their propensity to commit sins of vanity and that girls and females in general were in a position to be controlled.[31]

In the fourth chapter, I shift my attention to the connections between a new theological trend that emphasized the laity's roles as active members of the Mystical Body of Christ and the propensity of both the church and media outlets to project images of outfitted Catholics as patriotic Americans. Between the late 1930s and the 1960s, Catholicism's "arrival" in mainstream America and Catholicism's "preoccupation with dress" provided a visual symbol of the link between Americanism and Catholic religiosity.[32] Catholicism as represented by movie priests and real uniformed students throughout the United States became a metonym for America during its struggles against fascist dictatorships and the Soviet Union. The church and popular culture seemed to leave sisters behind as they embraced a modernized, militarized, and activist style of Catholicism. Nevertheless, sisters were quietly developing intellectual resources to understand the significance of clothing in their work and lives.

Chapter 5 documents the unraveling of what had become the Catholic clothing trademark. By the early 1960s, the unified presence that identifiable attire helped create in American society was reaching its peak. Social and political upheaval in American society, alongside theological reforms by way of the Second Vatican Council, encouraged a reconsideration of "antagonistic appearance," especially regarding women religious. What Catholics wore— priests, sisters, or students—communicated their political sympathies and religious priorities in an environment where bureaucratic allegiances and militarism were actively questioned by many Americans. Inspired by the civil rights movement and the Second Vatican Council, priests and sisters began to consider how their appearance could lend a powerful symbol to demonstrations against racial inequality or how a distinctive costume potentially hindered interaction in poor communities. For instance, they wondered if their uniform and antiquated clothing created distance between themselves and the people they wanted to serve. Aware of the politics of their dress, many religious communities decided, with what they perceived to be the Vatican's encouragement, that their clothing was both unnecessarily antiquated and ultimately a hindrance to performing their work. As a result, the majority of sisters and many male religious altered their habits and eventually ceased wearing them.[33] When the sisters took charge of their appearance, a firestorm of controversy spilled out into the popular press. Priests also donned ordinary menswear, but their change of attire drew significantly less publicity and criticism. Thanks to Hollywood, moviegoers, regardless of religion, understood that priests owned and wore secular clothing. Women religious, however, did not have the same clothing options. Women's habits conveyed many meanings, but I argue that one of the more significant intentions of the church was female submission, subordination, and denial of self. Reforming or rejecting the habit was accurately interpreted as a new understanding of women's place in the church and an assertion of self over bureaucracy—an expression that Catholics received with mixed reactions.

By the 1980s the politics of the church were varied and complicated. Under the leadership of Pope John Paul II, conservative Catholics who had lamented many of the reforms of the 1960s found support to bring back the Latin Rite mass and several pre–Vatican II dress standards. While sartorial neoconservatism increased with detailed dalmatics, chasubles, cassocks, and religious habits, so too did the vocal and visual liberalism of many women religious who stood on their own with independent attire. Although clothing remains a contested symbol, one garment retained unquestioned support—the school uniform. Religious orthodoxy and social justice teaching could find common ground in regulating students' clothing. Both political camps supported inquiries into the manufacture of Catholic clothing, denouncing sweatshop facilities. Campaigns for "No Sweat" purchasing policies spread throughout the country. Finally, the Catholic school uniform was no longer just for Catholics, as public schools and charter schools adopted the uniform look to address behavior issues and build a sense of community among socioeconomically diverse students. By the beginning of the twenty-first century, Catholic clothing moved away from expressing collective identity and came to represent the diversity in Catholic opinion on theological and social issues as well as the influence of Catholic educational culture on American society.

NOTES AND CLARIFICATIONS

There is no one repository or collection that expressly invites this sort of investigation. Nevertheless, with the help of several detailed secondary sources, most notably Mary Ewen's *The Role of the Nun in Nineteenth-Century America* and Joseph M. White's *The Diocesan Seminary in the United States: A History from the 1780s to the Present*, I was able to locate a trail of evidence that began to answer my questions.[34] My primary source material includes published, archived, and digitized materials such as ceremonials, prescriptive literature, pastoral letters, sodality magazines, and Catholic and popular newspapers. Unpublished material such as school yearbooks, annals, and meeting minutes rounded out my textual sources. Looking at pictures was indispensable. Carefully examining collars, hemlines, stockings, habits, guimpes, belts, and shoes often told me part of a story. Sometimes the first piece of evidence was a picture—as in the case of the Hallahan girls in ordinary dress. Other times my evidence began with the written text, and then I went about cross-referencing a statement by examining available pictures. Photos and written texts informed each other. The investigation would not have been possible without both. Fashion historians know this well, but as a more conventionally trained historian with a field in religious studies and a great curiosity about clothing, I had to learn along the way. Films, television shows, and interviews with a handful of people who wore, made, or required (and sometimes all three) a form of Catholic clothing illuminate the contours and details of the story as well. In the end this is a history of clothing that relies primarily on written sources and secondarily on visual sources.

Throughout the book, I've made certain word choices and inclusive references worth noting. America is frequently used to refer to the United States. Regarding the categories nuns, sisters, religious women, and women religious, I tend to distinguish between sisters and nuns through most of Chapter 2, but in keeping with the direction of papal pronouncements and other religious texts I blur the distinctions as I move into the twentieth century. By the 1920s the terms "nun" and "sister" became almost interchangeable despite the association of nuns with cloister and sisters with the laity. Most sisters were "semicloistered" after the turn of the twentieth century, which confused their status and thus created the frequently incorrect but commonly used reference to "nun" for any Catholic woman in a habit. Catholic writers, particularly but not exclusively, use an uppercase "S" when referring to the sisters. Sisters' status in the church certainly warranted an "uppercase" distinction. Nevertheless, in keeping with current usage I refer to the sisters using a lowercase "s" and simply retain all uppercase usages when quoting documents. When I refer to a specific sister by name, the "S" is capitalized. The term "church" frequently refers to the pope, sometimes refers to the hierarchy, and least frequently refers to all of the people who identify as Catholic. Again, keeping with current usage, I use a lowercase "c" when referring to the church and uppercase "C" when coupling it with Catholic, for example, Catholic Church.

Finally, in the interest of introducing the topic to readers, my project is exploratory rather than exhaustive. There are many Catholics, members of male religious orders in particular, and forms of Catholic dress I did not examine. The different collars associated with male religious, bridal gowns worn by women taking religious vows, and First Communion dresses and suits are not part of this study. Instead, this book focuses on the clothing Catholics wore over and again and which became the standard dress Americans associate with certain groups of Catholics. This study reveals the broader development of distinctive Catholic dress and its various meanings throughout American history. I hope my brief contribution will encourage other researchers to delve into this topic further to uncover the wealth of sartorial texts in the history of Catholicism.

CHAPTER 1

THE CLOTHES MAKE THE MAN

CLERICAL AND

LITURGICAL GARMENTURE,

1830S–1930S

"There are no Roman Catholic priests who show less taste for the minute individual observances, for the extraordinary or peculiar means of salvation, who cling more to the spirit and less to the letter of the law than the Roman Catholic priests of the United States," penned Alexis de Tocqueville in his oft-cited account *Democracy in America*.[1] De Tocqueville likely considered clerical mufti and perhaps even vestments in his observations. Catholic priests, the secular variety especially, were not particularly distinctive, ornamental, or peculiar in 1831, especially in their everyday attire.[2] Indeed they were difficult to distinguish from Protestant priests, ministers, and even ordinary men.[3] Vestments, considered by Catholics to be sacred garments and derived from antiquity, were also subject to irregularity and displayed less ornamentation than those worn in the well-established Catholic churches of Europe. A century later, observers of the American clergy would not have applied the same description to Catholic priests as de Tocqueville once did. Likewise, they would have had little trouble picking out the Catholic prelates, whether dressed in their clerics or their vestments. As the church waded into a century of political revolutions, modernism, and religious diversity, clerical clothing became a conscious, though not uncontested, tool for establishing both discipline over and authority for the priesthood. Priestly dress ideally conveyed bureaucratic allegiance at a time when the Vatican sought affirmation. Distinctive or religiously inspired clothing was not a new communication device for Catholics. On the contrary, it had a long-established place in the traditions and sacred consciousness of the church. In the American context, however, traditional ways did not necessarily transplant automatically or easily.

Historian John Tracy Ellis described Roman Catholic clerical life in the American colonies as a "long period of abnormal rule." According to Ellis, the British penal laws that applied to priests in the American colonies "not only deprived them of the sacraments of confirmation and holy orders but likewise left them with little or no knowledge of the traditional form of church government, an ignorance that caused some very strange notions among both priests and laity concerning episcopal office and its functions."[4] The church, however, had anticipated periods of "abnormal rule" as Catholic explorers and missionaries set out to claim both land and souls beyond Christendom. The church identified these foreign locations without stable Catholic populations and traditions as "missionary territories," and while obligated to obey papal laws, mission territories nevertheless enjoyed modest flexibility in maintaining religious practice. In this way, priests, sisters, and nuns could more successfully integrate themselves into society and ensure their daily existence. Regarding clothing, clergy and religious applied common sense. If displaying a distinctive habit would result in torture, death, or imprisonment, clergy and religious could choose not to wear it. Likewise, if wearing the local dress seemed appropriate, then that was another option. For instance, after traveling to China in the late sixteenth century, Italian Jesuit Matteo Ricci initially donned the dress of a Buddhist monk and later adopted the clothing style of a Confucian mandarin in an effort to appear adaptable.[5]

To guide the missionary territories in this new era, Pope Gregory XV permanently established the *Congregation de Propaganda Fide* in 1622 as a clearinghouse for questions regarding canonically approved behavior and religious practice.[6] Once Catholicism became rooted, then the *Propaganda Fide* would "relinquish its authority" and the former mission area would come under the common obligations of canon law alongside the established catholicized nations.[7] In 1908, the same year that the United States lost its missionary status, the Vatican also established a permanent office devoted to questions regarding the life of religious: the Congregation of the Affairs of Religious or, later, the Congregation of Religious. The church recognized the need for flexibility in the missionary years, but consistency and greater uniformity was its ultimate goal. Both withdrawing missionary status and placing men who had received Holy Orders and men and women who had taken solemn and simple vows under a designated office of the Curia would facilitate the achievement of consistency.

British penal laws, such as those cited by Ellis, did indeed influence clerical attire in the American colonies. In the colony of New York, for instance, the legislature severely curtailed the civil rights of Catholics and forbade priests from entering the colony under penalty of law. In terms of clerical dress, therefore, disguise was the order of the day. Jesuit priest Ferdinand Steinmeyer, more popularly referred to as Ferdinand Farmer, traveled from Maryland up through East and West Jersey and was known to "enter New York by stealth."[8] In his travels he "dressed soberly like a good Quaker."[9] Even after New York lifted its restrictions on priests, Farmer's clothing could have remained unremarkable, as there was no mandatory habit required of the Jesuits.[10] Although they are often associated with a black robe and cincture or belt, their constitution only required that "the clothing . . . should have three characteristics: first, it should be proper; second, conformed to the usage of the country of residence; and third, not contradictory to the poverty we profess."[11] Likewise, there was no ecclesial mandate operating in the American colonies or the new United States that would have required Farmer to wear, for instance, a Roman collar.[12] In Farmer's case, his freedom depended on his blending in even if it was only as another, albeit legal, religious minority.

A century later, in 1856 the acceptance of distinctive clerical dress was still not fully established. Father George Reš (Roesch), a priest from Carinthia in the Hapsburg Empire, came to New York to minister to Slovenian and German-speaking Catholics. Father Reš made his way to Poughkeepsie, New York, where he was dismayed to find his German speakers living in an atmosphere of mixed marriages and multiple faiths and worshipping in makeshift church structures. He mused that if "every diocese were as well-run as the Lavantine [in Slovenia], the Catholic world would be very fortunate."[13] Complaining to his former bishop, Father Reš went on to claim that in Poughkeepsie they could not "dress as priests as we could in Germany or Austria."[14] Although Father Reš did not specify why he and other priests could not dress as they had in Europe, he was writing at the height of the popular Know-Nothing movement, a political party that espoused nativist and specifically anti-Catholic sentiment.[15] Advertising one's Catholicism might result in harassment. Instead, wearing denominationally nonspecific (or less specific) attire would allow priests to appear closer to American male clothing standards and, by connection, American values. Projecting American-style manliness could come in handy for any religious minority.

Other conditions and inclinations, most of which had nothing to do with discrimination, also contributed to making a more uniform look unlikely. Diverse origins and seminary training contributed to a multifarious clerical population. The priests in Detroit, for instance, came from an array of countries, including France, Italy, Flanders, Germany, Switzerland, Ireland, and Hungary, among others. According to historian Leslie Woodcock Tentler, Detroit did not ordain its first American-born priest until 1850. As a result of this diversity, clerical behavior varied considerably.[16]

Some priests came to the United States for an opportunity to thoughtfully minister, but others came because they had damaged their reputations in their homeland. Ireland, specifically, contributed a large number of priests to the United States, and observers complained about the "erratic Irish-born priests" being a problem.[17] According to Cardinal Paul Cullen, a nineteenth-century Roman-leaning reformer of Irish Catholicism, St. Patrick's College at Maynooth was a school where "discipline . . . [did] not greatly prevail."[18] Echoing Cardinal Cullen, Peter Paul Lefevere, bishop of Detroit from 1841 to 1869, likewise bemoaned the Irish-trained priests. In a letter to a fellow bishop he explained that although he had over fifty "well recommended" priests from Ireland in his diocese, he found them all disappointing. "I am sorry to say," Lefevere wrote, "that I have not succeeded with one of them for all have done more harm than good, whilst many of them have given the most dreadful scandals."[19] The connection between dress and erratic or undisciplined behavior was twofold. Priests, although known to observers, attempted to travel incognito. Therefore they drew criticism for disguising themselves while acting freely. On the other hand, some priests were identifiable in their dress, and onlookers associated their undisciplined behavior with the Roman Catholic priesthood.

Sometimes priests were not misbehaving but merely on a vacation and, in that case, enjoying a respite from their clerical role. In those cases as well, a priest might attempt to "disguise" himself, attired as an ordinary man. In 1866 the bishops regretfully observed that in regard to appearance, "we fear that in this country we are drifting in a direction not altogether in harmony either with the spirit or the letter of ecclesiastical law. We have met priests who sought relaxation from their arduous duties on seashores, or in fashionable watering places dressed in every other conceivable way but as a priest."[20] Bishops worried that American priests did not view the priesthood as a transformative life commitment and instead saw it as merely a profession from which one could indeed take a holiday.[21]

While undisciplined, sociable, or vacationing priests could pose challenges to the bishop, a spirit of independence and practicality infected even the well-behaved and high-ranking clergy. American clothing sensibilities, which were simple and functional, attracted members of the clergy.[22] Father

John J. Williams, born in the United States in 1822 to Irish parents, went on to become bishop of the Diocese of Boston in 1866 and, later, archbishop. Williams maintained good relations with non-Catholics and downplayed Catholic distinctiveness. A fellow priest noted that Williams and other clergymen in Boston wore "brown hats and ordinary shirt collars," and this, he interpreted, showed an absence of "churchly bureaucratic trappings."[23] Williams, one might conclude, sought to present Catholicism as a religious faith that accommodated American values.

Father Richard Burtsell, arguably an even more "native" Catholic priest than Williams, descended from early-seventeenth-century Maryland Catholics, and his ancestors were settled in New York by the time of the American Revolution.[24] Born in New York in 1840, Burtsell studied for the priesthood and later became a canon lawyer. Similar to Archbishop Williams, Burtsell donned fashions that reflected his interest in blending in with his sartorial surroundings. He noted in his diary that he wore a "panama hat," bought his pants ready-made, and took baths at Coney Island.[25] Commenting on a disagreement he had with a priest after the Second Plenary Council of 1866, Burtsell wrote, "Fr. Quin and I had a sharp controversy on clerical dress. He thought that sleeve-buttons should not be tolerated in priests!!! I thought the church should not interfere with collars, buttons, beards, etc., etc."[26] Burtsell was among a small but vocal group of priests who saw church doctrine as separate from church discipline. Thus he believed American Catholic priests should develop an American, rather than Roman, style of behavior and discipline.[27] Likewise, his desire for clerical freedom reflected his sense of class. To be assigned clothing suggested a kind of livery of service in the mid-nineteenth century. As a free man who viewed his position as akin to that of an officer, Burtsell felt he should determine his own attire.[28]

More often than not, in the first half of the nineteenth century and especially in rural areas, priests would travel several miles to hear confessions and offer mass for Catholics in vastly spread out and isolated rural areas. These conditions presented clothing challenges as well. According to historian Mary Ewen, in Indiana, "the Sisters of Providence were shocked when their chaplain proposed hearing their confessions in the parlor of their back woods convent, without benefit of confessional or surplice."[29] Likewise, a bishop appeared "sunburnt, dusty, and with dry mud on his clothes." The clergy the sisters had known in France had given up what they considered to be the proper clerical attire and adopted the "flat lie-down collar and black string tie of the laity."[30] Priests and sometimes even bishops themselves chose decidedly non-

European clothing standards for their American ministry. To make matters worse, sometimes the laity referred to the clergy with a uniquely American address, calling priests "Mister" rather than "Father."[31]

Diminishing the familiarity between priests and the laity was a valuable endeavor in the eyes of the church leadership, as familiarity invited regular challenges to ministerial authority. In certain areas of the United States, particularly New York and Philadelphia, the scarcity of priests blending with the disestablishment culture of antebellum America inspired lay-controlled Catholic churches. Congregational-style churches were common among Protestants but novel for Catholics. Without a centralized diocesan system, the laity often had to purchase land, build the church, oversee prayers, and teach catechism to maintain their faith. Additionally, the leading men of the parish held "annual elections to choose the board of lay trustees."[32] This form of parish governance became known as "trusteeism," and with the dearth of priests in the United States and the far-flung settlements of Catholics, trusteeism flourished. After a few decades of shared power, however, pastors became increasingly frustrated with the laity's sense of rights. In Philadelphia, German Catholics in St. Mary's Parish decided to replace their English-speaking priest with a German priest whom they contracted on their own.[33] Another case arose in Norfolk, Virginia, when the pastor assigned to a parish in 1815 ran afoul of the trustees. The lay committee told their pastor they no longer wanted him to travel to Richmond to say mass.[34] To assert his authority, the pastor instead sought to remove a few of the troublesome trustees. Not accepting defeat, the trustees locked the pastor out of the church and eventually left him and established another church with a pastor from New York.[35] Lay assertiveness in matters of religion, while initially desirable in that it demonstrated a commitment to upholding Catholicism in a Protestant land, ultimately became problematic in issues of governance. Bishops feared that if the parishioners did not agree with what their pastor said or required, they would dismiss him. Trusteeism could, and sometimes did, lead to situations where the people were directing the church rather than the church directing the people.

Mindful of their freedom-loving environment, the bishops and clergy in the United States debated the appropriateness of a foreign and monarchical stamp on America. The separation of church and state, one of the hallmarks of liberal government, had, for the most part, served the American church and the priests who ministered in it well. Freedom of religion had in fact created the setting by which the church witnessed its growth and establishment throughout the country. De Tocqueville spoke to Catholic clergymen in his travels and found that although "they differed upon matters of detail alone . . . all attributed the peaceful dominion of religion in their country mainly to the separation of church and state." He continued, "I do not hesitate to affirm that during my stay in America I did not meet a single individual, of the clergy or the laity, who was not of the same opinion on this point."[36] Although de Tocqueville wrote in the 1830s, the goal or at least discussion of keeping religious peace in what Catholics rightfully perceived to be an anti-Catholic environment continued for several decades. According to historian Thomas McAvoy, Archbishop James Gibbons, the apostolic delegate at the Third Plenary Council of Baltimore and the most senior Catholic prelate in the United States, rejected the Catholic ornamentation that one in his position was likely to wear in Rome. An ascetic and a peacekeeper, he was a symbol of American Catholic accommodation.[37] Father Walter Elliot, a Paulist, expressed similar sentiments. In his 1889 sermon at the consecration mass of Bishops John Shanley, James McGolrick, and Joseph B. Cotter, he praised the exceptionalism of Americans. In his homily he "stressed the view that in the United States the ideas of manhood were not so much loyalty, obedience, and uniformity, but rather worthiness to be free. The aspirations of the American people were toward progress and intelligence and liberty, the dignity of man, and his capacity to govern himself."[38] While not outright schismatic, the American church appeared dangerously enamored with "freedom" and less concerned with Roman standards and submission. Critics and supporters alike identified this more independent style as "Americanism."

In summary, the American mission presented more challenges than anticipated, and unlike most other mission countries, the United States became the destination for an ever increasing number of Catholics. Between 1790 and 1866 the Catholic population had risen from 35,000 to 3,555,000. Immigration accounted for much of this rapid growth.[39] Therefore, regardless of America's status as a mission with Vatican-approved flexibility, the ecclesial leadership sought to address the American state of irregularity with haste. Clerical clothing was a logical focus. Diverse attire reflected individualism and liberty. Greater standardization, however, would convey consistency of belief and behavior. Although the bishops were unsure of how much European Catholic bureaucracy should be transplanted, they knew that in a democratic nation, guided by the "will of the people," they required a strategy to foster less willfulness and more compliance. Clerical attire was a familiar and powerful resource.

A single archbishop and four bishops convened the 1829 Provincial Council in Baltimore with the goal of imposing a modicum of regularity on church life, which they hoped would address some of the challenges facing the American priesthood and Catholic leadership more broadly. It is within this context that the bishops introduced the beginnings of a "regulated" form of dress.[40] The council explained in its "Pastoral Letter to the Clergy,"

> Many things that may appear trivial are to you important. The very fashion of your dress is, in the eye of the world, calculated to elevate or to depress your character, and to extend or restrict your usefulness. In almost every organized public association, such a subject is matter of regulation; the soldier who loves his profession is laudably exact in its regard; and however philosophism might speculate, every practical officer will feel that the character of the individual is generally ascertained from his appearance. You are the officers of the militia of Christ. You bear his commission. Is it possible that there can be found amongst you who would feel disposed to conceal the dignity with which he is invested? Such a renegade would be unworthy of his place. Can he presume to seek precedence in the Church who is disguised in the world? Is he ashamed of that station to which he sought, with so much earnestness, to be raised? He should be forthwith discharged to make room for one more worthy of the honor. The canons of the Church equally censure the thoughtless folly or censurable vanity which is made ridiculous by its efforts to be fashionable, and the unbecoming slovenliness which degrades the dignity of the order, by the meanness of the individual; the simple cleanliness of the attire should evince the plain-innocence of the wearer, and his conformity to the regulation of the Church should manifest the esteem in which he holds its authority.[41]

The bishops admonished the priests in their letter, suggesting that disguise, vanity, and slovenliness were common approaches to clerical dress. The prescription, however, was vague. In these early years, with relatively few priests and such diverse diocesan experiences, each bishop in attendance would have determined, independently, whether he wanted more specific guidelines and how he interpreted "conformity to the regulation of the Church."[42] It was also unclear with what role the priest should associate himself. As a "soldier" he would be issued clothing and be expected to follow orders, and as an "officer" he would obtain his own clothing and would give orders.[43] The bishops' use of both metaphors suggests they wanted the priests to see themselves filling the roles simultaneously. Priests would be soldiers under the command of the bishops, and officers in the eyes of the laity. In either case, clothing's appearance in the letter indicates that clerical presentation was a growing concern for the bishops.

The council took up vagaries of vestments and ceremonial techniques as well. At the gathering the bishops decided that a new ceremonial was needed. A ceremonial is a detailed description of the vestments, liturgical ordering, and altar assignments expected at specific religious occasions, such as the priest celebrating a low mass, vespers, or a Palm Sunday mass. According to Katherine Haas, the decision to publish a ceremonial for the United States conveyed a concern for more unification in the church and to encourage standard practices.[44] The book initially provided both historical background and procedural information, taking into consideration the lack of liturgical models available to the priests in America. One of the earlier versions, the 1852 *Ceremonial: For the Use of the Catholic Churches in the United States of America*, offered instructions in a collegial tone. On the topic of the liturgical vestments, Bishops Rosati and England submitted an essay that explained the inspiration for the various liturgical colors. "The Church also by the very color of the . . . vestments, teaches her children the nature of the solemnity which she celebrates." They continued, "Thus, for instance, white is used upon the great festivals of the Trinity, of the Saviour, of his Blessed Mother, of angels, of saints, who without shedding their blood gave their testimony by the practice of exhalted virtues; and on some other occasions. Red is used on the Feast of Pentecost when the Holy Ghost descended in the form of tongues of fire; on the festivals of martyrs and the like. In times of penance, violet is used, green on days when there is no special solemnity, and black on Good Friday, and on occasion of offices for the deceased."[45] The essay was instructive rather than legalistic but nevertheless laid out the church's expectations regarding the proper coordination of liturgical vesture with the church calendar. By the end of the century the collegial tone of the ceremonial would be replaced by a more legalistic style expressing requirements rather than explanations and inspirations.

Another way to encourage regularity was to simply give the proper vestments to a parish. St. Patrick's Church in Rochester, New York, received vestments for the various liturgical seasons and feasts from Bishop John DuBois. However, Bishop DuBois must have been unsure that the trustees would pay for the vestments because he provided valuable gifts to the church pending reimbursement for the vestments. Perhaps Bishop Dubois did not believe that the trustees would provide all the necessary vestments unless he commissioned the order. A substantial portion of his letter appears below:

New York, October 7th, 1827.

To Mr. Horan,
Dear Sir
    Inclosed I send you the Bill of the vestments-vizt–
    One white Vestment including all materials

and making	$14.77
One Green-Do-Do	12.71
One Black-Do-Do	13.80½
One Purple-Do-Do	13.71
One Altar Stone	3.00
	————
Amount	$57.99½

    I make a present to the Church on condition that it shall not be lent out or carried away by any Clergyman attending-of

A Chalice of Silver	Linen for the Chalice
The Body of a Crucifix	A Mass-book in folio
An Alb of Linen for every day	Altar cards.

    You will be so good as to present or send me the amount of the above articles I advanced out of my money Vizt $57.99½, for it is on condition of its being returned to me immediately that I gave the other articles.[46]

In the 1820s, without frequent diocesan oversight or regular communication, Bishop DuBois had to rely on the trustees as well as the priest in residence to appreciate that multiple vestments, which corresponded to the religious occasions, were a priority. After the Provincial Council of 1829, however, when the bishops moved to reject trusteeism, such direct reliance on the parishioners for particular vesture would not be as great a concern.

    In Philadelphia the city's bishop, Francis Patrick Kenrick, took up the issue of "ritual observances" and vestments with his clergy in 1831. Echoing the bishops at the Provincial Council, Kenrick asserted, "It is time that all our efforts should be combined, not merely to propagate the truths of faith, and perform the most important acts of our ministry, but by the uniformity and exactness of our ritual observances to practically exhibit, in a sensible manner, the unity, beauty, and majesty of our divine religion."[47] Bishop Kenrick contended that detail to ritual performance and vestments were an important aspect of visual instruction. He explained, "We should particularly take care, lest the neglect of the vesture and solemn rights prescribed to be used in the administration of the sacraments should occasion, in ourselves, or in others, a want of regard and veneration for the mysteries sublime and tremendous."[48] The presentation and performance, which critics of Catholicism saw as "seducing" congregants, Kenrick would argue were designed to enchant Catholics and inspire in them an awe and reverence of the blessed sacrament and, correspondingly, the priest who transformed the host and performed the rituals.

The recommendations of the Provincial Council at Baltimore made their way into other dioceses over the next several years.[49] At the Third Synod of the Philadelphia Diocese in 1847, Bishop Kenrick concluded that, regarding clericals, "a modest, serious dress is conducive to the preservation of morals in their integrity and to the edification of the faithful; hence We admonish the Priest of this Diocese that the coat which they wear when out of doors should approximate the cassock in cut, in such wise that it reaches below the knees; and let them carefully avoid all worldly fashions, especially exposure of the shirt upon the breast."[50] Once again, the cassock required in Philadelphia was not one that reached to the ground, as it would have been in Europe. Instead it was a modified cassock that could easily be concealed under a gentleman's frock coat. Covering the shirtfront would be accomplished with a waistcoat or vest that buttoned up to near the base of the throat. The item of distinction would have been a collar, but Bishop Kenrick made no mention of neckwear. Father John E. Fitzmaurice, the first pastor of St. Agatha's Church in Philadelphia, is pictured in 1865 with a bow tie and black vest (see fig. 1). While the collar is visible, it is an ordinary shirt collar rather than a clerical collar. His coat length is not visible, but his appearance from the waist up does not disclose his vocation.

Both Bishop Lefevere and his successor, Bishop Borgess, regulated their priests' clothing along with activities. The first diocesan synod in Detroit in 1859 issued a dress code that required priests to wear "a Roman collar in public and a black soutane that reached at least to the knees."[51] When Borgess took over in 1870, he retained the dress code and added other rules that would further distance the Detroit priests from the laity. For instance, he "allowed an occasional drink at the rectory, but never in the company of laymen."[52] He also forbade his priests from playing athletic games in public or attending music halls, theaters, or saloons.[53] What Borgess meant by a "Roman collar" is not necessarily what modern-day observers of clerical attire might assume. According to the Reverends John A. Nainfa and Henry J. McCloud, authors of approved reference books on clerical dress, the Roman collar was not Roman in origin. As Nainfa explains, "Ecclesiastics who have lived or studied in

Figure 1. Father John E. Fitzmaurice, 1865. Courtesy of the Philadelphia Archdiocesan Historical Research Center, Philadelphia, Pa.

Rome may have noticed that what we call a 'Roman Collar' is a collar indeed, except not Roman, except by adoption."[54] He pointed out that clerical tailors tend to have their own individual styles in terms of dressing the clergy, suggesting that there were several options for neckwear as well as other clerical garments. He went on, "Our Roman Collar, so-called, consists of two parts, a starched circle of white linen—the collar, and a piece of cloth or silk, to which the collar itself is fashioned by means of buttons or hooks, a sort of stock which has been given the strange name of 'rabbi' probably a corruption of the French word 'rabat.'" Nainfa suggested that "what is familiar to us under the name 'rabbi' is the true Roman Collar." However, tailors and priests in Italy referred to the linen collar as a *collaro*. Nainfa preferred and encouraged the adoption of the Italian terminology. "The Roman *collaro* is made up of a loose breast-piece and of a rigid circle of the same material. The rigid part is properly called the collar." Nainfa pointed out that "it is maintained stiff by slipping into it a piece of light cardboard or leather. In order to keep the collar clean, a changeable band of white linen (*collarino*) is placed over it and fixed behind with two silver clips. It is that small band of linen which has grown into, the stiff affair now worn, and has usurped among us the name of 'Roman collar.'"[55] What appears to have given the collar distinction as Catholic rather than "Lutheran neckwear" was the fact that it was worn with a cassock that had a standup collar and a square cutout in the center of the throat.[56] Without the cassock (and this we know was only required to be worn in the church at this time), therefore, the collar would not have been distinctly Catholic or "Roman." In a footnote, Nainfa cites the other popular collar: "The 'single band Roman collar,'" which, he observed, "seems to be in favor in some parts of the country, and is advertised as a 'specialty' by certain clerical tailors." Nainfa concluded that this collar "should be left to the clergy-men of the 'Episcopal Church.'"[57] Returning to Bishop Borgess, what he was demanding of his clergy in 1859 was at least a "collar" that would identify his priests as members of the ministry. To make it "Roman," he would have had to require that the cassock, or soutane, as he referred to the gown, included the proper standup collar with cutout style; but the cassock of the priests of Detroit, as in the rest of the United States, was only required to come to the knee, and there was no mention of the cutout. Therefore when considering the nineteenth century, we should focus more on "collar" than "Roman."[58]

Ideally, identifiable dress could also render priests more accountable for their behavior. Attending dances, enjoying a drink in a tavern, and fraterniz-ing too closely with the laity were all considered inappropriate pastimes for priests. Some bishops had stricter rules than others regarding the leisure ac-tivities of their priests, but monitoring their behavior was, to some degree, on the agenda of every bishop. Wearing clerical garb reaffirmed for the priests, in an intimate way, that they should not become too engaged in the trappings "of the world," and it reminded those around them to look upon the priests differ-ently. At the Council of Trent, the church leaders had determined that "there is nothing that continually instructs others unto piety and the service of God more than the life and example of those who have dedicated themselves to the divine ministry. For as they are seen to be raised to a higher position above the things of this world, others fix their eyes upon them as upon a mirror, and de-rive from them what they are to imitate. Wherefore clerics called to the Lord . . . ought . . . to regulate their whole life and conversation as that in their dress, comportment, gait, discourse, and all things else, nothing appear but what is grave, regulated, and replete with religiousness."[59] Distinctive cloth-ing would ideally express a priest's virtuousness and obedience, providing an exemplary model for his parishioners and anyone who observed him. Uni-formity also reminded the priest of his commitment and submission. He did not have the unrestricted "right" to choose any clothing he wanted, as Father Burtsell had hoped; instead, he was bound to wear what he was told he could wear, and the church expected him to do so without reservation.

By the close of the Second Plenary Council in 1866, not a great deal had changed regarding the specific regulation of clerical attire. Chronicler Father Sebastian Smith, a former professor of sacred scripture, canon law, and ecclesiastical history at Seton Hall Seminary in New York, provided a detailed account of the council's conclusions in the form of explanatory text he hoped would be accessible to seminary students, clerics, and even "intelligent perusers of the laity."[60] On the subject of clerical garments, he explained that the bishops reiterated the desire of earlier meetings, stating that priests "should observe the law of the Church, wearing the cassock at home as well as in church, as being the distinctive dress of ecclesiastics."[61] Smith explained, "At present," the clerical habit "consists chiefly of the cassock reaching to the ground. . . . In Catholic countries this attire is used at all times and in all places; at home or abroad. A transgression of this custom is punishable with privation of ecclesiastical immunities."[62] Smith then offered an account for the American exception. He pointed out that "in America this law does not bind in so unlimited a manner. Living among non-Catholics, clergymen would be constantly exposed to ridicule and annoyance, should they appear in public places vested in cassock. Yet nothing hinders them from doing so in the house or in church. This, in fact, is made obligatory on all clerics, as we saw, by the Fathers of Baltimore. Nor do we think that their prescriptions on this point can be set aside continually without betraying contempt, more or less sinful, for a grave ordinance of the Church."[63] Therefore, at home and in church the long cassock had become the requirement. However, for traveling, a short cassock or simply the black-colored clothing identified with the ministry would suffice. He implied, however, that the exceptions made in the United States should not be used as an excuse not to wear ecclesial garments when possible.

It was at the Third Plenary Council, held in 1884, that the bishops developed specific instructions for the priests of all dioceses. Father William O'Connell, the future archbishop of Boston, provided a sort of accounting of the council's proposed plan in a falsely identified "letter home" published after his elevation to cardinal.[64] According to O'Connell, American clergy were congregating to meet with the Roman Curia in preparation for the upcoming Third Plenary Council scheduled for Baltimore the following year.[65] Reflecting on the visual presentation the collection of priests offered, O'Connell told his reader, "Of course we understand well enough that in America the street costume of our clergy until now has been nothing especially distinctive, because of conditions. But they say that is one of the matters the Council will take up, requiring the Roman collar and long black coat." He went on to write, "One of the prelates, speaking about this to the students, pointed laughingly at Father Daley, who wore an open vest displaying a great white shirt front, decorated with three enormous emerald studs, and said, 'This sort of array will end pretty soon.' Well most of us agreed it was time."[66] While the veracity of O'Connell's account is certainly questionable, the conclusion O'Connell conveyed is nonetheless accurate. Over a century of sartorial flexibility was about to end.

The agenda of the Third Plenary Council in Baltimore came together in Rome several months before the council meeting itself. This was the first time the cardinals of the *Congregation de Propaganda Fide* required the American bishops to consult Rome before a provincial or plenary meeting. Rome's summoning of the bishops was significant. Pope Pius IX watched the United States with growing interest in the second half of the nineteenth century. For his own part, Pius IX found himself on the less popular side of the wave of liberal reform that was coursing through Europe and, most importantly, on the Italian peninsula. He took up a position against a campaign for an independent Italian republic that at different times called on him to support a war against the then-Catholic monarch in Austria, Franz Joseph I, and to relinquish temporal power over the Papal States. Pius IX, who had gradually expanded his intolerance of secularism, pluralism, and liberal government since the revolutions of the 1840s, culminated his discontent by introducing the doctrine of papal infallibility in 1870, a reminder to all Catholics of his supreme authority.[67] In 1871, after suffering defeat in the capture of Rome, Pope Pius IX shut himself in the Vatican and declared himself a "prisoner." He and his papal successors refused to negotiate with the Italian government until 1929. Defeated by secular political agitation, the pontiff demanded allegiance to himself and everything Roman. For several decades to come, one's "Romanism" became the litmus test of being a truly devoted Catholic priest.[68]

The Catholics of the United States were offspring of the kind of liberalism that had forcefully taken the Holy See's earthly kingdom. As a result, Pius IX and subsequent popes carefully watched their transatlantic brothers for signs that "national spirit" might overwhelm religious allegiance. For the American bishops, a uniform appearance linking Catholic priests to the institutional church was one way of signaling that allegiance to Rome. And the planning session prior to the Third Plenary Council confirmed that the issue of clerical dress in America had won Rome's attention.[69]

Once back in the United States for the meeting in Baltimore, the council decreed, "We wish therefore and enjoin that all keep the law of the Church, and that when at home or when engaged in the sanctuary they should always wear the cassock [*vestis talaris*] which is proper to the clergy."[70] The bishops went on to specify, "When they go abroad for duty or relaxation, or when upon a journey, they may use a shorter dress, but still one that is black in colour, and which reaches to the knees, so as to distinguish it from lay costume. We enjoin upon our priests, as a matter of strict precept, that both at home and abroad, and whether they are residing in their own diocese or outside of it, they should wear the Roman collar."[71] The long soutane or cassock was more common in Europe. When the priest was walking on paved streets or riding in a carriage, the length of the cassock did not inhibit his movement or draw negative attention. In America, however, the likelihood of having to negotiate a frontier environment or rely on a horse and, later, a bicycle to travel around one's parish rendered an abbreviated dress more practical. The short cassock, black and distinguished from the attire of the laity, as noted by Father Sebastian Smith, was a compromise, but the Roman collar was a new and distinctive addition. In the eyes of the European and Canadian priests, American clergy looked more like "Protestant priests," but with the regular use of the Roman collar and black clothing, as well as donning the European-style cassock at home, priests now would set themselves off with ministerial authority.[72]

SEMINARY EDUCATION AND THE LIVERY OF THE PRIESTHOOD

Despite the promulgation of definitive rules regarding everyday clerical appearance, discussion on the topic of clerical attire and the message it conveyed continued. The United States, after all, was still a missionary territory until 1908. Written sources about seminaries and for the seminarians reveal some of the contours of the dialogue.

In his study of the development of diocesan seminaries, historian Joseph M. White contends that commentators on clerical life in America generally encouraged seminarians and priests to conscientiously adapt to American society. James Gibbons, archbishop of Baltimore; John Ireland, bishop of St. Paul; Father John Talbot Smith of New York; German-born Father William Stang; and Belgian-born Camillus Maes, bishop of Kentucky, all advocated a practical approach to the clerical life in America. Gibbons for instance, disapproved of severe discipline meant to break seminarians of their love of freedom or harsh admonishments in sermons.[73] Ireland argued for "truthfulness, honest[y] in business dealings, loyalty to law and social order, temperance, and respect for the rights of others." Without these qualities, Ireland believed, the church would not be successful. "An honest ballot and social decorum," Ireland stated, "will do more for God's glory and the salvation of souls than midnight flagellations or Compostellan pilgrimages."[74] Smith proposed that an athletic, well-spoken, and gentlemanly priest would best suit America. And Bishop Maes proposed that "the priest . . . to exert a salutary influence over his own people as well as over non-Catholics must live in the world, though he may not be of it." He went on, "This is especially true of our own country. . . . Doing good to others is a greater source of merit and a greater safeguard to virtue in the world than the state which makes the ministry of the World subservient to personal sanctification." Catholic priests needed to be out among the people mingling and performing good works. Maes questioned "the young man who from his tenderest years has been kept entirely away from the world, who has never known its temptations. . . . Will he do effective work under the modern conditions in which his life is cast?"[75] Maes doubted isolated seminarians would flourish and suggested that seminary students not wear Roman collars in public until they began their theological studies. Until then, Maes believed young Catholic men should attend college in ordinary street dress and with those who did not intend to enter seminary. At the Catholic University of America, a seminary founded in the United States in 1887 for the training of American priests, philosophy professor Father Joseph Pohle made a democratic proposal. He suggested having "the students themselves work out a code of rules by which they should be governed, to give them back that feeling of personal freedom." Pohle saw "freedom" as "an essential and important . . . element of a free country and of an American citizen."[76] Pohle's recommendation implied an older student body, unlike the European model, which often began vocational grooming in childhood.

John Talbot Smith devoted an entire book, published in 1896, to the topic of seminary reform. Smith argued that a clergyman should not only adapt to American life but also exude the qualities of a professional and a gentleman. To attain these goals, he surmised, required a certain attentiveness to dress. "We are cautioned to avoid singularity in appearance," Smith wrote, "and at the same time to adhere strictly to the clerical dress; and yet how often has the writer seen a whole street and a whole village convulsed with laughter at the sight afforded by priests on dress parade. One has only to stand on Barclay Street in New York, where the priests of half the country pass in procession, to admire the wondrous raiment in which they have bagged themselves. Men grow careless with years, but priests ought to grow more careful."[77] Barclay Street in New York City was famous for its purveyors of religious wares.

Smith reiterated the importance of grooming seminarians for social acceptance. After seminary training, the American priest, he wrote, should be "a gentleman. . . . He is a failure otherwise. But what the writer desires to express here by the term gentleman more particularly refers to the externals of a cultivated and presentable man. Americans are the best-dressed people in the world; they naturally look for the same taste in their teachers. . . . In public ceremonies they are impatient of the ornate and Oriental, but are more than severe in exacting from the functionaries the dignity of manner suited to the scene. The priest who is to enjoy the fullest influence over all classes of citizens must have the manners, habits, and appearance of a gentleman."[78] Seminarians, he suggested, should cultivate a taste for linen. Father John Burtsell identified the priest as a gentleman as well. While shopping in Montreal, he complained that the clothing sold there "was too rough, made for working people or too thick." Burtsell looked for the fabric that reflected his station in life as a gentleman and professional.[79]

Complicating the image of the priesthood was the dual identity of the gentleman-minister in society and the transcendent proxy of Christ in the church. American society interpreted male professionals as virile, and the American Catholic priest, dressed in presentable mufti and in good health, would fit that ideal. However, a collection of cassocks, capes (mantle), tuft-bearing birettas, and lacy surplices, alongside a more European religious sensibility of pietism and complete with a vow of celibacy, left some priests appearing sexually ambiguous. Referring to the French traditions, Timothy Holland, a young American who joined the Society of St. Sulpice in 1904, complained that in France, the priests' piety "tends toward effeminacy and becomes insipid." He likened the French Sulpicians to "prudish old women." John Talbot Smith, too, decried the unathletic and overly ascetic European style of priestly training. In the American seminaries, he found that one of the "problem personalities" was the "Miss Nancy," or "girl-boy." This was a seminarian who was "giggling in place of laughing" and had "feminine delicacy of gesture, of movement, nicety of inflection in speech, facial motions, and peculiarities in sitting and walking." A priest, in Smith's summation, could not afford to raise questions about his sexuality.[80]

William O'Connell of Boston implied that effeminacy was an issue when he wrote about his fellow seminarians in Maryland being pious. He explained, "All the chaps who I have met here are genuinely pious. Strange I don't like that word applied to a boy. But there is no other. They are not what we used to call pi-is. They are as jolly and boisterous a lot as you could wish. But in their quiet hours and in their general behavior they somehow show another influence, which is underneath all the time. When a young fellow goes to confession every week and receives every Sunday, well you know it must get all into him and all over him in time. And it does without in a least spoiling him for football or any other game in the field or making him petty or fussy or finicky with his comrades."[81] Even if the authenticity of the letters is questionable, O'Connell wanted his readers to understand that although seminarians might appear to be effeminate due to their piety, they were nevertheless still both masculine and heterosexual.

The surest route to social acceptance for a priest, as a member of a religious minority in America, was a manly bearing. However, the social discourse on virility was in flux toward the end of the nineteenth century. Gail Bederman contends that in an effort to defend their racial and social superiority in the age of imperialism and Jim Crow, white men combined ideas about the physical prowess associated with working-class and "primitive men" with attributes such as self-restraint and strength of character that middle-class men believed characterized themselves. Upper- and middle-class white men threw themselves into competitive sports and came to revere the physically conditioned and athletic man. Thus wealthier white men could defend their positions of power over other, physically strong but intellectually and morally weak men. Historian Kevin Murphy also examines the shifting definition of masculinity in the late nineteenth century. Murphy contends that middle-class reformers, borrowing military rhetoric and organizational models from the working class, promoted a "civic militarism" in order to claim an acceptable expression of masculinity and to "defuse the threat of class warfare and promote social unity." Using Edward Bellamy's "industrial army" as an example, Murphy argues that people were attracted to the military model because it "offered an antidote to the unbridled 'self-interest' that many believed had produced corporate monopolies, wide-scale political corruption, and consequently, horrendous working and living conditions in industrial cities."[82] Militarism denoted sacrifice and duty rather than success and ambition.

John Talbot Smith's suggestions regarding seminaries support both Bederman's and Murphy's arguments. Smith recommended that the American seminaries model themselves after the U.S. Military Academy at West Point. In an institution shaped by American values, European-style priests could be replaced by American priests with "all the popular virtues of the manly as well as the priestly standard; a gentleman in polish and education, chaste and pious, and of good physical presence, with a taste or appreciation for the athletic sports of the nation."[83] Likewise, with careful attention to every facet of his behavior, the "Miss Nancy" could be "cured" and become a priest fit to serve in America.[84]

While Smith and other writers considered the character of future priests and what their clothing suggested about their masculinity, other clergy focused on how the seminary curriculum could be used to direct ministerial behavior. The Reverend William Stang, vice rector and professor at the American College in Louvain, Belgium, published a textbook in 1897 on pastoral theology, or "the science which teaches the proper discharging of the various duties of the priest in the care of souls."[85] An interdisciplinary subject, pastoral theology drew on "dogmatic teaching, moral theology, ascetical theology, and canon law" to instruct seminarians on how to apply their religious training to their practical ministry and the administration of the sacraments.[86] Stang began his text on a defensive note, perhaps anticipating criticism for writing a book that seemed to lay out several commonsense attributes and behaviors expected of a priest. The preface explained that "this volume on Pastoral Theology is published primarily as a text-book for the Students of Louvain College who are completing the last year of their theological course. Pastoral Theology is taught at our College as a special branch of the sacred sciences. Most of our Candidates are destined for American dioceses where, immediately after their arrival, they are placed in charge of Missions, no opportunity being afforded them to study the proper management of Mission and Parish work under the guidance of experienced Rectors. Therefore they must needs be introduced to the practical work of an American Missionary and be prepared for their apostolical life before they leave our College."[87] He stated frankly, "If further apology be necessary for the publication of this book, the author would respectfully state: The students wanted a text-book of Pastoral Theology; there was none in English. His esteemed Superior, the Rt. Rev. Rector, Mgr. Willemsen, requested him to write one, and here is what he could gather from reliable sources and from personal experience of nearly seventeen years on the American Mission."[88] Such an explicit defense suggests another American compromise. An English, rather than Latin or French, sourcebook assisted in standardizing the behavior of a diverse and less widely educated population of Roman Catholic priests.

Catholic ministry in the United States was, Stang suggested, a unique experience. He pointed out that "local customs, special conditions and circumstances are so various and manifold in America that they could not be noticed singly in a manual which has to deal with more general principles."[89] Nevertheless, clerical educators attempted to meet the challenge by publishing more guides for seminarians and priests in English. These books became readily available at the turn of the century as priests prepared to live and practice their ministry in English-speaking countries, particularly America, and Rome began to care more about priestly appearance and behavior. The Reverend Frederick Schulze's *Manual of Pastoral Theology* was in its second edition by 1906. Schulze, too, identified the necessity of such a manual, since "the newly ordained priest needs a guide to steer him safely past the rocks and shoals which lie in his course. . . . This applies particularly to our own country, for here a priest's pastoral duties extend over a vastly wider sphere than elsewhere, and we have none of the traditional usages and laws by which clerical life is regulated abroad."[90] Schulze, writing from Milwaukee, Wisconsin, concurred with Stang's observation that "often the young priest, almost immediately after his ordination, is sent to a mission where he is entirely alone. Comparatively few are fortunate enough to be able to serve for a while as assistants to experienced pastors, by whom they are gradually introduced to parochial work."[91] Without the guidance of a pastor, these priests needed a reference to inform their behavior, including how to dress.

Pastoral theology texts and guides for priests frequently addressed the issue of clerical attire, both mufti and vesture. F. Benedict Valuy, SJ, author of *Directorium Sacerdotale: A Guide for Priests in Their Public and Private Life*, suggested,

> On no account neglect to wear any portion of the ecclesiastical dress. Never appear without the Roman collar, and when you wear the cassock see that it is buttoned throughout. The clerical costume, if it be such as it ought to be, forces the wearer to remember his position, and secures for him the respect of the people. To convince yourself of this, think of two military officers in a place of public resort, one in his uniform, the other in plain clothes; and ask yourself which of the two would receive most marks of honour and consideration, which of the two would be the more observant of the rules and etiquette of the profession of arms. S[aint] Bernard asserts that the inclination, observable in some Priests, to lay aside the glorious livery of the priesthood is "a sign of mental and moral deformity." Even people in the world share this opinion. To dress with too much or too little care is equally blameworthy; the former because it argues a vain and frivolous mind, the latter because it provokes contempt and wounds the lawful sensibilities of your parishioners.[92]

Although guides for priests are prescriptive literature and do not reveal the choices priests made regarding dress, the concerns raised—for instance, of "lay[ing] aside the glorious livery of the priesthood" or dressing with too much finery—suggest such problems existed. A comparison to the military, once again, provided both an identifiable and a masculine model for priests, who, it was hoped, would project respectability and dignity. Finally, the uniform would command authority among the parishioners. Concern for seminarians and their lives immediately after receiving Holy Orders vacillated between dressing for the approval of the non-Catholic onlookers and appearing authoritative to garner obedience and respect from lay Catholics. The two goals were not at odds. On the contrary, the guides left no excuse for neglecting appearance.

RAIMENTS OF THE LORD

The church accepted a certain level of artistic flexibility for vestments; nevertheless it provided specific guidelines for their usage. Regarding a priest's religious garb, Schulze wrote, "For the celebration of the Holy Sacrifice you need proper vestments. Let them be neat and clean. . . . See to it that the vestments are made of the prescribed material. The amice and alb, must be of linen, the chasuble, stole, etc., of some material not inferior to silk. For Sundays and holydays you should have a few more costly vestments. Take care that they be strictly liturgical in regard to both shape and color. Every mission, even the poorest, we believe, should have at least one set (five colors) of sacerdotal vestments. Vestments must be blessed before they are used."[93] While the early missions made do with the vestments available to them—for instance, an itinerant priest likely borrowed the vestments at the chapel he visited or wore the vestments his own church could afford to procure—by the late nineteenth century, the vestmentary expectations had increased, and episcopal oversight of the correct sacramental items and actions associated with the items brought closer scrutiny. The greater number of bishops and decreasing area of dioceses resulted in more episcopal visitations and inspections.[94] Bishop McQuaid of Rochester, New York, explained the new spirit of vigilance he would practice in his diocese by way of a pastoral letter read at every mass in the Diocese of Rochester on 11 May 1884. He wrote,

> Bishops are commanded to visit in person, if possible, all the churches of their diocese once a year, or at least once in three years. . . . Your attention is called to these teachings of the Church, because, owing to the exceptional condition of the Church in these United States in past years, the Episcopal visitations have been well nigh impossible. Dioceses, covering one or more states were too vast to be reached often by bishops; parishes, spreading over several counties, gave the pastor little time to do more than to administer to the spiritual wants of his flock in the simplest form possible. Churches were . . . scantily furnished with the utensils and ornaments needed for worship and the sacraments.[95]

Pleased that the era of "mission living" was coming to an end, McQuaid stated that "these days of small and rude beginnings are rapidly passing away. Dioceses of more contracted limits enable bishops to visit pastors and missions with facility. . . . Our pious people have shown the warmth of their faith by their readiness and generosity in providing whatever could be reasonably asked of them for the adornment of the altar and church."[96] McQuaid's message was for the pastor as well as the people; churches had to be equipped correctly and tastefully. He specified, "No laxity is allowed to creep in, that registers and records are well kept, that vestments and linens are suitable and sufficient, that altars, confessionals and the baptismal font are in order and becoming, and that the church is in a good state of repair and ample for the accommodation of its members."[97] In order to bring the American church closer to Rome, the Vatican expected it to adopt the practices long adhered to in the European countries. The financial responsibility for the material aspects of the church fell to the parishioners, and it was the pastor's job to compel parishioners to make the necessary monetary contributions for those procurements.[98] Ecclesial visitations would reveal whether the pastor was persuasive enough with his congregants to raise sufficient funds for building and adornment, and if the pastor used those funds to comply with the bishop's expectations.

Episcopal visitations not only assessed accurate record keeping and the pastor's spending for the necessary sacramentals and supplies; they also provided an opportunity for the bishop to check other requirements, such as the 1884 mandate that priests wear the Roman collar in public and the long cassock at home. While much of the nineteenth century was characterized by independence for the priests, and Americanist priests held discussions about priests' "rights," that independence was receding in the face of tightening bureaucratic control. Archbishop Corrigan of New York, delighted by Bishop McQuaid's pastoral letter on visitations, referenced the advocates of clerical rights in a letter to McQuaid on 14 May 1884. In his correspondence Corrigan chortled, "I would like very much to see a copy of it in the hands of every Bishop. Our good friends who want Canon Law will have reason to say that they will be treated to it in abundance. The tradition of making Visitations will be started and enforced, and this will do good."[99] In 1883 an anonymous author published a pamphlet titled *The Rights of the Clergy Vindicated, or, A Plea for Canon Law in the United States*, by a Roman Catholic Priest. Likely authored by New York's Father Richard Burtsell, his basic goal was "to promote 'obedience to properly framed laws,' and to end 'submission to caprice and whim, or merely personal standards of propriety.'"[100] In America, priests had shown assertiveness by challenging bishops in their speeches, behavior, and attire, and even in civil courts. Sometimes they took their cases directly to the pope.[101] On the matter of legal cases, the Vatican determined that any use of civil courts by a priest against a bishop "will *de facto* incur suspension *a divinis*."[102] In other words, to attempt to expose a church matter or dispute to the extra-Catholic world would result in a loss of clerical privileges. The bishops' power was more clearly defined, and the bishops' new authority to oversee their dioceses encouraged greater exactness in presentation and the detail of vesture. Proper attire provided priests with an "opportunity" to demonstrate their compliance with both the pastor and the bishop. The ordering of the American church was fully under way, and sartorial submission became a visual sign of that new order.

While vestments had always been significant, displaying a stylistic link to the early church and allowing the visual transformation of the priest for his sacred functions in the mass, they had not always been particularly ornate. The mid-nineteenth century, however, was a turning point in the artistry of the vestments—a period when the church, particularly under the leadership of Pope Pius IX, sought to promote greater devotionalism, tie the devotions to parishes, and identify priests as the mediators of the devotion's spiritual gifts.[103] According to Katherine Haas, "As the temporal power of the pope and bishops declined, they increasingly focused on maintaining spiritual control within the church. The main enemy of the nineteenth century church was no longer a rival monarch, but the omnipresent threat of secularism."[104] Eager to make a strong case against New York's Father Burtsell in a dispute he had with Archbishop Corrigan, an ally of Corrigan's, Monsignor Thomas Preston, wrote to Archbishop Domenico Jacobini in Rome about the threat to the church that was lurking in America. Preston offered that the problem was "a few priests who are really disloyal to the Holy See. They minimized all the declarations of His Holiness. They were opposed to the Infallibility until its definition, and now are disposed to make it as little as possible consistent with a profession of faith. They are opposed to parochial schools. . . . They have spoken in favor of saying Mass in the English language, of doing away with the vestments and ceremonies prescribed by the church, of getting rid of what they call medieval customs and obsolete practices, and of Americanizing the Catholic Church here, and adapting it to our liberal and republican institutions."[105] What Preston described, Rome feared, and greater regulation of and reverence for the ceremonies and traditions of the church as defined by Rome would convey the power of the papacy in America.

Further reinforcing the significance of the priest, the church "promised an ever-increasing number of indulgences and blessings for worshiping in a church-approved and church-controlled fashion."[106] In his 1902 encyclical, *Mirae Caritatis* (On the Holy Eucharist), Pope Leo XIII lamented the religious critics and spiritual disbelief of the age. He instead emphasized the "docility" necessary to receive grace.[107] He went on to explain the mysterious benefits derived by the faithful in the sacrifice of the mass. Among the blessings was access to the power of the saints. Even though a layperson could pray for a saint's intercession, it was through the sacrifice of the mass that communion with the saints became most attainable. All of the arousing, distribution, and acceptance of grace required a correctly vested priest.

Educating the laity about the significance of the vestments and why they should revere them became an important aspect of devotional literature and catechism in the nineteenth century. In *Instructions for First Communicants*, Jacob Schmitt explained, "The priest goes to the altar in the service and in the name of the Supreme Lord; therefore he needs a particular holy dress. . . . He wears, as it were, the uniform of Jesus."[108] Other sources associated vestments with the Passion. One such book asserted, "See the priest at the altar: the chasuble recalls the mantle at the praetorium; the tonsure, the crown of thorns. Nothing is wanting, not even the cross; see it, drawn large upon the chasuble; the celebrant like his Master, carries it on his shoulders."[109] Still other interpretations focused on the virtues and morality represented by the vestments. According to Katherine Haas, "In the most common elaboration of the scheme, the amice represents divine protection, the whiteness of the alb represents purity of life, the cincture represents the restraint of lust, the maniple represents patient suffering, the stole represents immortality, and the chasuble stands for charity and perseverance under the yoke of the Lord."[110] The church took great care to instill in both priests and the laity a deep sense of reverence for the sacerdotal vestments and the priestly role. Additionally, as parishioners gained knowledge of proper vesture, the church enlisted them "as norm enforcers" who, like the bishops, held certain expectations for how their priests would be dressed.[111] Therefore, although greater embellishments and attention to vestments raised the status of the priest, they simultaneously made him more accountable to his congregants as they learned about the rules and significance of priestly attire.

CLERICAL JOURNALS AND GUIDING GARMENTRY

As a more exacting clerical ensemble came together at the end of the nineteenth century, journals designed for clerical audiences also conveyed the importance of priestly attire. Catholic publications such as the *American Ecclesiastical Review*, a conservative publication established in 1889 and edited by Father Herman Heuser, a professor of scripture at St. Charles Seminary in

Philadelphia, and the *Homiletic Monthly and Catechist* (later the *Homiletic and Pastoral Review*), established in 1899 and edited by a New York priest, Father John F. Brady, provided explanations of policies, answers to questions, and essays regarding clerical clothing and character in the late nineteenth century while "discussion" regarding appearance was still ongoing. Although diverse positions on clerical attire and presentation found their way into publication, clerical journals tended to reinforce the standardization of dress and most definitely rubric-determined vestments.

The journal readers would have come across the value of proper clerical dress in subtle ways. For instance, at the beginning of an issue of *Homiletic and Pastoral Review*, a priest could find "Notification of Deprivation of Ecclesiastical Garb."[112] Writers referred to priests being "defrocked" or having the specific clothing that represented the priestly office taken away or the privileges to use the garments revoked. Certain clothing was required to perform the different functions of the priesthood, and the sacred rituals would not be complete without the garments themselves being blessed. The stole, for instance, was required for the distribution of the host, while performing blessings, any time the Eucharist was carried, and at burial rites. Without the stole, the one blessed garment that was often worn both inside and outside the church, the benefits of a blessing would not be conferred.[113] Likewise, without the necessary blessed items, a priest could not perform the sacrifice at mass. In other words, a blessing would be invalid without the appropriate ensemble. Clerical clothing was also associated with services that came with remuneration as well. Catholics paid "collar fees" or "stole fees" to priests who performed specific ceremonies such as marriages, funerals, or baptisms.[114] In essence the clothing bestowed professional privileges and confirmed the legitimacy of the priestly service.

Priests learned about appropriate dress in the Answers to Questions section of the journals. For instance, in a letter to the editors of the *American Ecclesiastical Review* in 1897, a priest asked, "How far may a priest conform to the fashion in dress suited to the convenience of bicycle-riders?" The priest's inquiry was accompanied by an explanation of his observations and understandings on the matter. He wrote, "The 'sweater' and the Roman collar are hardly compatible forms of dress; yet in some dioceses, at least in the Eastern States, it is statute law to wear the Roman collar and a coat reaching to the knees. In view of this fact some priests maintain that if the bishop permits the use of bicycles he implicitly sanctions the use of a suitable dress, and such sanction takes away the obligation of the diocesan law to wear the Roman collar and long coat. 1. Could such a position be defended? 2. Could a bishop

forbid his clergy to use the ordinary bicycle garb worn by the laity, and to retain the Roman collar?" The reply suggested a measure of discomfort that this
question would be posed. The editor corrected the questioner, stating that all
regular priests were obligated to wear the Roman collar, not just those in the
"Eastern States." And although a bishop might "tolerate" bicycles, tolerance
in no way implied that a priest could forgo the distinctive clothing associated
with his office.[115]

The next year, a priest wrote in inquiring if he had wrongly criticized the
woman who was responsible for the church linens for taking the lace border
off one of the parish's albs and replacing it with fancier and more expensive
lace. The inquiring priest's complaint was about what the woman did with
the old border. She used it for curtains and a tidy (perhaps armchair covers)
in what was probably the rectory's parlor. The *American Ecclesiastical Review* took
a decidedly Roman approach in its response and stated that the woman had
been wrong and it was "simply a question of reverence." The editor then included a poem by Father Clarence Walworth, titled "The Priestly Robe," that
he believed would answer any similar questions that might arise in the future.

I.
Touch it lightly, or not at all.
Let it not fall!
Let not a fabric so august
Trail in the dust!
'Tis a costly thing,
Woven by love in suffering.
'Twas Jesus' parting gift to men.
When the Lord rose to heaven again,
His latest breathing fell on it,
And left a sacred spell on it.
A mystery hides within its folds.
Quickened by sacramental breath,
It holds
The power of life and death.
Would you sully it? Would you rend it?
Is there a Christian would not defend it—
A robe so costly and so rare,
So wonderfully rare?
Woe to the hand profane,
Woe to the heart ungracious,

Woe to the tongue unheeding,
Would dare to cast a stain
On a vestment made so precious
By such costly bleeding!

II.
I know this robe and its history,
And what strange virtue goeth forth
From its hem to bless the earth;
And I adore the mystery
That gives it grace,
In Jesus' name, to soothe and heal.
With more than human tenderness
I prize the priestly order;
And, while with reverent knee I kneel,
I do not see beneath the border
Frail feet of clay,
But seek to find, if so I may
By feeling,
Some gracious thread which will convey
To my sore spirit healing.
Vicars of Christ! Deem me not rude,
If nearer than is wont I press me;
But turn and bless me
Amid the kneeling multitude.[116]

The editor contended that it was "a question of reverence." Father Walworth, a convert to Catholicism who became a Redemptorist priest, took the matter of the vestment even further. He elevated the garment to clothing specifically associated with Jesus — "His latest breathing fell on it, / And left a sacred spell on it." Walworth contended that priestly robes held supernatural value. An Answers to Questions entry published in 1933 reiterated the significance of the priest's presentation. A priest wrote inquiring as to whether the Sacred Congregation of Rites had issued any decrees regarding the appropriateness of priests wearing wristwatches when they attended sacred functions or distributed Holy Communion. The writer was concerned that a watch was "apt to be offensive to the eyes of the communicants," because it "savors of the world." Although the Sacred Congregation of Rites had not issued a decree, the editor agreed that the wristwatch could certainly be a problematic distraction. The sight of a clearly mundane object would diminish the solemnity of the priest's actions. The response took into consideration the perspective of the parishioners. In order to maintain the congregants' acceptance, the priest had to communicate transcendence, and the watch could potentially compromise that message.

In 1903, Pius X (1903–14) assumed the papacy. While his predecessor Pope Leo XIII had admonished the United States for its "Americanist" tendencies, Pius X was determined to squelch any behaviors that he perceived threatened the authority of Rome.[117] In his 1907 encyclical, *Pascendi Dominici Gregis* (On the Doctrine of Modernists), he condemned the broad and amorphous teaching of modernism.[118] Many freedoms evaporated in quick measure. While priests had openly debated the topic of priestly formation and seminary reform through the turn of the century, debate was now closed. The Vatican required its *imprimatur* (approval to print) and *nihil obstat* (clearance from a church censor confirming that a publication does not offend the Catholic faith) "on all books touching religious subjects"; rectors removed popular reading material from seminaries; bishops forbade clerical meetings or "congresses" without special permission; seminary administrators mandated that all professors who taught in seminaries take "anti-modernist oaths"; each diocese created a "vigilance committee" to report on errors; and the pope demanded Quinquennial Reports from all provinces outside Europe.[119] This was not a backlash against the American church specifically, but modernism's easy association with Americanism and the Americanist controversy less than a decade before made Rome more demanding, and the American hierarchy more eager to demonstrate their compliance.[120]

The Pius X and post–Pius X years welcomed a visibly Romanized leadership in America, and to project a "Roman aesthetic" the American hierarchy employed extravagant pageantry. Most of the leaders chosen for bishoprics in prestigious dioceses, such as Cardinal William O'Connell of Boston (1907–44), Cardinal Dennis Dougherty of Philadelphia (1918–51), and Cardinal George Mundelein of Chicago (1915–39), received their start with a Roman education, and they imbued their dioceses with a Catholic culture they felt reflected the values and significance of Rome.[121]

William O'Connell, future archbishop of Boston, was a keen observer of clerical appearance and costume. As a student at the North American College in Rome, beyond noting the clothing faux pas of Father Daley and his "enormous emerald buttons," he provided descriptions of the prelates whose appearances he admired. Monsignor Conroy, the bishop of Ardagh in Ireland and the papal legate to Canada, for instance, was "very handsome, very stately, rather portly, and extremely dignified," according to O'Connell's letters. "As he came out . . . the first thing I saw of him was a beautiful foot encased in patent leather pumps with gold buckles. The next was a plump leg in long purple silk stockings, which had got free from his soutane as he reached out for the carriage step. Then lightly out of the door with a single spring appeared a stalwart, noble figure, a fine head and a shapely, handsome, pleasant face with a crown of beautiful silvery hair." [122] Archbishop Gibbons was a "conspicuous figure," and coadjutor of New York, Archbishop Corrigan, was "young, and even boyish." Bishop Patrick Feehan was a "stately figure," while Bishop Ryan of Cincinnati had a "rather pompous and dramatic style." [123] O'Connell and his classmates picked their favorites, and for O'Connell it was his own archbishop of Boston, John Williams. O'Connell described him as having a "majestic walk,—so regal in his manner." O'Connell continued, "Faith and good blood make a regal combination. I cannot take my eyes off him, he fascinates me so. His face is a strange combination of severe dignity and genuine goodness." [124] The descriptions and appraisals O'Connell offered are revealing. Gold buckles on pumps were the courtly style of shoe wear prior to the French Revolution. The pumps harkened to a time when the church had greater status and the dignity of the episcopal office won unquestioning respect. Stockings corresponded to a prelate's position, and sometimes so did his soutane. Bishops, as in the case of the bishop of Ardagh, wore purple silk stockings, the bishop's color. The assignment of color and even material and garment was based on position, a sumptuary designation that announced a person's place in society and the church. The soutane mentioned by O'Connell, and worn publicly, was relatively new, at least by Roman standards. According to writer Maurizio Bettoja, prior to the loss of the Papal States in 1870, it was common for clergy in Italy, even those of high rank, to wear an austere form of court dress when they traveled outside their homes. Knee britches, stockings, pumps with buckles, a knee-length coat, and a hat made up the main features of the ensemble. The *abito corto* (short dress) or *abito d'abate* (priest's dress) distinguished its wearers as clergy due to its simplicity and black cloth. Cassocks and choir cassocks, or cassocks with a fastenable train, were saved for formal and liturgical affairs. Frustrated with his diminished political and territorial status, Pope Pius IX chose to project strength through formalism. Thus he abandoned informal clerical attire in Rome and embraced a state of perpetual ceremony requiring cassocks at all times. [125] When it came time to craft an image for himself, O'Connell adopted one that was also regal and conspicuous. In this way he hoped to convey Catholic triumphalism, Roman orthodoxy, and personal power.

According to historian James M. O'Toole, the future cardinal of Boston, William O'Connell, honed his public image as bishop of Portland, Maine. There O'Connell led the first-ever public procession, in commemoration of Pope Leo XIII's golden jubilee.[126] Once in Boston, he kept up his public image. O'Connell's emphasis on dress was recorded in a less-than-flattering poem penned by a fellow Bostonian, Father Hugh O'Donnell, pastor of St. Anthony's Church in Allston, on the occasion of O'Connell's elevation to cardinal. The poem was titled "History is Made, 1912." O'Donnell's sentiments become readily apparent in his verses:

> The journals produced illustrations
> Of red Hats and garments galore;
> And this most democratic of nations
> Saw princes in print, by the score
>
> The supplement sheets issued photos
> Of churches and palace hotels,
> With His Eminence riding in autos,
> The Prince of America swells
>
> We are told in a way that convinces
> How blue blood now flows in his veins
> How, ranking with royalty's princes
> This prince over governors reigns
>
> In fine, it is hardly surprising
> That people exclaim—quite aghast—
> "For lime light and big advertising,
> Old Barnum is nailed to the mast!"[127]

In Father O'Donnell's view, O'Connell had achieved the royal appearance he was aiming for, but the display was akin to a royal circus and was clearly at odds with the nineteenth-century Americanist position of Catholicism's compatibility with American democracy. O'Connell's aesthetic was "Roman to the core," a trait O'Connell once admired in Archbishop Corrigan of New York.[128] Nevertheless his delivery was thoroughly modern. Newspapers, "supplement sheets" with pictures, and an auto procession assisted O'Connell in projecting his own power as well as that of the Vatican.

At St. John's Seminary O'Connell removed Sulpicians, whom he perceived

Figure 2. Cardinal Dougherty (in front, wearing top hat) and others at the 1926 International Eucharistic Congress, Chicago. Courtesy of the University of Saint Mary of the Lake/Mundelein Seminary.

to be "less Roman" in 1911. He had questionable reading material taken out of the reading room, and he returned the seminarians, who had in the late nineteenth century exercised without cassocks, back to their cassocks for sports.[129] In addition, O'Connell had the "grand promenade" of chaperoned seminarians, lined up in pairs and "in full clerical dress, including biretta and cape," walking around the area near the seminary. Discipline and distinction were on display.[130] Practices common at the seminaries in Rome had found their way to America.

Cardinal Dennis Dougherty shared O'Connell's concern for appearance. All priests in Philadelphia had to wear clerical garb, including the three-flanged (Roman style) biretta whenever they were out.[131] According to writer Charles Morris, "Priests working in the chancery were required to have frock coats and silk top hats, for formal events. (In fact, they bought a few generic sizes and kept them behind a door in case Dougherty ran a drill.)"[132] To be a successful priest in Philadelphia, one had to accept the discipline that was so central to Dougherty's sense of Catholicism, appearance, and organization. In a photo of Cardinal Dougherty and a priest who appears to be traveling with him at the 1926 International Eucharistic Congress celebration in Chicago (see fig. 2), all of the priests are wearing Roman collars and proper priestly attire, but Dougherty and two companions stand out further in their top hats. One priest holds his top hat in his hand.

Priests who did not follow the discipline associated with the post-*Pascendi* church were dealt with swiftly. New York priest Father John Mitty, future bishop of Salt Lake City and archbishop of San Francisco, was recalled from his studies in Munich when the rector of the North American College learned that he had been living independent of a religious house and that he and others had been seen "with turn down collars and red and white neckties."[133] Black, by the early twentieth century, was the only color deemed appropriate for clerical attire.

THE MAN OR THE MESSAGE

The debate over everyday clothes for priests ended with America's missionary status. American priests knew what they could wear and when, and although American priests donned trousers much more often than the priests of Italy, they were nevertheless identifiable as Roman Catholic priests. Daily clerical attire became rationalized, and predictable differences of opinion suggestive of an old/new theology turned up in the United States, under a new guise, after simmering for several decades in Europe. The European Liturgical movement of the nineteenth century embraced the inclusive, early church theology of the Mystical Body of Christ, which identified a role for all members of the church in the liturgy. Originating among the Benedictines at Solesmes, France, in the 1830 and 1840s, it eventually made its way to the United States after the turn of the century. The Liturgical movement generally promoted monastic practices among Catholics. Thus lay Catholics could be part of the Catholic community in a way that the more hierarchical model of bishop, priest, religious, and congregant denied them. The Liturgical movement included practices such as participation in the Liturgy of the Hours; offering vernacular translations of the Latin missal; introducing the Missa recitata (a mass said in Latin, but with prayers recited by the whole congregation); offertory processions that included the laity; shorter dietary fasts; and religious architecture that promoted congregational involvement.[134] In the United States, proponents of the Liturgical movement also emphasized lay participation in the mass, which could ultimately reduce the clerical status so carefully cultivated by the secular hierarchy.

E. A. Roulins, author of *Vestments and Vesture*, a widely circulated book on the church vesture, was a Benedictine monk who attacked priestly garments from a theological perspective. He contended that vestments suffered from royal

Figure 3. Cardinal Bonzano (censing the altar) saying mass in ornate vestments, 1926 International Eucharistic Congress, Chicago. Courtesy of the University of Saint Mary of the Lake/Mundelein Seminary.

and materialist influence and unfortunately emphasized opulence over solemnity. The vestment styles he denounced most vehemently were the board-back and fiddleback chasubles, which derived from the early Renaissance and provided a surface adequate to support heavy ornamentation and privileged a period when church leaders presented in princelike attire.[135] Cut away at the sides with seams on the shoulders, the square-shouldered chasuble resembled decorative armor on the priest's back and chest.[136] In figure 3, Cardinal Bonzano wears an ornately decorated board-back chasuble and a generously laced alb. In antiquity, the chasuble had one seam and draped over the presbyter like a tent or "little house." Roulins opined, "We may say, speaking generally, that vestments of full and generous dimensions are still to be found in the fourteenth and fifteenth centuries, but they do not achieve that high quality of which we have spoken. . . . Simplicity of spirit had given place to complexity, simplicity of taste to a desire for elaboration; and so, under the influence of this secular evolution and simultaneously with it, the antique simplicity of ecclesiastical vesture passed away."[137] He went on to explain,

During the three centuries next after the Gothic period, tailors, embroiderers and manufacturers did worse still. They diminished the length and width of vestments, and on the other hand exaggerated the accidental ornament. We have a riot of elaborate orfreys and crosses, on which are embroidered numerous figures in theatrical postures and with pathetic expressions. Every sort of applique work is used, sometimes not inelegant, often very complicated. Gilt and lace and other finery—these things are used to excess, and ecclesiastical vesture groans under a heavy mass of ugly elaboration. . . . In their worth, or rather in their wretchedness, the chasuble, copes and other vestments of their period go hand in hand with the swaggering costume worn by the exquisites of the Renaissance, or with the elaborate dress of the great lords of the eighteenth century in its monumental affection and pride, or with the lace frills, embroidered waistcoats and rose-tinted coats of the Revolution. And so we come to the end of the eighteenth century. The decadence is complete. The liturgical vestment has ceased to be a vestment and has become an ornament, an ornament in a style either of pompous affectation or of stilted ugliness.[138]

Despite his uncensored criticism, Roulins and other representatives of the Liturgical movement were somewhat careful. "But let us never forget," Roulins added, "that a return to the usages of the ages of faith should be submitted to the guidance and approval of the Church, which has the right and power to legislate even in matters of the least importance." Roulins hinted that the appropriate direction—historically and theologically—was "back to the glories of the Middle Ages, and, better still, past them to that first Christian period when the faithful lived a life of charity in an atmosphere of simplicity and dignity."[139] In his chapter "Materials and Colours," Roulins continued his attack, rejecting both gold fabric and watered silks. The ideal chasuble for Roulins took its model from antiquity and aimed for graceful draping rather than stiff fabrics and complicated compositions and embellishments.[140] Arguably, by drawing inspiration from even further back in time, the priest would appear even more distinct in his conical chasuble, but including the congregation and inviting them to chant in Latin moved the church closer to Martin Luther's concept of a "priesthood of believers" and the Second Vatican Council's concept of the church as the people of God. The ecclesiology did not demote priests, but it did elevate the people. Cardinal Dougherty in his watered silk cappa magna (see fig. 4) demonstrates the regal presentation that Roulins wanted to leave behind.

The ultramontanists prioritized visibility and sought to communicate

Figure 4. Cardinal Dougherty (center) in watered silk cappa magna, 1926 International Eucharistic Congress, Chicago. Courtesy of the University of Saint Mary of the Lake/Mundelein Seminary.

discipline and order for the everyday and elaborate pageantry and hierarchical stratification in ceremonies. The priest was the one man among many people who, they argued, should stand out. The Liturgical movement challenged ornate display and the singularization of the priest in Catholicism. This did not go unnoticed by ultramontanists. In an exchange regarding "Gothic vestments" versus "Roman vestments," one can pick out how the "man over the message" conflict was played out in chasuble style. Important to note is that both Pope Pius IX and Pope Pius XI rejected the use of what they thought at the time were Gothic style vestments. Nevertheless they both could have been simply condemning the designation "Gothic," without a real sense of style differences.[141]

In correspondence with Cardinal Dougherty of Philadelphia, the Reverend Salvator M. Burgio, CM, reported that the cardinals of the Congregation of Rites had resolved the issue of "Gothic vestments" in a way that would please Cardinal Dougherty. Burgio attached a summary of the congregation's decision along with a fellow priest's commentary for Cardinal Dougherty. The report explained,

I need scarcely tell you that the wearing of these vestments and propagating the use of them in spite of the position of the Holy See has taken is the work in considerable part . . . which passes under the name of the liturgical movement. It is one thing to help our people to understand better in as far as it is possible the sacred liturgy in its dogmatic aspects and in its helps to Catholic piety, it is entirely another thing to carry on a propaganda blatantly and boldly in the form of try to do the things which the church has either forbidden or restricted their practice. Yet this is the very thing the liturgical movement does. Take the matter of the Gothic vestments. Read Roulin in the French in his work, "Vetements" etc. or in its English translation. "Vestements and Vesture," and see the labored effort to disparage the decrees of the Holy See to which I have already had occasion to refer.[142]

He added more offenders to the list: the *Liturgical Arts* magazine in 1937, Father Michael Andrew Chapman, the Reverend Harold Gonder, Raymond James, and the Reverend Adrian Fortescue. He lamented that in James's *Origin and Development of Roman Liturgical Vestments* and Fortescue's *Vestments of the Roman Rite* a person can "go cover to cover without reading one word to tell you that the Gothic vestments which they show in the pictures in their books are not the Roman vestment that they profess to be writing." Furthermore, "to hinder the reader from catching the real state of affairs is to avoid the use of the word Gothic and to call the vestments which they strive to propagate ample vestments, as though the real Roman vestments are not ample and very dignified." Cardinal Dougherty wanted to "know the facts," according to Burgio. The "Holy See has twice in recent times condemned the form of vestments known as 'Gothic'"—what more could be said on the topic? Finally, it was these same advocates of Gothic vestments who "have striven to introduce the so-called dialogue mass in spite of the decree of the Congregation of Rites of 1922 showing in the plainest terms that the dialogue mass is not in accord with the mind of the church and can be tolerated by the local ordinaries only within very narrow limits."[143] The ultramontanes had signed on for triumphalism, but almost as soon as they succeeded in finding a sartorial formula to convey it, concern arouse from the monastic side of Catholicism to question it. Nevertheless, for the time being, the abbreviated, often ornate, and most definitely imperial style chasuble prevailed.

■ When America was a new and less welcoming home, the Roman Catholic clergy did not display a set uniform, nor did they doggedly maintain European vestmentary practices. Instead priests, with the support of the church, evaluated their surroundings and made adjustments. They wore various collars, hats, and coats. Some likely wore long cassocks, but they were not required in public, and most clerics wore black for everyday affairs. The "Roman" collar was not a trademark of the Catholic clergy until sometime after 1884. Bishops did not want their priests to face antagonism from their mostly Protestant neighbors, and many Catholic leaders admired American freedom and supported its influence in the lives of the clergy. Nevertheless, the indistinguishableness of priests presented the bishops with challenges. Clerical discipline was inconsistent, the laity challenged clerical authority, and the clergy questioned episcopal prerogatives. In the bishops' desire for accountability and control, sartorial regulation found its major proponents. Gradually, American Catholic leaders regulated clerical attire to promote discipline within the priesthood and establish the clergy as authority figures within the church. Greater uniformity among the clergy communicated priestly allegiance to the institutional church and adherence to its teachings, while rubric-regulated and increasingly ornate vestments elevated the stature of the priests in the eyes of their congregants.

The bishops desired to exercise control over those pastors and priests under their watch, and they were also eager to communicate allegiance to those above them, particularly the pope. Facing off against liberal reforms and secularization, Pope Pius IX and his successors condemned many of the freedoms Americans enjoyed and the modernist sentiments that accompanied them. Out of loyalty and ambition, the ultramontanist bishops maximized clerical visibility, requiring Roman aesthetics and strictly regulated attire for their ranks of clergy. Discipline and pageantry replaced the casual and inconspicuous approach to clerical dress. As the Reverend John Nainfa advised in 1925, "The time is now passed when a good-natured disregard for the formalities of ceremonial was accepted by many as a sign of broad-mindedness and loyal Americanism. Too long have some priests and Prelates seemed to regard a display of accurate ceremonial and etiquette as savoring of 'Old World traditions'; the much misunderstood and misquoted 'Jeffersonian simplicity' belongs to an age that is past, and allusions to it are nowadays permissible only to political orators. Now, as in all ages, the human eye is fond of color, and we have in the ceremonial of the Catholic Church a treasure which is envied by outsiders and has been entrusted to us that we may open it to all and spend it lavishly."[144] Therefore not only the clothing, but even alluding to the years of varied attire was discouraged.

The United States did, however, retain some sartorial distinction, a bit of a compromise. Although cassocks that touched the heel were the common dress of seminarians and priests on church property, trousers and suit coats remained the clerical attire of the priest on the street. Regimented, identifiable, and professional clothing on priests was enough to allow the bishops to gain greater control over their clergy and laity in a century marked by Catholic growth, diversity, and debate. It likewise signaled to the Vatican that America, despite being a land of revolutionary origins and democratic ideals, was home to loyal priests ready and ultimately willing to wear the livery of Rome.

CHAPTER 2

WOMEN RELIGIOUS ON

AMERICAN SOIL

ADAPTATION OR AUTHORITY

IN NINETEENTH-CENTURY

AMERICA

Not long after the bishops decided that priests must don more distinct ecclesial attire and wear Roman collars, sisters too came to the conclusion that
their habited appearance would, for the foreseeable future, be central to their
complex religious identity.[1] The sisters did not initially choose to emphasize their dress because the local clergy or bishops wanted them to be more
noticeable. On the contrary, the clergy in the United States, both conservative
and liberal, seemed to encourage greater flexibility and adaptability regarding
the women's habits.[2] But, the sisters *chose* to fully embrace their distinct and
rapidly antiquating dresses. Considering both societal and church cues, the
sisters recognized that the clergy, with the endorsement of Rome, had staked
their own professional and religious status on a more uniform appearance.
Indeed, the sisters enjoyed a certain amount of "choice" throughout the nineteenth century; but as the century drew to a close, they opted for a full-time
habit, and Rome stepped in to codify this practice soon after.

GENDER, JURIDICAL STATUS, AND RULES

Generalizations about religious sisters are admittedly problematic, especially
in the history of the United States. To begin with, while sharing several simi-
larities with the secular priests of the previous chapter, they are nonetheless
significantly different. The most obvious difference is their sex, but there are
other differences as well. The Catholic Church is and has throughout most of
its history been notably hierarchical. And nuns and sisters, despite having renounced marriage and future reproduction and having committed their lives
to the service of God, did not fully overcome the second- (or third-) place
position of their sex as a result of their commitment.[3] Nuns and sisters occu-

pied a lower status in relation to men but a level of superiority above ordinary Catholic women, at least until the Second Vatican Council in the 1960s. For instance, if we made up a Catholic classification system, all Catholics would be part of the same family, then the sexually mature Catholics could be divided into a "genus" based on a committed celibate or noncelibate lifestyle. The "species" could divide Catholics further. Among celibates there are priests, monastic men (monks), brothers, monastic women (nuns), and sisters. Sisters are also "laity," but their simple vows of poverty, chastity, and obedience and their adoption of common dress, for all intents and purposes, elevate them above women who did not make a similar commitment to a virginal life.[4] Marriage vows did not compare in "value" on the Catholic scale to solemn or simple vows, again, until the 1960s, when the Vatican deemed all commitments and vocations of relatively equal value.

Clerical sources from the nineteenth century, in preparing seminarians and priests for future contact with these pious women, provide a sense of the gendered in-betweenness, or "unwoman" position, nuns and sisters held in Catholic society.[5] In his 1898 reference book, *Directorium Sacerdotale: A Guide for Priests in Their Public and Private Life*, F. Benedict Valuy, SJ, discussed women in his chapter "Rocks and Shoals." Drawing support from the church fathers, Valuy asked, "What is woman? S[aint] Jerome gives the answer: 'She is the gate by which the devil enters, the road that leads to sin: she is what the sting of the scorpion is.'"[6] St. Anastasius the Sinaite offered, "She is the viper clothed with a shining skin, a comfort to the demon, a laboratory of devils, a flaming furnace, a javelin wherewith the heart is pierced, a storm by which houses are overthrown, a guide leading to darkness, a teacher of all evil."[7] St. Bonaventure agreed, adding, "A fair woman tricked out with her finery is a keen and sharp-edged sword in the hands of the devil."[8] In his footnotes Valuy explained that these characterizations of women were not even the worst offered. He referred his readers to scripture, specifically the book of Ecclesiasticus, for an even harsher evaluation of women's nature.[9] While Valuy treated readers to a particularly damning view of women, Father William Stang, author of *Pastoral Theology*, was much less condemning. Stang warned, for instance, that "a dangerous rock which the priest encounters in the stormy sea of the world is the hearing of women's Confessions. The knowledge of this fact and a sense of dread are his best safeguard. . . . He must keep his heart hermetically sealed against human sentiments of affection and avoid every sign of familiarity, though cherishing a holy respect and reverence for the sex of our mothers."[10] Both Valuy and Stang, to varying degrees, concurred that women were a dangerous "other" having the potential to undermine the priest's perfect state by leading him to sin.

While Valuy and Stang did not include nuns or sisters in their portraits of women, the problematic nature of women potentially cast all women, with the exception of Jesus' mother, Mary, in a negative light. Nuns and sisters, however, garnered a position well above ordinary women but clearly below clergy. Valuy directed his readers to "show honour to religious women on all occasions, taking their part against all their enemies. In everything that regards the government of the Community and the interpretation of the Rule, stand aloof. Never try to influence the votes of the Sisterhood during their elections, and never side with subjects against the Mother Superior."[11] Stang warned his seminary readers about disregarding the nuns and sisters. He urged, "Always show a sincere respect for the *consecrated virgins* of the Church. The priest who looks upon them merely as troublesome women, as a necessary evil in the parish, has lost sight of the supernatural in them, and fails in one of his important pastoral duties which obliges him to care first for those who are nearest and dearest to God. . . . Never quarrel with them; never show your displeasure with them. If anything is to be corrected, do it in so quiet and friendly a way as to make them feel your good intentions for their own welfare. Have no preference for any member, but treat them all alike as Sisters."[12] These clerical recommendations illuminate the Catholic perspectives on women religious. The sisters by no means fell into the sinful category in which ordinary women might find themselves—the sisters were not "tricked out with . . . finery," but they were not co-equals with priests either. In describing sisters as the "nearest and dearest to God," Stang portrayed them as childlike. Historian Amy Koehlinger explains that sisters held "interstitial gender" status and argues that "most Catholics (including women religious) considered sisters to be a category unto themselves in the structure of the church, distinct from both laity and clergy and positioned somewhere between them."[13] Although many priests infantilized women religious in nineteenth-century America, the church expected priests to be dutiful, tolerant, and tempered in their dealings with them.[14] Beyond that, equitable treatment to all and distance appeared to be the recommended approach to both nuns and sisters.

Historically, orders, congregations, and institutes came together inspired by the charism of an individual.[15] Women such as Angela Merici, Elizabeth Ann Seton, and Catherine McAuley established followings among the women of their time that eventually became church-sanctioned communities. The groups' good works or apostolates often included teaching, feeding the poor, providing care for orphans, or contemplative pursuits, and they could change based on context; but for each order and congregation an original charism existed.[16] Despite the similarity in the various religious groups' work, there was nevertheless a great variety of orders and congregations.[17] By 1900 the United States was home to almost 50,000 sisters claiming membership in over 100 religious communities.[18] Their origins were scattered over the centuries. The Dominican Nuns of Perpetual Adoration, for instance, began in 1206 under the organization of St. Dominic de Guzman in Prouilhe, France.[19] These women retained the title "nun" and took solemn vows, lived in a cloistered community, and devoted themselves to prayer. The church distinguished nuns from pious sisters based on the nuns' profession of solemn vows, claustration, and life of contemplative devotion. The Sisters of the Third Order of St. Dominic and the Sisters of St. Mary of the Third Order of St. Francis were tertiary groups.[20] These Third Order sisters, although following many of the spiritual exercises of the stem order, were not cloistered women and had permission to be active in society. The thirteenth century also witnessed the organization of women in Europe who wished to live in poverty and work on behalf of society. Their communities became known as Benuinages, and while they adopted a veil, the clothing requirements varied from house to house.[21] The Ursulines, started by Angela Merici in 1535, began as an institute devoted to educating young girls and shifted to a pontifical order obligated to observing cloister while administering their schools. And the Company of the Daughters of Charity, organized by St. Vincent de Paul in 1633, performed charity among the poor of France. Bands of Catholic women established communities throughout Europe and eventually in the United States as well, but their juridical status was an ongoing discussion. For instance, a pontifical order had primary accountability to the pope and secondary accountability to the bishop.[22] A diocesan community had primary accountability to their diocesan bishop. Accountability, however, did not always mean obedience. Arguably the most important layer of leadership for women religious was the mother general of the community. Until 1846, for instance, the Sisters of Charity took a vow of obedience to their order, not to the pope or the bishop.[23]

Despite the variety of orders and their unique charisms, locations, and leaders, each order had a "rule" that set out required behaviors, and all of these rules eventually included approved clothing or a habit. The rule could be and often was written by the women leaders within the congregation, but rules required approval from the Vatican. In his 1298 bull, *Periculoso*, Pope Boniface VIII declared that all women religious were from that point forward "perpetually enclosed within their monasteries."[24] These cloistered women took solemn vows of poverty, chastity, and obedience and donned a veil as a symbol of their chastity and renunciation of the world. Although the veil was not required by the pope until 1889, it was nonetheless closely associated with convent life and was included in the rule of each order.[25]

Following the Council of Trent (1545–63), Pope Pius V issued the bull *Circa Pastoralis*, which established the expectations and procedures for communities of women to gain papal approval: They must live in community; take solemn vows of poverty, chastity, and obedience; and renounce all claims to family property.[26] The church considered these contemplative orders "pontifical." Once again, while many had a female foundress, their recognition and any subsequent permission to change their rule came from the pope.[27] According to historian Silvia Evangelisti, religious habits were required by religious orders; "the habit, as well as the veil and cloak, was a sign of their definitive departure from the world and their inclusion in the spiritual family of the monastic community."[28] An important symbol of virginity, "the habit had to cover the whole body from head to toes, and be made of rough and unrefined fabric of bare colours. Together with the habit, their short hair . . . marked their condition of eternal chastity as brides of Christ."[29] Habits, nevertheless, were not uniform. The requirements and restrictions, such as the rejection of ribbons, did not result in an identical display but simply provided general guidelines on what could and could not be worn. Likewise, contemplative orders were enclosed, so while there were vestmentary requirements, few people ever saw the nuns.

Complicating the understanding of congregations of women religious were bands of active uncloistered women who organized themselves for work in a community, such as Angela Merici's Ursulines. According to historian Mary Ewen, these women "were dependent on local bishops and tacitly tolerated by Rome because of the obvious good which they did."[30] St. Vincent de Paul insisted that his Daughters of Charity were not "religious" (having canonical status) and could not and should not be cloistered. He contended that "no monastery but the houses of the sick, no cell but a hired room, no cloister, but the streets of the city or the wards of hospitals, no enclosure but obedience, no grate but the fear of God, no veil but holy modesty" would be associated with these pious women.[31] The Daughters of Charity, at least initially, wore the dress style that ordinary seventeenth-century French women would have worn, along with a *toquois*, or tight-fitting skullcap, while they went about their work in the hospitals or in their parishes.[32]

Therefore, there were two main lifestyles for Catholic women who devoted their lives to God. The first route was the cloistered life. This required women to take solemn vows and lead a severely restricted existence cut off, for the most part, from the outside world. For their sacrifice, the nuns gained religious or canonical status and were officially recognized by the pope as "religious" women. The second course was an active apostolate. These sisters or groups of pious women took simple vows and functioned as nurses, teachers, and social welfare providers. They did not necessarily wear a habit, nor did they have religious status.[33] In the mid-eighteenth century, Pope Benedict XIV diminished the difference between the two groups of Catholic women. He extended "juridical existence" to those institutes whose members were not cloistered and did not take solemn vows. These active women were still not "nuns," but Benedict XIV expected the women to adhere to most regulations that bound cloistered women.[34] Despite the pope's greater acceptance of these active communities—after all, they offered some of the best public relations the church could ask for—the sisters' lifestyle, by church standards, was still considered inferior to that of the nuns who had renounced the world completely.

ADAPTATION AND ANTI-CATHOLICISM

Similar to early-nineteenth-century Catholic priests, sisters believed that a certain amount of adaptation was necessary if they were to successfully settle in the new United States. The hierarchy concurred. Bishop Rese of Detroit wrote to Rome in 1835, "Every religious order in America must unite the active life to the contemplative; otherwise the Americans would reject them, and we do not have means to support them in any other way."[35] Without a tradition of Catholicism, monasteries, or nuns bringing dowries, the United States presented nuns and sisters with a unique set of challenges. The sisters would have to devise reliable methods of sustaining themselves. Begging was a temporary solution, but sisters found teaching and hospital work monetarily more reliable.

Other bishops agreed with Rese, arguing that flexibility was the key to the sisters' survival. Bishop Rosati believed that the austerity that some orders observed, for instance, was not conducive to life in America. In the case of the Sisters of Loretto, their founder, Belgian priest Father Nerinckx, established severe rules that did not account for frontier conditions. Referring to the Sisters of Loretto in an 1823 letter to Bishop Dubourg, Bishop Rosati of St. Louis commented, "They go barefooted, have no other dresses but what they make themselves, of dyed linen in Summer and of wool in Winter, and they sleep upon a straw tick, spread on the bare floor. Their fare is no more delicate: no coffee, tea, or sugar. It is true pleasure to witness their fervor, which equals that of the strictest communities of Europe in the palmist days of their first establishment."[36] While Rosati praised the band of hardworking Sisters of Loretto, other clerics became concerned, concluding that such extreme deprivation and arduous labor endangered the sisters' lives. Eleven Lorettines perished during the first seven years of a mission in Bethania, North Carolina, due to the austerity and exposure.[37] Bishop Benedict Flaget of Louisville, Kentucky, lamented that "going barefoot, and sleeping with their clothes on and then praying in oratories open to the wind . . . made the sisters prone to contract tuberculosis." Flaget wrote to Bishop Rosati, "In the space of eleven years we have lost twenty-four religious, and not one of them had yet reached the age of thirty years. Besides, of the eighty religious of the same family, that we have in Kentucky, there are at present thirty-eight who have bad health and who are perhaps not yet four years in vows. I learned that in your convent you have five or six whose health is almost ruined. All these deaths and other illnesses so multiplied, do not prove . . . that the rules are too austere?"[38] Flaget, with Rome's endorsement, saw to it that the rule of the Sisters of Loretto changed. Thereafter the rule required behaviors less destructive to the sisters' health.[39]

The sartorial appearance of sisters and nuns also concerned both priests and sisters. In a nativist climate, neither wanted the sisters to become unhealthy or to attract negative attention to the church. Anti-Catholic literature, popular in the mid-nineteenth century, targeted the sisters and their unusual garments. Salacious publications such as *Awful Disclosures of Maria Monk, or, The Hidden Secrets of a Nun's Life in a Convent Exposed* offered a fictional tale of alleged convent debauchery. Less sensational, but nevertheless condemning, the 1845 book *Cecilia*, by Benjamin Barker, depicted sisters as attention seekers. "There are thousands who daily dispense charities of various kinds," Barker wrote, "yet they do not term themselves Sisters of Charity, neither promenade the streets in a garb so antiquated and peculiar as to excite attention, or elicit encomiums on their marvelously holy lives and charitable deeds."[40] Beyond literary attacks, the sisters suffered from physical and verbal assaults. Philadelphians threw mud at School Sisters of Notre Dame, and on another occasion observers "taunted" traveling sisters "for their black clothing during a stage coach ride from Pittsburgh to Milwaukee."[41] Once the sisters reached Milwaukee, crowds threw stones at them, and children drew crosses on the sisters' backs. In Baltimore, people yelled "papist," "cross-back," and "pope-lover" at the sisters.[42] Personal experiences or rumors of harassment made sisters wary of drawing attention, and many communities dispensed with their habit if they traveled away from the convent.[43]

For some orders, the habit had been the focus of harassment either before they came to the United States, within the United States, or both. The French National Assembly banned religious habits in 1790, and the revolutionary government dispersed communities such as the Sisters of St. Joseph and killed other religious at the guillotine.[44] As a result, the Sisters of St. Joseph did not reorganize until 1836 under Mother St. John Fontbonne.[45] Religious women and men in the Kingdom of Piedmont and what would later become the southern area of a unified Italy in 1871, while not experiencing the Reign of Terror that befell French nuns and sisters during the French Revolution, nevertheless lived through political revolutions that targeted religious. In the years leading up to the unification of Italy, political leaders suppressed nuns who did not offer a useful service—the government targeted contemplative orders specifically.[46] And, after the unification of Germany in 1871, during the Kulturkampf, Otto von Bismarck expelled orders of women religious such as the Poor Handmaids of Jesus Christ from schools.[47] Therefore, for many active orders, even if their service to society spared them from being disbanded or expelled, they nevertheless experienced or heard stories of anti-Catholic and more specifically antireligious behavior.

In America, when women religious believed harassment was a possibility, they took off their habits and put on ordinary street clothes. According to historian Mary Ewen, "There seems to have been little questioning, or referring to Rome or to a European motherhouse, before deciding to disregard it. In what concerned the religious habit . . . American social and political conditions compelled sisters to adapt."[48] The Ursulines in New Orleans "advised all who stopped there to don a cap and the heavy veil of widows before proceeding up the Mississippi, so as to avoid being taken for escaped nuns."[49] Other communities made adjustments as well. On the street, the Sisters of St. Joseph "added a black bonnet and cloak . . . to their regular habit," and the School Sisters of Notre Dame in Milwaukee would not even cross the street in their habits. "They found it expedient to curtain off a corner of the classroom for use as a dressing–room, where the sister-teacher could change from secular dress to habit and back again."[50] The Sisters of St. Joseph of Carondolet traveled in "disguise" to avoid harassment as they made their way to St. Louis, Missouri, to start a school for the deaf in the 1830s. Because the sisters arrived late and were indistinguishable from ordinary women of the day, the bishop of St. Louis, Bishop Rosati, "had them demonstrate their ability to communicate in sign language before he was convinced they were indeed his long-awaited nuns."[51] In the 1860s at least one member of the Congregation of St. Joseph in Buffalo also traveled anonymously. Visiting Philadelphia to study education techniques for teaching the deaf, Sister Mary Anne Burke wore "the dress of a widow of the time" instead of her habit.[52] The Mercy Sisters likewise altered their public appearance and "wore the broad-brimmed black straw bonnet, thick crepe veil, and simple cloak that had once been the fashionable walking dress of elderly women and widows."[53] In the 1870s, the Sisters of Mercy in Batavia, New York, continued the practice of traveling out of habit. Due to their spare living conditions, the sisters were sometimes compelled to obtain money from relatives or the motherhouse. In order to do so, however, they had to travel. In these instances, "whoever was appointed for the task, laid aside her religious habit and dressed in secular clothes in order to travel without attracting attention. . . . This custom was . . . known as 'going McCracken.'"[54] Sisters especially adopted a flexible approach to the habit. Old fears and new locations encouraged caution.

Despite their secular disguises, the sisters had limited and undeveloped fashion sense, so their identities were often obvious. While they moved about "McCracken," the Sisters of Mercy in Batavia were known to the train conductor, who would let a sister on to beg for her train fare from the other passengers.[55] The "Sisters of Notre Dame de Namur . . . wore their night robes — loose 'mother hubbards' of violet calico — topped by huge white sunbonnets," while riding to California in 1851. Although the goal was to complete the trek undetected, people were able to identify the women as Catholic nuns everywhere they stopped.[56] And the Kentucky Dominicans were so obvious with their secular costume that they "dropped their practice of wearing secular dress while traveling after two of their number, having aroused suspicion in their outdated clothing, were arrested as spies."[57] The sisters, regardless of order, had taken a vow of poverty. Secular dress presented a formidable obstacle when styles continued to change, and there might only be a small selection of everyday women's clothes available in the convent.

It was not just the nuns and sisters who thought about what to wear; there seemed to be no shortage of clerics willing to offer their opinions on religious women's dress. Bishop Henri wrote to the Racine Dominicans in 1862, "Naturally the Sisters must have permission to walk to the schools. I wish, however, that they would endeavor to keep their white habit concealed as much as possible on the street."[58] Allegedly, the apostolic delegate to Puerto Rico and Cuba, Archbishop Chapelle, weighed in on altering the religious habits of women during the Spanish-American War. A writer, Alice Worthington Winthrop, criticized the sister-nurses for their clothes, claiming,

Figure 5. Mother Theodore Guerin in habit, 1855. Courtesy of the Sisters of Providence Archives, St. Mary-of-the-Woods, Ind.

As a rule, the surgeons condemn the woolen habit of the Sisters. It was unnecessarily heavy and warm in the severe heat to which they were exposed; and modern science teaches that it is most favorable for the growth and retention of disease germs, thus rendering it a menace to the health of nurse and of patient as well. The orders would naturally be unwilling to make changes in the essential character of their habit, endeared to them by their symbolic meaning and by historical associations; but there seems to be no good reason why the material of which they are composed should not be altered—why woolen stuffs should not be replaced by linen and cotton, especially as these may be frequently washed and can be renewed at less cost.[59]

Winthrop cited Apostolic Delegate Chapelle as favoring the modifications.

While disguises met the immediate needs of the sisters, they were eager to get back to their habits when circumstances allowed. Likewise, they began to resent intrusions into their dress choice. The foundress of the Oldenburg Franciscans simply refused when the chaplain "suggested they wear similar secular dress for work and study, and reserve the religious habit for prayer time."[60] The foundress argued that "giving up the religious habit meant relaxing religious discipline."[61] Mother Guerin of the Sisters of Providence of St. Mary-of-the-Woods (see fig. 5) wrote from Indiana to her French superior in

1840, "This holy habit, which we had given up, we resumed at Philadelphia to quit again. But at Vincennes we put it on again never to give it up, I hope. . . . Monseigneur wishes to make one change today, another tomorrow, but we have held firm, and nothing, absolutely nothing, has been changed."[62] In Kentucky, "Bishop Flaget suggested that the Sisters of Christ Nazareth switch the color of their cap from white to black." Mother Catherine Spalding was adamantly opposed. She wrote,

> We attach little importance to the article of dress in itself, yet we think changes so striking as that which you propose in our cap would be hazardous and calculated to arouse public observation, to elicit surmises and occasion of prejudices which may be highly detrimental to Nazareth and perhaps to Religion in Kentucky. Had we worn the black cap for twenty-five years, as we have done the white one, we should feel equally reluctant to [make] so remarkable a change as that of the color; which undoubtedly would subject the community to animadversion and ridicule, and thus might tend to diminish respect and confidence, which St. Vincent de Paul considered as most essential to the success of the Sisters' labor.[63]

Priests tended to see the sisters' habit primarily as a modest dress whose uniformity symbolized community, while sisters' understanding of the habit went much further. Mother Catherine Spalding recognized the far-reaching implications of even a minor change. As the sisters were women on display, one little reform could expose them to accusations of vanity and raise suspicion regarding their public efforts. In addition, assuming that all eyes were upon them, Mother Catherine suggested that the sisters played a role in bringing "Religion" to Kentucky. If they sullied their reputation, Catholicism itself would be threatened. According to Mother Catherine, the visual consistency of the habit protected the reputation of both the sisters and the church and encouraged religious observance. Significantly, Mother Catherine infused the habit with metonymic qualities that necessitated continuity for the health of the faith—certainly a bold interpretation to offer a bishop.

Finally, after decades of concealment, sisters' social contributions became more well known, and critical reactions to their unique costume greatly diminished.[64] During the Civil War, Sisters of Charity and several other religious congregations nursed wounded soldiers, both Union and Confederate. Katherine Coon's examination of the efforts of the Sisters of Charity over the course of the Civil War reveals that "the sisters' religious status and symbolism were critical."[65] She argues that their discipline, charity, and spirituality marked by their actions and symbolized in their habit made them valued contributors to the war effort. Surgeons, military leaders, soldiers, and many Protestant nurses came to admire the sisters' work.[66] Mary Livermore, who had one time refused to staff hospitals with Catholic sisters, withdrew her prejudice and admitted, "If I had ever felt prejudice against these 'Sisters' as nurses, my experience with them during the war would have dissipated it entirely. The world has known no nobler and no more heroic women" than the Catholic sisters.[67] Newspaper accounts of the war praised the sisters as well. A story in the *Cleveland Daily Herald* offered, "[Sisters] have taught [the public] many things. Their life-long sacrifice in the hovels of the poor, and at the bed-sides of the sick, has endowed them with a skill which no other class of persons possessed, and which has given them the deserved reputation of the best nurses in the world."[68] Another news piece appearing in the Newark, Ohio, *Advocate* painted the sisters as an "oasis" shortly after the Battle of Stones River in Tennessee. The combined casualty record was over 23,000, but despite the carnage, the reporter saved a few words of praise for the sisters. "There is a sect called Roman Catholics," the writer described, "—a sect, that in my young days I was taught to look upon as monsters, capable of any crime in the calendar of human frailties, who have hospitals under their own charge, attended by 'Sisters of Charity.' . . . If a soldier is dangerously sick, you will see . . . one of these heaven-born angels, ministering to his every want. With the tender care of a mother or sisters they glide. . . . No one who has the heart of a man can help loving them with a holy, sisterly love."[69] Not only were writers heaping praise on the sisters, but they were identifying their former anti-Catholicism and repenting for it. The sisters' contributions performed in an identifiable costume made them that much more knowable.

Along with a change of heart among critics came an acceptance of the sisters' peculiar dress. The Sisters of Charity in Emmitsburg wore the winged cornette of the French Daughters of Charity. "One man described the coronet [cornette] as 'a white bonnet in the shape of a scoop shovel . . . the ugliest piece of furniture I ever saw."[70] Nevertheless, others saw the winged sisters as reassuring, and Ambrose Kennedy portrayed the sisters' cornette as "familiar." He remarked admiringly, "Their black and white robes harmonized picturesquely with the military surroundings."[71] A former patient even tried to buy a sister a new cornette, since the one she had was bloodied. The millinery shop, however, did not supply the unique headcovering.[72] Therefore, as habited sisters in the United States demonstrated their professionalism, bravery, and kindness, they began to win acceptance for their most obvious distinction, the habit. The antiquated dress became a public relations tool distinguishing the sisters as charitable women who did not give in to convenience, fashion, and even the whims of their bishops.

Beyond staffing the Civil War infirmaries and hospitals, sisters contributed to the public school system as well. And in this case too, Americans who were initially uneasy about sisters in peculiar garments appeared to adopt a more accepting attitude when they recognized the significance of the sisters' work. In states such as New York, "compromise plans" were common. Catholic pastors and school boards established compromise plans in towns such as Poughkeepsie, Watervliet, Corning, Lima, Ogdensburg, Plattsburg, and Allegany. One could also find them in other areas of the country, such as Milwaukee, Wisconsin; Gallitzin, Pennsylvania; and Stillwater and Faribault, Minnesota. According to the Reverend Edward M. Connors, "John Jay, a militant opponent of the Catholic Church, in 1889 cited instances in Connecticut . . . Georgia, and New Jersey, where Catholics had made similar arrangements with school authorities."[73] Finally, while not a compromise plan per se, the federal government paid sisters to teach Native American children in states such as Oregon, North and South Dakota, and Oklahoma.[74] The Sisters of St. Francis of Penance and Christian Charity taught Native American children at the Holy Rosary Mission in South Dakota, which was at times funded by the U.S. government. In figure 6, either the photographer or the sisters chose props to convey the sisters' goals of teaching the students academics, religion, and industry.

New York State in particular sustained several compromises: the Sisters of St. Francis in Allegany from 1864 to 1906, the Grey Nuns of the Cross in Plattsburg from 1869 to 1906, the Sisters of Mercy (Batavia) in Corning from 1867 to 1898, the Sisters of St. Joseph (Rochester) in Lima from 1875 to 1903, and the Sisters of Charity in Poughkeepsie from 1873 to 1898. The arrangements usually involved the Catholic pastor leasing one or more school buildings to the local trustees of the board of education for a nominal fee. In exchange, the school board agreed to hire religious sisters with the necessary teaching qualifications. Often, to determine qualifications, sisters sat for written and sometimes oral examinations.[75] The board controlled the curriculum, and it would frequently select the textbooks for the classes.[76] Likewise, the arrangements commonly stipulated that during school hours sisters would refrain from giving religious instruction and that all religious items,

Figure 6. Sisters of St. Francis of Penance and Christian Charity, 1885–95. Courtesy of the Department of Special Collections and University Archives, Marquette University Libraries.

such as statues, pictures, or crucifixes, would be removed from the classrooms. The sisters could, however, recite prayers and hold catechism classes outside regular school hours.[77] School boards, pastors, and families put aside sectarian differences in order to find a solution to the expense and demand for schools. The most frequently cited and most well-known compromise plan was the one established in Poughkeepsie, New York, just sixty miles north of New York City in the Hudson River Valley. The school arrangement became known as the "Poughkeepsie Plan."

The historical record reveals that the compromise plans generally worked well. They utilized a reliable workforce in the form of sister-teachers; Catholic sisters were single women who in many cases wanted to teach and needed to earn a living.[78] Allowing Catholic children to attend public schools provided financial relief for Catholic pastors and families who otherwise would have had to shoulder the financial burden of building and maintaining separate Catholic schools. And compromise plans allowed for cooperative use of school buildings. All of the arrangements demonstrated just how adaptable Catholics could be in the American milieu.

Despite these quiet successes, the school compromise form of adaptation was not universally popular. Prelates had become increasingly concerned about the negative characterizations of Catholics found in public school texts and the use of the King James Bible in public school classrooms. In 1829 the bishops felt it was enough to require that parishes offer religious education for their young congregants to at least guarantee that the Catholic children would be inculcated with Catholic religious teaching. By 1852, however, the bishops' concerns about Catholic children and the educational opportunities in America had grown more serious. The First Plenary Council of that same year recommended that all parishes establish elementary schools. Furthermore, the council concluded that the bishops should "begin these schools whenever possible in their dioceses, since Catholic boys and girls are in grave danger in educational institutions which are not directed by [Catholic] religious motives."[79] To offset the expense of maintaining separate schools, a few bishops, such as Bishop John Hughes of New York, sought public funds to support Catholic education. "Catholic tax dollars" could be allocated for Catholic education, he proposed. Sectarian government allowances for Catholic education did not garner much support among non-Catholics, however. After the Tammany political machine voted to provide the Diocese of New York with $1.4 million to educate Catholic children in 1875, an alarm sounded in the nation's capital. Critics saw collusion between the political machine and the pope's minion in America. James Blaine, an opponent of government money for Catholic schools, sponsored legislation which would require that "no money raised by taxation in any State for the support of public schools . . . shall ever be under the control of any religious sect, or denomination," thereby denying the distribution of government money for sectarian education.[80] Despite the bill's defeat, thirty-seven states adopted similarly worded legislation into their state constitutions, thus denying schools taxes for sectarian education.[81] Therefore, local successes aside, neither the church nor the majority of the states encouraged compromise in the case of education.

A storm began to brew on the topic of Catholics and education in the last few decades of the nineteenth century, and sisters and their distinctive dress found themselves at the center of the controversy. Within Catholic circles, there was disagreement regarding the benefits of compromise plans specifically and the larger issue of Catholics accommodating American society and values more generally. The promoters of compromise plans tended to be Americanists. Father James Nilan, whose name is most closely associated with the Poughkeepsie Plan, certainly was. There was significant variety among so-called Americanists, but most of these priests endorsed a form of Catholicism that reflected the uniquely democratic character of the United States. As he appears in figure 7, Father Nilan does not give a distinctly clerical impression, despite being the pastor of a Catholic parish. In fact, the shadow that dark-

ens his neck is a rather unusual beard. Facial hair was uncommon for Catholic prelates and at times apparently regulated, but Father Nilan seems to have worked around the expectation of a clean shave by maintaining a "neck only" beard.[82] The fact that he is not wearing a Roman collar is less noteworthy, since the bishops did not require the collar until 1884 and this photograph was likely taken before that date, as Nilan took over the pastorate of St. Peter's Parish, Poughkeepsie, in 1877. Men such as Father Patrick McSweeny, who first initiated the compromise plan in Poughkeepsie; Father Richard Burtsell, the canon lawyer who defended clerical rights and disagreed with the bishops' aim of controlling clerical appearance; and Father Edward McGlynn, an active supporter of Henry George's campaign for mayor of New York City and an independent-minded priest, were all included among the ranks of the Americanists.

After the vicar general of the New York Archdiocese gave a lecture at Cooper Institute in which he "criticized public schools for outlawing religious instruction and recommended state support for Catholics schools," McGlynn, for instance, gave an interview to the *New York Sun* contradicting "his superior's statements."[83] McGlynn declared the public schools the "pride and glory of the Americas." He went on to suggest that in the common school system, "an infidel, a Jew or a Mohammedan would have the same rights as a Catholic."[84] He even suggested a constitutional amendment "to guard against the union of Church and State and to protect liberty of conscience."[85] The position McGlynn adopted on schools was not exceptional, but his willingness to vocalize it was. Other Americanists, of varying degrees, included Father John Keane, rector of the Catholic University; Archbishop John Ireland of Minnesota; and Cardinal Gibbons of Baltimore.[86]

Outspoken opponents of Americanism were Bernard McQuaid, bishop of Rochester, New York, and Michael Corrigan, archbishop of the Diocese of New York, who promoted strict hierarchical order, parochial school education, and ultramontanism, or complete devotion to Rome. Writing on the subject of educational injustices aimed at Catholics, McQuaid opined, "When in large cities such as New York and Rochester, a third of the children turn from the open door of the public school, on conscientious grounds, and seek schooling in other buildings, put up and paid for by citizens the least able to open their slim purses to a second taxgathering, it becomes a duty to proclaim the existing system a failure and a cruel wrong."[87] Public schools could not offer religion, and Catholics could not send their children to schools that were "godless"; therefore they ideally wanted their tax dollars directed to Catholic education. Support for compromise plans came in at a distant second. Bishop McQuaid complained that the school-sharing arrangements ultimately "weakened and deadened the Catholicity of our school rooms," but he tolerated them as long as the habit-draped sisters instructed.[88] Distinctive clothing was clearly the preference of the opponents of Americanism. A teacher in uniform linked the sisters to the church and projected at the very least a minimal form of religious education.

While neither Americanists nor ultramontanists addressed the role of women in their disputations on education, implicit in both of their arrangements was an understanding that sisters would do what they were told where they were told. If there were to be more compromise plans, then sisters would be agreeable. However, if a diocese was determined to have separate Catholic schools, then the sisters would teach in them. Within the restrictive context in which they lived, the sisters found the ultramontanists offering more than the Americanists, and so they embraced the habit. The habit gave sisters a rank or identifiable position, however insignificant, in the church leadership. Likewise, even though it was diametrically opposed to its purpose of rendering the sisters unnoticeable, the habit set the sisters off as extraordinary. To wear mundane clothes while teaching would have left the sisters appearing ordinary. In a patriarchal church and society, aligning with everyday women would reduce the sisters' access to authority and power. Finally, it was the sisters' experience with Americanists and these priests' lack of regard for the sisters' unique role that helped move the sisters toward ending their long century of vestmentary adaptation.

Readers can gain a sense of Americanists' perspectives on Catholic sisters through the personal writings of the priests. In his diary, Father Richard Burtsell, a friend of Father James Nilan, lamented what he perceived as the haughtiness and "convent piety" of the sisters.[89] He viewed them as overly concerned with appearances and sadly unconcerned about American principles and Catholic theology.[90] He included men in his critique as well. While Burtsell had once revered the Jesuits, by 1866 he found them "wishing to fossilize us with the habits of the middle age. . . . The superiors are Frenchmen of very cramped minds, who denounce our institutions as they would denounce the revolution of 1793."[91] The Jesuits were not alone among Catholics who anathematized the French Revolution and all subsequent liberal revolutions—the popes did as well. Burtsell also recorded his friend Nilan's views on the problems with religious orders. Nilan argued that the "Catholic religion is like the human race, adaptable to every climate and form of government whilst the sects [religious orders] are like the brute creature, only fit for a limited number of climates and forms of government."[92] Burtsell did not want the American Catholic Church associated with the political and sartorial antimodernism he saw exalted by some religious orders.

Other possible objections Burtsell likely had for the nuns and sisters would have been the class consciousness of certain orders and the strictness with which the sisters upheld their rule. According to historian Mary Ewen, the sisters were upper class or lower class, depending on where their members came from in society and which class they tended to serve. Ewen explained that "the Visitandines (Visitation nuns), Ursulines, Religious of the Sacred Heart, and the Irish Mercy Sisters were connected in the popular and ecclesiastical minds with the upper classes, while the Sisters of Charity were thought to be daughters of the 'people,' as were the members of most other indigenous American communities."[93] Upper-class orders made distinctions among themselves. Choir nuns chanted or recited the Divine Office in Latin throughout the day and night.[94] Financial means and education likewise distinguished the choir nuns. Girls and women who joined elite orders but did not have education or wealth could become lay sisters. Their role was to cook, clean, and mend. Beyond their different roles, choir and lay nuns were also distinguished by dress. A longer veil and wimple, a different-colored headdress, a gold rather than a silver ring, and a train on the choir robe were among the unique features often found in the wardrobe of a choir nun.[95]

While class distinction may have contributed to Father Burtsell's impression that sisters were "haughty," Archbishop Ireland believed the class consciousness of the nuns to be downright un-American. Referring to the Josephite Order, who made the lay sisters eat separately from the choir nuns and allowed the choir nuns to treat the lay sisters as servants, Ireland remarked, "It's a wonder they don't burn the house down."[96] Although the secular male clergy employed a rigid hierarchy, it appears they expected the women of the church to readily adjust and maintain a more democratic and classless community.

Choir and lay distinctions, however, were part of the sisters' and nuns' heritage, especially for those that originated in prerevolutionary France and other parts of Europe. And although "family" was still the operative metaphor, the ranking within a religious order was not unlike the military model of the priests. In the ecclesial ranks the garment or at the very least the trim of the garment indicated a cleric's place in the church's hierarchy: White is reserved for the pope, while cardinals wear scarlet red, a bishop is assigned amaranth red or purple, and priests appear in black.[97] The Ursulines' constitution spelled out their differences in attire: "The Lay Sisters shall dress as the Choir Sisters. Their Choir robe shall be without a train, their veil shorter than those of the Choir Religious. For work these can be replaced by veils of white cotton. Their wimples shall be shorter; their rings of silver. Their Communion Veils shall only reach about ten centimetres below the waist."[98] Employing a hierarchy implied that someone or some women had greater status than others. In the eyes of the Americanists, such ranking appeared both undemocratic and unnecessary. After all, in the end, religious or lay, they were all women (or at least not men), and that specification was nonnegotiable. Likewise, assuming a place of power was inappropriate, as "power" in the church and society was also reserved for men.

Americanists did not have to concern themselves too much with the sisters initially, but eventually the distinctive religious garb and the battle over religion in schools or whether tax proceeds could go to denominational schools became part of the same conversation. In New York, the first case of concern about the sisters' habits arose in the town of Suspension Bridge, Niagara County. There St. Raphael's, which had been in operation for twenty years, placed itself under the control of the local school board. The school board retained three of St. Raphael's teachers, who were all Sisters of St. Joseph. Responding to a local appeal, both the superintendent of common schools and the state superintendent, Andrew S. Draper, found the arrangement an unfair discrimination in favor of Catholics.[99] Draper concluded, "The wearing of an unusual garb worn exclusively by members of one religious sect, and for the purpose of indicating membership in that sect, by the teachers in a public school, constitutes a sectarian influence which ought not to be persisted in. . . . The conclusion is irresistible that these things may constitute a much stronger or sectarian influence over the minds of children than the repetition of the Lord's Prayer or the reading of Scriptures at the opening of schools."[100] Unless the sisters were willing to conform to a secular dress style and forgo their habits, as they had in the past, the compromise plans seemed doomed.

In 1894, New York held its constitutional convention and determined that schools controlled by a specific religious denomination were not eligible for financial appropriations. At the time of the decision, St. Bridget's Parish and the West Troy Board of Education were marking their fifth year with a compromise plan. The state convention ruling, however, invited challenges to the arrangement. At the beginning of the next school year, a group in West Troy "protested against the action of the Board of Education in leasing St. Bridget's School. Their challenge took the form of an appeal to the State Superintendent of Public Instruction."[101] The citizens' complaint explained "that six of the fifteen teachers appointed to teach in the First Ward School of West Troy were known as 'sisters' who resided in St. Joseph's convent; that these sisters all dress in a garb peculiar to their religious order and are usually addressed in school, not by their family name, but by the names assumed by them as members of the religious order to which they belong, prefixed by the term 'sisters.'"[102] Furthermore, the protesters claimed that the sisters had not passed the teacher exam and that since the sisters were under the control of a particular denomination, the "denominational doctrines or tenets are taught therein."[103] From past experience, it appeared that the sisters had the power to address all of the citizens' concerns. But times had changed in America and in Rome, and while Catholicism was still embattled, the sisters, even in their peculiar garb, had won a level of acceptance among Americans.

Armed with the legislation from the state convention, the state superintendent of schools, Charles R. Skinner, issued a decision in 1896 and found the West Troy school district maintaining a sectarian school in violation of the state constitution.[104] Galvanized by both the state constitution and Skinner's decision, citizens critical of the compromise plans had the power to undo them. The Poughkeepsie Plan came under fire in 1898 and was found illegal. The school board gave the sisters an ultimatum: Lay aside your habits or leave the schools.

Historians of the school controversy years tend to see the end of the compromise plans as a foregone conclusion once citizens complained about the sisters' habits and states issued "garment laws." Nevertheless, as I have established, sisters in various orders outfitted themselves in secular clothing on many occasions throughout the nineteenth century. The compromise plans did indeed begin to disappear, but why at this time? Why did the sisters lose their willingness to make more adjustments? The Poughkeepsie Plan offers a few insights into why sisters came to invest the habit with such importance.

In 1898, Father James Nilan, pastor of St. Peter's Church in Poughkeepsie, made a last desperate attempt to maintain the compromise plan that he and his predecessor, Father Patrick McSweeny, had negotiated with the local school board. For twenty-five years, the Sisters of Charity, New York, had taught in public schools no. 11 and no. 12. The sisters wore their habits when they taught, but according to the arrangement determined by Father Nilan and the school board, they did not make reference to religion, display any religious statues or images, or provide Catholic instruction. Despite the success of the arrangement, State Superintendent Skinner determined that the plan could not continue as long as the sisters wore their habits. The appearance of the distinctive costume constituted a form of "visual education," which Skinner concluded violated the separation of church and state.

Alarmed by Skinner's decision, Father Nilan wrote to the mother superior, "It appears to me judicious to ask for a dispensation for the four sisters teaching in our schools to be allowed to wear another dress during school hours. If you have no objection I would petition Rome with the most Reverend Archbishop's approval. It can do no harm and may lead in several ways, to much good."[105] The response of the mother superior is lost to historians, but inferences can be drawn from the tone of Father Nilan's next letter to her: "Your love of God's children and your desire to explain his Kingdom by teaching of His doctrine," he declared, "must surely be deeper than your veneration for a particular style of dress. So, I hold you in higher esteem and think better of your Christian spirit, than what the tenor of your note conveys." He went on to point out, "You will kindly bear in mind the alacrity with which your pious predecessor submitted to the opinion of the representative of the Holy See, when she assented to the retention of Sister Alphonse in one of our schools although no sister was employed in the building. The strong objection to her continuance in the school gave way immediately to the wish of the apostolic delegate. The incident is only a clear evidence of the submissive spirit, which I am sure lives today in you as lively as it did then in her humble heart. As to the inhibition not to mention the matter anymore, this will be determined by my sense of duty. This you will heartily commend."[106] He concluded his letter reiterating his position on the habit: "I judge the work done by the sisters of more value than mere outward symbolism and I know that their personal influence is more in molding the character of the pupils, is far more effective than a style of dress. Human favor or sentiment must ever yield, in the Catholic mind, to the essential work of God."[107] As an Americanist who likely questioned the wisdom of regulated clothing, Nilan was not sympathetic to the sisters.[108] The sisters' rigidity regarding clothing appeared illogical, considering the good that might result from laying the habit aside. Therefore the sisters were working against Americanist ideals. As a man and a pastor, Nilan also expected a "submissive spirit" regarding his plans.

Despite Father Nilan's admonishment, the mother superior had the final word. The day after she received Father Nilan's second letter, she convened a council meeting. The council members were a select group of professed sisters with whom the mother superior discussed issues and made decisions.[109] The sisters voted on whether they would "lay aside their religious habit during school hours," as Father Nilan had suggested. The council, with the endorsement of Archbishop Corrigan, unanimously voted against Nilan's proposal. The archbishop was well known for his anti-Americanist opinions, and therefore the mother superior retained a valuable and strategic ally in Corrigan. The Poughkeepsie Plan ended shortly thereafter.

This brief exchange illuminates a significant cast of characters as well as a critical historical period regarding the importance of religious habits in the lives of Catholic sisters in the United States. For Catholic nuns and sisters, religious habits could and did represent marriage to Christ, in some cases emulation of the foundress and spiritual mother, and commitment to a community of sisters. The habit did not, however, signal their allegiance to earthly men or clergy. For the most part, sisters controlled their lives and convents. Nevertheless, they were still part of a patriarchal family with a "father" who was ideally distant but still corporeal. Archbishop Corrigan, if the sisters' arrangements were unchallenged, would not have been needed. However, when a pastor attempted to assert authority over a motherhouse and influence the outfitting of the sisters, the mother superior called on the archbishop to assume the role of the patriarch and reinforce the decision she and her council had already made. The archbishop was certainly higher than the pastor in the bureaucratic hierarchy.

As Nilan pointed out to the sisters, he would "petition Rome with the . . . Archbishop's approval" because, as he saw it, "it can do no harm and may lead in several ways, to much good."[110] The habit, to Nilan, had historic and symbolic significance, but in the end it was not "sacred." And even if it had become arguably more sacred as the difference between nuns and sisters became less distinct, in the American milieu the habit was a potential obstacle to the successful promotion of Catholicism in a mission territory.

The rule and habit, while standardized, were changeable, as Nilan knew. Beyond the Sisters of Charity, whose decision to retain their habit during the school day was chronicled in their archive, evidence reveals that the other religious orders involved in compromise plans could also have complied with orders to teach without wearing religious habits. Histories of the orders of women religious who participated in the compromise plans reveal several episodes of sisters in secular dress. The stories of sisters wearing secular dress for travel, begging, or receiving an education from the 1830s through the turn of the century suggest that during the years of the school compromise plans, a practice of wearing secular dress for encounters "in the world" was common across religious communities and could have been established. The Mercy Sisters of Omaha "wore what their rule book described as a 'cottage bonnet of fine twilled woolen stuff or straw with a veil of thick silk gauze or crepe tied on it according to their season'" when they traveled. These Mercies kept the traveling disguise until 1907.[111] Nevertheless, multiple forces propelled sisters toward a habit-bound identity. For a variety of reasons, some shared by priests, and others uniquely experienced by religious sisters, the women tenaciously embraced the habit, with the Vatican's recognition close behind.[112] And because sisters *chose* the habit, it became the primary symbol of religious life for women for almost three-quarters of a century.

HABITS, HISTORY, AND HIERARCHY

Each religious order has its own heritage. There was a foundress who was inspired by a charism or offering to society, a male sponsor among the clergy who encouraged the foundress and provided spiritual direction, and a rule that was determined to be the nuns' or sisters' "right—and obligation" and which assisted the sisters in keeping their vows.[113]

The habits of sisters were varied. The Company of St. Ursula, founded by Angela Merici in 1535, for instance, began without a habit; there were "no requirements of public vows, enclosure, common life, unique apostolate," or a "uniform dress."[114] However, the habit came with the Tridentine reforms. In 1612, the Paris community of Ursulines became monastic, "adopted the Rule of St. Augustine, pronounced solemn vows, and were bound by the strict rules of papal enclosure."[115] Other communities of Ursulines then followed the lead of the Paris community. The dress regulations were based on the Rule of St. Augustine. The constitution instructed sisters to

Keep your clothes in common, in care of one or two Sisters, or as many as may be necessary to keep them clean and from bother. As your food is given out to you all from one and the same place, so let it be with your clothing. As far as possible you will not concern yourselves with the choice of what you are to wear according to the different seasons, whether one receives the garments she had before or those worn by another. . . . If disputes and murmurs arise among you on this subject . . . judge thereby how greatly you lack the interior clothing of holiness in your hearts, since you dispute on the subject of clothing for the body. . . . Your progress may be measured, therefore, by the preference you give to what is in common over your personal advantage, so that with regard to all things of passing utility, charity, which never passes away, may be pre-eminent. . . . Your clothes will be washed either by yourselves or by others, as the Superior thinks best, so that excessive seeking of cleanliness many not cause you to contract any interior stain.[116]

Focus on clothing invited sin, as did undue emphasis on cleanliness. Even cleaning the clothes could promote "interior stain" or sin. Clothing, therefore, could be a path to either holiness or wickedness, depending on the motivations of the wearer. The monastic model, which inspired virtually all women's habits, perhaps with the exception of the Sisters of Charity, likewise inspired symbolism and interpretation. The orderliness of the exterior ideally conveyed the perfection of the inward state. The community's near-universal use of black symbolized death in the world, while uniformity reflected a rejection of individualism. The church told the sisters that only their divine spouse should be able to distinguish among them.

Among the orders that taught in public schools in the nineteenth century, the Sisters of St. Joseph wore what French widows wore in the middle of the seventeenth century. Women religious or nuns were cloistered and "respectable" women who only went out in public with chaperones. A widow, however, had more freedom, and therefore adopting the widow's dress enabled the sisters to perform works of mercy in public without reproach. The sisters wore a black habit. On their head they wore a white cornette draped with a black veil. A white band covered their forehead, and a cincture belted their waist. Accompanying their dress, a crucifix hung around their neck and lay on their chest. A rosary hung from their cincture.[117] In the seventeenth century, the Sisters of St. Joseph would not have been distinct, nor would they have been encouraged to be. Mary Catherine McAuley, founder of the Sisters of Mercy in Dublin, Ireland, in 1834, started out wearing a simple black dress with her "sisters."[118] However, compelled to obtain canonical status, Mc-Auley eventually took on the seventeenth-century habit style, adding a coif or linen cap to cover the head, hair, and ears; a guimpe or broad and long collar to cover the chest; and a black leather belt from which she hung her rosary.[119]

The Sisters of Charity, founded by a convert, Elizabeth Ann Seton, in 1809, were able to adopt a more "modern" habit. Mother Seton considered modeling her order after the French Daughters of Charity, an order that wore a blue dress and a high white cornette with winglike folds pointing out from either side of the sister's head. Nevertheless, she concluded that religious life had to adapt to the American environment.[120] Therefore she chose the "widow's weeds" of early-nineteenth-century Italian society, with a simple black dress, cape, and bonnet, and a white collar and a rosary. The Sisters of Charity remained less distinctive until the late nineteenth century, when women's fashions became more diversified and shirtwaists or blouses and skirts became a common feature of women's apparel.

Once the storms of revolution in Europe and nativism in America began to settle, the sisters looked forward to returning to their own rule or perhaps a less altered one. And they likewise looked forward to some semblance of family order within their communities. Nevertheless, pressure to keep adapting continued. When a woman chose religious life, she also chose to commit to modesty in a unique way. Her appearance was not intended to draw attention. The compromise plans, when they came under fire, challenged one of the primary goals of the habit, in that the dress, and therefore the woman's body in it, became the center of the controversy.

In Watervliet, New York, when the members of the school board came to the convent of the Sisters of St. Joseph of Carondolet to tell the women that they would have to dispense with the habit or the teaching position, the sisters whom the news would affect did not allow the visitors to serve them the decision. The board members had to leave the news with a sister portress. A portress was a designated position among the sisters in the convent—she was the keeper of the door. So concerned were sisters about visitors violating enclosure or semi-enclosure, or simply perceived impropriety, few women were entrusted with the position. According to the Ursuline constitution, the prioress would "choose from amongst the Community one or more sensible and prudent Religious, confirmed in their vocation."[121] By not receiving the visitors, the sisters were reminding the school board members that the vicissitudes of the board or the state superintendent of education did not alter the propriety to which women religious subscribed.[122] The sisters were not ordinary citizens who received male visitors in the evening—they had retreated from the world. In the eyes of the sisters, their garment choice should have removed their bodies as a primary form of social identification elevating them beyond their sex, but the courts were insisting that their choice to wear a habit had done just the opposite: Habits supplied a kind of "visual instruction" of their own and promoted a distinct visibility.

The "body" as a focus of attention had come up in another way as well with the compromise plan. According to historian Louis Zuccarello, in 1884 the Poughkeepsie, New York, board of education decided that all teachers had to take a hygiene exam. The mother superior of the Sisters of Charity refused on behalf of the order. Once again, the compromise plans challenged convent standards of modesty. According to Zuccarello, Father Nilan, pastor of St. Peter's, "frantically wrote to his archbishop asking him to tell the Mother Superior to tell the nuns to take the test so that they wouldn't ruin the relationship."[123] Therefore, in Poughkeepsie, compromise plans challenged the sisters' view of modesty on two fronts. The debate put their bodies and clothes in the headlines, and the teaching requirements mandated academic attention to the body. If St. Augustine deemed focus on cleanliness an occasion for sin, talking about hygiene certainly seemed equally problematic.

Another reason to reject compromise plans had to do with jurisdiction and politics. Who had authority over the sisters? It was always the mother superior, often the bishop, and then still, the pastor. The compromise plans added another layer of authority: school boards. The 1873 school board minutes regarding the Poughkeepsie Plan clearly stated, "The teachers for these schools to be selected, employed, paid and subject to dismissal by the Board in the same manner as the other teachers in its employ; the teachers and pupils at all times during the school hours to be subject to the control and authority of the Board and its rules and regulations; the schools to be open for the attendance of pupils and visitations by members of the Board the same as the other public schools."[124] In public schools, school boards had the right to unscheduled classroom inspections. When the compromise plan ended in Corning, New York, the Sisters of Mercy were relieved to put the fear of unannounced inspections to rest. According to historian Robert F. McNamara, "There was no great regret in the parish at the passing of the Corning Plan. It had worked many inconveniences and hardships. However well they cooperated with the agreement, the sisters never quite got over the nervous fear that some Board member might suddenly drop in to see if they were perhaps teaching catechism at a forbidden hour."[125] An unexpected visit from the pastor could happen at parish schools as well, but what seemed like "religious education" to a non-Catholic school board member and to a person who had undergone religious formation and lived in religious community would likely be very different.

In addition to causing concern over unannounced inspections from the board, compromise plans put the sisters' credentials up for scrutiny. In some cases, sisters had to sit for both written and oral examinations for their positions. This was not the case in Catholic schools. Membership alone in the religious order responsible for education in the parish had been credential enough for teaching in the nineteenth century. Teaching materials, too, might vary between the Catholic schools and the public schools, and as the school board reserved the right to choose the books used in the curriculum, the sisters might have to utilize unfamiliar books.

Therefore the arrangements were not simple for the sisters. The school boards watched them and directed them. All the while the pastors continued to expect sisters to teach catechism, but outside the typical school hours. In order to meet the requirements of both the school board and the pastor in Corning, New York, the Sisters of Mercy had to keep the 1898 First Communion and Confirmation class "long after school" to cover the necessary material. According to the parish history, it "was hard on both the teachers and the pupils. . . . Father Bustin . . . was not long in arriving at the conclusion that such annoyances were too big a price to pay for public support."[126] In addition to all of these inconveniences, the school boards now wanted the sisters to put aside the habit.

As the aforementioned example of the hygiene test attests, mothers superior and clergy did not always see eye to eye. Their disagreement extended to the habit. When the garments of the Sisters of Charity threatened to undo the compromise plan in Poughkeepsie, Father Nilan wrote directly to the mother superior. In his letter he requested that the teaching sisters be allowed to wear alternate apparel. Mothers superior saw themselves as "mothers," who protected and disciplined, and "superiors," who made the decisions. Compromise plans had the potential to unsettle and excite young sisters and undermine maternal authority. In a letter to the mother superior of the Sisters of Charity, Mother Mary Rose, one sister working under the compromise plan in Poughkeepsie wrote,

On Sunday night, Fr. Nilan told us, he made the Board the proposition that they rent No. 12 for $1000.00 a yr. He told us we were to have No. 11. This morning, Monday, the Board were to meet and consider the matter. Fr. Nilan called this noon and told us he sent a note to the members of the Board this morning reminding them that in the contract the agreement was to give thirty days notice and desired them to keep the contract. The Board have accepted the thirty-days and all the teachers are back in the school and we four have neither No. 11 or 12. We thought it better to send you word at once. It was quite a shock to us for Fr. Nilan left us so hopeful this morning that we were to be back in—schools tomorrow. Now Mother we await your directions. You may picture our little home tonight.

Your obedient and affectionate child, Sr. M. Bertille[127]

The letter from Sr. Bertille reveals how sisters looked toward their mother superior for direction. It also suggests why any mother superior might have felt the need to protect the sisters under her care. If the mother superior did not assert herself, others, including clerics and even the sisters under her, might challenge her more often.

In 1900 Pope Leo XIII delivered his papal bull, *Conditae a Christo*, in which he provided a provision for congregations to become pontifical, a status above diocesan. The *Normae* published a year later set out the regulations that accompanied this new status. It addressed the cloistral issue and deemed that the sisters desiring pontifical status would be semicloistered by having a section of the convent open only to them, travel with a companion when outside the convent (a requirement of nuns), and refrain from work that involved "care of babies, the nursing of maternity cases, management of clerical seminaries, and staffing in co-educational schools."[128] Obvious distinctions between sisters and nuns were now significantly less clear. The Vatican's priorities, however, were recognizable: To be associated with the pontiff, a woman's behavior had to be impeccable. Her actions required curtailment, and she had to be kept out of situations where she could be tainted.

Habits were a form of vestmentary claustration. Monastic orders invested nuns with their habits in solemn ceremonies, and this investment provided the nun with her clothes for life. The clothing was a central feature of her identity—it transformed her. When the Vatican blurred the lines between religious nuns and lay sisters, the habit then became more significant to the lay sister than ever before. The charism that was originally the most important feature of the sisters' lives was replaced by codified behavior and dress, rendering the habit the most important symbol of religious life, both active and contemplative, in twentieth-century America.[129]

In the case of the compromise plan and the Sisters of Charity, even though they were not an upper-class order, they made a strategic decision in the wake of the Americanist/ultramontane debate—they chose sides. The party that viewed them with the most sympathy and seemed to represent their interests most closely was the ultramontanes or anti-Americanists. Fathers Nilan and Burtsell and Bishop Ireland wanted the sisters to accommodate the American milieu more and more, diminish distinctive features of their identity, and all the while remain submissive to clergy and school boards, whatever the case might be. If sisters were to gain the status of "religious" like the nuns who took solemn vows, drawing closer to Rome seemed more logical. Mary Ewen pointed out that "the religious habit assumed a greater importance after 1889, when 'Ecclesia Catholicia' made it one of the essential characteristics of bona fide religious. The element of public witness in the religious habit was emphasized."[130] I would add to Ewen's observation that based on the value Rome placed on the habit, women religious saw only promise in their decision to embrace the unique dress. What little power was available to women in the church appeared to be more attainable if one was dressed in uniform.

■ If there were any question about the ordering of vowed Catholics, the 1917 Code of Canon Law clarified the hierarchical sequence that applied to men as well as women. The law reads, "Religious precede laity; clerical religious [precede] other regulars[, who precede] religious Congregations; Congregations of pontifical rite [precede] Congregations of diocesan right. . . . But a secular cleric precedes both laity and religious outside of their churches and even in their churches if it concerns lay religious."[131] Ordering was fundamental to the Catholic view of the world, and sisters were under no illusion about where they ranked despite their charity and devotion. The sisters' position as active bands of pious women, institutes, or congregations was certainly near the bottom of the chain. The hierarchy of the church holds theological significance in that one's closeness to God was at this time directly related to one's position on the hierarchical scale. Kissing a bishop's ring, for instance, is a sign of sincere respect for the value of the man who knows God's will so intimately. Sisters, too, wanted to gain status or value in the eyes of the church, which were in their minds also the eyes of God. Of course, ecclesial recognition also had temporal benefits. Habited sisters, quite against St. Augustine's designs, would certainly attract attention to their ministry as teachers, hospital workers, and social welfare workers. The uniform, as Michel Foucault points out, is a sign distinguishable from far away; it shows disciplined allegiance. And while sociologists tend to emphasize uniforms as an element of institutional or bureaucratic control, within the gender strictures of the Catholic Church, agency is nevertheless apparent. The sisters *chose* the habit and ritualized conformity. It was a logical decision informed by theological motives and context. Sisters improved their religious value; gave visual evidence of their allegiance to the Vatican, thus inspiring trust in their activities; and enjoyed the protection vestmentary claustration offered them as working women. As vowed Catholics who wore a unique garb that was identifiable in public, they seemed to convey religiosity above the male clergy. Therefore, there was much more to gain in wearing the habit than in laying it aside on public occasions. At the beginning of the twentieth century, in the context of living in what the Vatican condemned as a modernist era, adherence to the habit ultimately freed the sisters to perform their ministry. Intentionally or not, it also shifted America's attention to women religious. The sisters were the most prominently outfitted representatives of the church and outnumbered priests approximately three to one. Although priests and bishops stood out at the pulpit and cut a professional appearance on the street, it was the sisters who came to dominate the visual landscape, at least until they outfitted their pupils.

CHAPTER 3

SCHOOL UNIFORMS

A NEW LOOK FOR

CATHOLIC GIRLS

A reader self-identified as "No Catholic" wrote to the *Boston Recorder* in 1837 responding to a published charge leveled at Catholics in Boston. The accuser contended that the Catholics were more focused on educating wealthy Protestants than poor children of their own religion. The critic stated, "We hope they will furnish the means and appropriate a building in connection with this establishment, for giving a useful education to the numerous poor children of the Irish in Broad Street and other parts of the city. Whilst they are offering to educate the children of rich Protestants, we should be pleased to see their benevolence exercised towards their own poor, who are perishing in a state of ignorance." Responding to this condemnation, No Catholic then offered a correction by way of a question. "Now, Sir, I want to ask, if you are not aware that an establishment for poor children from Broad St. and other parts of the city has been in existence some time, and that they not only instruct gratuitously, but clothe them?"[1]

Beyond the nativist tension brewing in Boston, the aforementioned complaint identified two Catholic educational models frequently employed in the nineteenth century: the tuition-supported select school and the asylum for those in need of charity. Other types of Catholic educational institutions such as the industrial boarding school, free day school, and local parish school were also available throughout the nineteenth century and into the twentieth century. In each of these schools, the clothing of the students, while a concern, was nevertheless an unremarkable aspect of the Catholic school culture. The schools most likely to have a dress code or "uniform" were the asylums or industrial schools.[2] Less than a century later, however, uniform attire became an almost standard dress for Catholic girls. This chapter explores the forces that raised uniforms to a "Catholic look" for girls in the late nineteenth and early twentieth centuries and how various Catholics participated in infusing this new mobile symbol with meaning.

Tuition-supported select schools, also referred to as convent schools or academies, were among the first Catholic schools. Both Catholic and Protestant families sent their daughters to these private boarding academies, which offered girls full academic and finishing school–style curriculums. Students studied academic subjects such as arithmetic, algebra, history, rhetoric, and languages as well as ornamental writing, needlework, and embroidery.[3] In New Orleans, the Ursulines established a convent school "for the daughters of the wealthy" in 1727.[4] The Visitandines opened their own academy in Washington, D.C., in 1799. And two decades later, in 1819, the Ursulines arrived in Boston and taught catechism classes in their convent next to the cathedral. In 1826 Bishop Benedict Fenwick relocated the Ursulines to a spacious hilltop compound in Charlestown, Massachusetts, nicknamed Mount Benedict after Bishop Fenwick.[5] The institution cited in the *Boston Recorder*, which complained about Catholics educating "rich Protestants" of Boston, was likely the convent school run by the Ursulines.[6]

The other unnamed institution referred to by No Catholic was probably St. Vincent's Asylum for Girls. Three Daughters of Charity from Emmitsburg, Maryland, came to Boston at the bequest of Bishop Fenwick in 1832 and established an asylum for "innocent" girls from ages four to sixteen who came from poor but respectable families.[7] At St. Vincent's, these immigrant daughters received a "useful education" and learned basic school subjects such as arithmetic, reading, and writing, along with catechism, sewing, and housekeeping.[8] Most girls were not adopted. Instead, young residents usually stayed in the asylum until they reached age fourteen, at which time they were old enough to take jobs in factories or in the homes of other women, where they worked at domestic tasks.[9]

Similar to asylums, but identified specifically as "schools," were the boarding schools Catholic religious orders worked in and established for Native American children after the passage of the Dawes Severalty Act in 1887.[10] The new policy established by the act ended the practice of making treaties with Native Americans and instead encouraged them to accept 160 acres of land and U.S. citizenship. Although "garment laws" restricted sisters in public school by the end of the century, Catholic sisters, brothers, and priests were able to continue working in asylums and Indian schools with government support. Religious women and men taught in North and South Dakota, Oregon, New Mexico, and Arizona, among other states. The church believed that Native American children, similar to poor orphaned or semi-orphaned children of immigrants, required a Catholic education to encourage a disciplined, productive, and religiously observant future.[11] A Catholic missionary contended, "The same reasons that render . . . asylums necessary for white Catholic children apply with greater force among the savage and semicivilized Indian Tribes."[12] Catholic missionaries aimed to "civilize" and convert Native American children while primarily training them for manual and industrial work.

Another type of Catholic school was the free school. A free Catholic day school, administered by religious sisters or nuns, provided a Catholic education for local children of ordinary or little means. The tuition revenue from the same religious order's adjacent private Catholic academy supplied the financial resources necessary for the sisters to carry out their "good works" on behalf of working-class children. Both the Ursuline Academy in New Orleans and the Visitation Academy in Washington, D.C., provided day schools, free of charge, on the grounds of their convents.[13] In Chicago, the Sisters of Mercy likewise offered a free school alongside their select school, St. Francis Xavier Academy for Females. In some cases, what historians may have identified as "free" might have been a lower-cost day school. At the Sacred Heart Academy in Rochester, New York, local families could pay $40.00 a year to send a daughter to the day school instead of $159.00 a year for the basic curriculum along with room, board, and fees.[14] The Sisters of St. Dominic opened another convent boarding school in Rochester in 1857, but their day school was free.[15]

Finally, as the nineteenth century wore on, Catholic children could increasingly attend parish schools. These schools eventually came to be known as parochial schools. When possible, a pastor established a parochial school for children of the parish. Depending on the location, the school might be free, charge a modest tuition, or have the tuition costs offset by collections at Sunday mass. To staff these parish-based institutions, pastors hired lay teachers or invited orders of women religious to teach classes. Procuring an order of sisters or nuns resulted in a significant savings for pastors and ultimately for the families who sent their children to the parish school. Figure 8 shows the students, teachers, and pastor of St. Charles Borromeo School in Bucks County, Pennsylvania, in 1920. Neither the girls nor the boys are in uniforms at this time. However, the pastor appears to be wearing his cassock and biretta, while the two teachers, Sisters of the Immaculate Heart of Mary, are dressed in habit, as one could expect.

Figure 8. Pastor, teachers, and students, St. Charles Borromeo School, 1920. Courtesy of the Philadelphia Archdiocesan Historical Research Center, Philadelphia, Pa.

SCHOOL RULES AND APPEARANCE

Regulating clothing, when it was the policy, occurred for different reasons in the multi-model Catholic school system. Whether a student was rich or poor, Catholics considered human depravity a universal affliction and dress as an area where this weakness could be, and often was, displayed.[16] Young girls, the church believed, were particularly prone to the sins of vanity and immodesty, and girls who gave in to these vices frequently led men to sin. As St. Bonaventure warned his priests, "A fair woman tricked out with her finery is a keen and sharp-edged sword in the hands of the devil."[17] Ultimately, the church believed that wealthy girls had to resist "finery" and ostentation, while girls with little money had to be provided with the resources and moral instruction to present themselves neatly and respectably.[18]

The select schools, often hidden away on remote campuses, initially sought to accommodate the modest fashion standards of wealthy society while encouraging the students to adopt an appreciation for simplicity.[19] School administrators required dress codes to curtail obvious displays of wealth and to limit wardrobe costs. Also, the sisters, acting in loco parentis, often took inspiration from their own habit guidelines. Thus several schools went so far as to require dark-colored dresses.[20] Students at St. Ambrose Female Academy, conducted by the Sisters of Loretto, for instance, wore dresses of "any color" during the weekdays, but on "Sundays and festivals [the] winter uniform consist[ed] of a black dress, with a black cape and apron. The summer uniform consisted of a black dress, with a white cape and apron."[21] The Sinsinawa Dominicans required modest dark clothes, as did the Sisters of Charity of the Blessed Virgin Mary and the Sisters of Mercy.[22] Girls at Mount St. Joseph on-the-Wissahickon in Philadelphia (hereafter identified as Mount St. Joseph) had a more specific uniform beginning in 1864, but one that kept within women's fashion standards. Girls wore a "mazarine blue" dress in the winter and a "pink delaine, with white body" and basque jacket, or button-up bodice jacket that covered the hips, in the summer.[23]

Administrators of private schools walked a careful line regarding recruitment, class, and clothing. On one hand, Catholics promoted austerity and charity as avenues to holiness. Nuns and sisters exemplified those attributes in their habits. On the other hand, without wealthy Catholics and at least a few well-to-do Protestants, institutions that served the faithful could not be sustained. Moderate "dress codes" therefore attended to the potentially conflicting forces bearing on school administrators. Dress rules distanced students from their parents' authority, which was the first step in cultivating vocations that came with a lifetime of poverty, chastity, and obedience. But making only minimal restrictions on students' attire was not too great a departure from parental standards and therefore did not likely concern tuition-paying parents and potential benefactors. Parents, it should be noted, while often eager to offer their daughters a Catholic education under the auspices of pious women, were frequently uninterested in their daughters following the women into religious life. Simplicity and dark hues allowed administrators to stir a potential vocation, keep order, and retain the support of the parents.

Directors of nineteenth-century Catholic asylums and Native American boarding schools did not have wealthy or influential parents to accommodate or contend with. The asylum, in the church's estimation, offered training and protection that the families or the government, in the case of Native Americans, decided families could not supply themselves. The schools in these cases outfitted students with clothing or with a type of uniform. St. Vincent's Asylum for Girls in Boston gave out clothing to residents and adopted a specific uniform by 1890.[24] The school-issued clothing also provided a form of social and moral direction, in other words, guidance the "benevolent" element in society presumed poor children lacked. Therefore, the clothing that the sisters required sought to elevate as well as educate students from less respectable backgrounds about good hygiene, presentable dress, and modesty. It also confirmed the students' institutional identity—as some students ran away from the asylums.[25]

For Native American children, both girls and boys, the first step in the "civilization process" was to remove traditional clothes and jewelry.[26] A Catholic missionary described the scene when Indian girls arrived at the school for the first time. "Thick and fast fell the tears," wrote an observer, "when the Indian clothing was removed, when the tight bangles were taken from their scarred arms, and their ear-rings were laid aside, and these little red skins had to taste the poison of soap and the water, and their hair to feel the torturing comb!"[27] The expectation of a European-American style of dress was not specifically Catholic, however. While Catholic Indian schools required European-American dress and sometimes a uniform, the Carlisle Indian School and other Indian schools did as well. According to archaeologist Owen Lindauer, "Wearing school clothing and marching uniforms was mandatory."[28] The superintendent of the Phoenix Indian School, Harwood Hall, wrote to the commissioner of Indian Affairs in 1887 regarding the benefits of discipline and uniformity. He explained, "Too much praise cannot be given to the merits of military organization, drill and routine in connection with the discipline of the school; every good end is obtained thereby. It teaches patriotism, obedience, courage, courtesy, promptness, and consistency; besides, in my opinion, it outranks any other plan or system in producing and developing every good moral, mental, and physical quality of the pupil."[29] Both Catholics and Protestants agreed that educators had to discipline the bodies of Native American children through regulation in order to cultivate a European-American standard of civilization.

The fact that some attempt at uniform clothing came into asylums and industrial schools first reflects the role society assigned to these socially marginalized resident students. The first "ready-to-wear" clothing, almost a prerequisite for standardizing clothes, predated the introduction of the sewing machine in 1846.[30] As early as the mid-1830s, clothiers in cities such as Boston, Philadelphia, and New York sold men's premade clothing that could be adjusted for size. A man, clothing manufacturers concluded, needed to purchase clothing because he might not have a mother, wife, or sister to make his clothes for him, nor, again as a man, would he be inclined to deliberate over details of style, since his goal was simply to perform his job. Men's ready-made clothing, therefore, was thought of as functional—it enabled men to move about in public and perform their work or serve in the military while allowing them to be presentable and manly.[31]

Although Catholic asylums and industrial boarding schools did not view their female charges as "men" they did consider "true femininity" to be a privilege of race and class. Girls of color and "uncivilized" girls, although not masculine, were decidedly not feminine either. Their race combined with their lack of education and finances distinguished them from white middle-class children. Manual labor, industrial and asylum school administrators believed, "civilized" children and prepared them for their future employment.[32] Catholic or nonsectarian industrial schools did not attempt to educate the destitute of the city or the children of the reservations in order to provide them with social and economic mobility or to recast the working girls into ladies. Instead, school administrators determined that the function of these students, whether girls or boys, would be to work, and they considered it the schools' responsibility to equip the social and economic outcasts with skills that would allow them to be manually productive.[33] At the Phoenix Indian School, for example, the boys "worked and learned in a variety of shops on campus (wagon making, shoemaking, harness making, blacksmithing, carpentry, tin working, cabinetmaking), as well as in the school's bakery and on its farm, which included a dairy. The education of girls focused on training for the household (sewing, cooking, and laundry). The girls worked with the school's doctor in providing care in the campus hospital and later in a tuberculosis sanitarium a mile from campus. For girls, caring for one's doll (baby) was a way of introducing socialization skills and gender-role identification at an early age."[34] Administrators at Catholic asylum and industrial schools sought to convert children to or reinforce their Catholicism, but race and class, they believed, undermined the children's eligibility for marrying well and becoming the patriarch or matron of a middle-class home. Thus Catholic asylums and industrial schools sought to equip girls and boys for gender- and class-specific labor, but labor nonetheless. Again, the belief in racial and economic determinism was not unique to Catholics. On the contrary, it was perhaps even more pronounced outside the church, but Catholics also assisted in reproducing class and race oppression by dressing the children in "functional clothing."

Photographs and descriptions of free and parochial schools are silent on the issue of uniforms in the mid-nineteenth century. This makes sense in that pastors and sisters would have likely been careful about adding any financial burden to the parents. Children wore the clothing their parents provided them with for attending school. Parochial schools, in fact, frequently failed to remain open in the mid-nineteenth century due to the inability of native and immigrant Catholics to fund both the church and the school. Likewise, creating any distinguishing mark of Catholicism on children who walked to and from school could ignite nativist antagonism, as seen with women religious. In the case of St. Rose, a Catholic girls' school in British Guiana, the Ursulines required a dress code for day students, but it was not a dress beyond what young girls typically wore. Day girls dressed in "plain washing calicos, black stockings and soft house shoes," which the children changed into upon their arrival at school. The unique aspect of the students' clothing was perhaps the apron to protect their dresses.[35] Girls donned black aprons over their dresses during the day. And "for special occasions, such as the Exhibition and Prize-Giving, white dresses, stockings and shoes had to be worn."[36] Aprons and house shoes could be left at school, and white dresses for graduations, once again, were not unique to Catholics. Therefore regarding uniforms, free and parochial schools did not initially promote them. And caution due to stigma and cost rendered them an illogical choice for a socioeconomically diverse church.

For Americans, clothing was a symbol employed to express their independence and freedom. Those in America who did not or were assumed not to be able to enjoy the full freedoms the country offered were more likely to be found in prescribed dress—a European carryover when clothing classified a person.[37] For instance, sumptuary laws in colonial America restricted residents whose estates were valued under £200 from wearing any gold or silver lace, gold or silver buttons, and silk hoods or scarves.[38] Slaves and indentured servants often had their clothes given to them. And one of the injustices suffered by the girls of Lowell Mills was the enforcement of a dress code that many Yankee daughters saw as a violation of their liberty.[39] Therefore, although uniforms existed, society primarily reserved them for institutionalized children, or classified children, who did not always have access to presentable clothing and whom both Catholics and non-Catholics alike considered to need charity, discipline, and often a "useful education."

NEW INFLUENCES INSIDE AND OUTSIDE THE CHURCH

The late nineteenth century witnessed a confluence of forces that promoted the adoption of distinct uniforms primarily for girls in select Catholic schools. The decision of the Catholic hierarchy to require Catholic education; increasing opportunities for women in work, education, and athletics; and advancements in technology related to clothing production all contributed to a new interest in uniform dress. Although not a consistent requirement across all Catholic schools for girls, uniforms nevertheless became a noticeable and a distinctly Catholic wardrobe item.

As we saw in Chapter 2, compromise plans could be found throughout the United States in the nineteenth century, but the Catholic Church did not always seek to make a compromise. Church leaders participated in contentious exchanges about how public education should accommodate Catholic children. Archbishop Francis Kenrick in Philadelphia and Bishop John Hughes in New York, most notably, attempted to remove Protestant features from the public education curriculum. Kenrick, for instance, wanted to relieve Catholic children of the requirement of reading passages of the King James Bible in school. In the case of New York, Hughes sought nothing less than to see all religious education omitted from the public schools and then let Catholics use their taxes to educate their own children. Other Catholic educational spokespersons such as Bishop Ireland in Minnesota and Father James Nilan of Poughkeepsie encouraged compromise plans with Catholic sisters teaching in public schools. Ultimately, many in the church, including the sisters, decided that the fight was not worth the trouble.[40] The American hierarchy determined that the church and its teachings would be more consistently sustained, and the faith of Catholic children protected, through the creation of a separate school system. Ideally, these schools would be staffed by women religious, who, through their prayerful and disciplined demeanor, would instill order and Catholic values in the lives of their pupils.[41]

The bishops to varying degrees had encouraged pastors to create Catholic schools and parishioners to send their children to these schools throughout the nineteenth century, but in 1884 the recommendation to educate one's child in a Catholic school became a mandate. At the same Plenary Council that ruled on Roman collars for priests, the bishops determined that each pastor must provide a Catholic school (or Catholic education, in the case of compromise plans) in his parish. Once the school was available, the church obligated parents to send their children to it.[42] In Detroit, "Bishop Borgess . . . as early as 1877 instructed his priests to deny the sacraments to parents who sent their children to public school" unless they had a good reason, such as the Catholic school was prohibitively far or a non-Catholic father was adamantly opposed to Catholic schools.[43] The perceived quality of education, while perhaps a concern for the parents, was not considered a legitimate reason by the pastors. Religious education automatically assumed a place of superiority in selecting a school. The Third Plenary Council's decision was a partial step toward reforming the heretofore piecemeal approach to Catholic education and its oversight. Rather than depending on the willingness and dedication of women religious to open a private school or free school, bishops expected pastors to take responsibility for providing an education for the children of their parish. Nuns and sisters, therefore, would not lead the development of these new parochial schools. Instead they would be the "employees" of the pastors and bishops. Decentralization had characterized primary Catholic school education until the late nineteenth century, but as the bishops moved to make education the required work of pastors, it began to become more rationally organized and systematic.

With the bishops demanding parochial schools, Catholics across the country experienced new expectations and dilemmas on the education front. Pastors had to find orders of women religious to staff their schools, and sisters who may have had some choice in what activity or good works they devoted themselves to were more often than not called on to teach in parochial schools. Parents who had sent their girls to select schools to board or to free and/or day schools for Catholic education would have other options. And teaching orders that relied on the revenue from select schools would face competition and possibly depleted ranks for staffing their own schools.[44] In the case of a parish school in Canandaigua, New York, Bishop Timon of Rochester decided that the Sisters of Carondolet should close their select and free schools so that the parish school would thrive.[45] Significantly, in the decade after the Third Plenary Council, the number of Catholic girls' academies in the United States dropped from 624 in 1890 to 609 in 1895.[46] The growing emphasis on parochial schools presented the sisters with a dilemma. If the sisters chose to maintain their academies, which were a wise economic investment, they would have to market their select schools differently from the parochial. Uniforms on the girls would ultimately assist women religious in cultivating "convent school" exclusivity.

While the hierarchy and the sisters were revising their approach to Catholic education, other educational changes were under way beyond the church. One of the most striking was the growing availability of college education for women. A few equal-opportunity colleges such as Oberlin, Antioch, and the Universities of Iowa, Wisconsin, and Michigan were educating women in coeducational environments before 1871. However, colleges exclusively for women took their lead from Vassar College, which opened its doors in 1861. Within three decades the educational options for young women increased rapidly: Smith and Wellesley (1875); Harvard Annex, later Radcliffe (1879); Bryn Mawr (1885); Mount Holyoke (1888); and Barnard (1889) joined Vassar in providing a college education exclusively for women.[47] The growth in higher education for women indicated society's willingness to provide the necessary academic credentials women needed to enter professions or to continue on to graduate school. Access to higher education was a significant step in expanding women's rights and opportunities in the years before women won the vote.

The emancipation offered to women through college education raised the issue of a new dress to mark the occasion. Before colleges opened their doors to young women, girls received an education "suitable to their sex," and one that "embraced every useful and ornamental branch" appropriate for young women.[48] Colleges such as Vassar, however, offered young women a curriculum equivalent to the studies found at any men's college. The founder of Vassar, beer baron Matthew Vassar, considered signaling the liberation of the scholar with a distinguishing costume. He consulted Sarah Josepha Hale, editor of *Godey's Lady's Book* and a champion of higher education for women, on the issue. In response to Vassar's query about a possible "student costume, perhaps along the lines of the Bloomer suit, which would blur distinctions between richer and poorer students," Hale objected.[49] Taking a view decidedly different from that of the Catholic educators, she discouraged the distinct outfit, asking, "Would it be well to enforce an equality of personal appearance . . . which cannot be found in life?"[50] She also thought the outfit was ridiculous and might harm the college's reputation. Instead, she counseled mere simplicity. Since the education was no longer ornamental and sex specific, so too the female students should not become ocular curiosities.[51]

Vassar College did, however, adopt uniforms in the 1860s for physical education, another curricular innovation that promoted women's equality and improved health through exercise.[52] From physical education the young women eventually moved on to organized sports. Women's basketball became a popular game in the 1890s, as were bicycling, baseball, and rowing. Students at Wellesley even designed their own uniforms for their many crew teams. Uniforms for athletic teams, while still feminine, nevertheless incorporated masculine sensibilities such as team camaraderie, discipline, and greater functionality.[53]

As opportunities for young women expanded in education, Catholics had to determine whether these educational opportunities would attract Catholic girls and, if so, if they would help or harm Catholic girls' religious identity. There was little disagreement that schools like Vassar were the wrong colleges for Catholic girls. A priest wrote to the editors of *American Ecclesiastical Review* in 1900 asking how he should handle Catholic parents who send their daughters to Vassar College. He lamented, "Apart from the evils or dangers of association with companions of every shade of belief or unbelief, and of every variety of moral sensitiveness, there exists for these girls the obligation of regular participation in non-Catholic forms of divine worship."[54] The priest wondered whether "their presence as pupils in such an institution constitute[d] grave peril at least for the faith of these young people." Should he, the priest asked, deny the parents the sacraments until they relent?[55] The respondent recommended "prudent" leadership instead. Once again, pastors had to be careful about offending wealthy Catholic families and potential contributors to the church. Likewise, in cases where parents chose not to send their children to the Catholic school, Pope Leo XIII forbade the punishment of withholding sacraments. Nevertheless, some clergy found this method both acceptable and effective.[56] The church had to keep in mind that Catholic girls and their families might be looking for the same opportunities in higher education, athletics, and eventually jobs that their upper-class non-Catholic peers enjoyed.

Considering internal pressure coming from the rapid expansion of parochial schools for the earlier school years and the lure of non-Catholic college education on the latter end of the educational spectrum, Catholic academies found a schooling niche with the help of their uniforms. Convent school girls, simply by appearance, could distinguish themselves from other everyday Catholics. Likewise, these privileged girls could enjoy an expanded curriculum as well and therefore enjoy at least a portion of the "liberation of the scholar" while making a vestmentary statement about their "qualified brand" of female emancipation. Girls in uniform would share the opportunities of education and ideally direct their heightened intellect toward proper womanly pursuits as well as defense of the Catholic faith.[57] Eventually these preexisting academies would provide the "unobtrusiveness" that was so convenient when women religious decided either to add college courses to their academies' curriculums or to turn their academies into Catholic colleges for women without drawing the attention of church leaders.[58]

A final influence contributing to more uniformity in Catholic girls' clothing was simply that it was possible. Men's apparel, with its simple lines, made a relatively quick transition to ready-made production. The demand for uniforms during the Civil War accelerated tailors' willingness to adopt mass manufacturing for menswear. Women's clothing was far more detailed, however, and its delicate fabrics did not lend themselves to manipulation by a sewing machine. Likewise, male tailors, who made the transition to ready-made first, did not initially make women's clothing. Dresses were the purview of the dressmakers, who often employed seamstresses to complete their sewing tasks.[59]

While the technology necessary to produce ready-made was available in the United States, and men had demonstrated the convenience and presentableness of ready-made clothes for decades, it was the efforts of clothing designers and reformers that completed the shift to making clothing that was more efficient and suited to the purposes of females. This "rational clothing" could be ready-made, and the "new woman" who had to appear fresh and neat each day for work or college could wear a simple shirtwaist blouse and a dark skirt. Inexpensive simple blouses could be changed each day, while the skirt remained the same. It was the nearest female outfit to a man's suit, and it reflected women's interest in enjoying similar or in some cases the same opportunities in education, employment, and society as men. Inspired by the popular illustrator Charles Dana and his Gibson Girl, young women embraced a "uniformish" look with their shirtwaist, dark skirt, and jacket. Therefore, women's and girls' fashions gravitated toward both practicality and ready-made as the nineteenth century drew to a close.[60]

AN EMERGING "LOOK" FOR CATHOLIC GIRLS

By the 1880s, students attending Maryville, a school run by the Society of the Sacred Heart, wore "long black cashmere uniforms with black alpaca aprons and white collars." A decade later, the Maryville uniform had shifted to a "black wool skirt, with a black and white checked gingham blouse."[61] The Sisters of Charity opened Mount St. Vincent on-the-Hudson in 1847 with no mention of a uniform, but they adopted one by the late nineteenth century. Girls wore the required combination of dark dresses and removable white collars. The Sisters of Charity likewise instructed girls to bring six linen collars, "a black reception dress, and two dresses of dark woolen texture, one winter balmoral; for summer: three dresses of thin material, (one black); and a dark reception dress, one summer balmoral; three black aprons, (silk or alpaca); for all pupils over nine years of age; and six white aprons as high in the neck as their dress, for all pupils under nine years."[62] For the distribution day or end-of-the-year ceremonies, Mount St. Vincent's specified, "a white French Lawn, or pure white Swiss Suit, plainly and neatly made, with high neck and long sleeves. No lace or ribbon trimmings, or train, allowed. One pair white hose; one white corset cover, with high neck and half sleeves; white kid gloves, black boots; black ribbon for hair; all jewelry, except brooch and ear-rings prohibited."[63] Notably, the Sisters of Charity asked families to provide several

Figure 9. Mount St. Joseph's uniform, 1899. Courtesy of the Sisters of St. Joseph Archive, Philadelphia, Pa.

dresses for the year—the sisters no longer seemed to be accommodating non-tuition-paying students. The children from working-class families now had the parochial schools, and the private academies could focus on promoting a greater sense of Catholic exclusivity and school identity. And if the sisters cultivated a few vocations in the process of educating their girls, then that was all the better for the sisters.

The Sisters of St. Joseph in Philadelphia mandated a more exacting uniform by the late 1890s as well. Rather than the "mazarine blue, in the winter and the pink delaine, with white body and black silk basque, in summer" required in 1864, Mount St. Joseph adopted identical black shirtwaists and black skirts (see fig. 9).[64] The brochure for students included a front and back postcard picture of the uniform as well as a sample of the fabric the dressmaker should use. The instructions stated, "Two dresses of Black Serge-Waist, three plaits front and three back, each two inches wide—Collar, three and a half inches wide. —Cuff, three and a half inches wide—Belt, two inches wide—Skirt, perfectly plain gathered into band." The instructions went on to say, "Please follow Model and Sample of Material exactly, otherwise Uniform must be returned for alterations." [65] The beheaded black dress in the photograph rendered the model "faceless"; there was no individuality, which was one of the goals of the religious habit. Nevertheless, the tightly drawn waist and leg-of-mutton sleeves anchored the uniform in late-nineteenth-century contemporary fashion.

Mount St. Joseph also provided instructions for the distribution or graduation attire:

> White Serge Dress made exactly like Model. White kid gloves. White silk gloves for children 12 years of age and under. One yard of black velvet for hair, 2 inches wide. Plain black shoes or ties; black stockings

> White Skirts, Aprons or Cuffs, are not to be worn; however white aprons are allowed to children under ten years of age.

> No Jewelry allowed except plain breast pin, small ear rings, and watch with black guard, no chain.

Concerned over the girls' and families' desire for extravagant display at graduation, the sisters included a warning for the distribution garments: Violators risked forfeiting "Honors and Premiums."

Mount St. Joseph's instructions reveal a significant consideration regarding uniformity.[66] It was a challenge to obtain ready-made women's clothing at the turn of the century, and therefore the more uniformity a school wanted, the more precise the directions would have to be—to the point of plait measurements, fabric swatches, and designations about what could be worn at a specific age. In the near future many academies would turn to selling the desired uniform at the school or identifying a specific shop that made the uniform they had in mind. Greater uniformity reflected the discipline that women religious sought to display on the outside and cultivate on the inside. Likewise, the uniform normalized the idea of a single dress style such as the solitary habit worn by the women religious.

Finally, another compelling consideration for a more overt commitment to a school uniform was the elevation of sisters to women religious. Where sisters, historically, were often public, activist, and diocesan, Pope Leo XIII invited them to "improve," so to speak, their canonical status and become officially "religious." The details of religious life were different from those of lay life, and exactness of behavior was certainly more closely associated with religious life. Nuns recited the Divine Office each day, wore veils that indicated their status as choir or lay, always traveled in pairs, removed themselves from public access, and might have several other rules, depending on the order. That this religious "promotion" might transfer over to the pupils of the convent schools and elevate the students seems reasonable. The days of disguising the habit were coming to an end; Rome elevated sisters to the level of nuns; and the girls in the care of the sisters would be the ladies of society or the members of the sisters' orders. Distinct uniforms encouraged an esprit de corps among the girls and linked the students to the religious status of their teachers. The Sinsinawa Dominicans even included the students in their rule. "Nothing should be allowed the children," explained the sisters' constitution, "either in their clothing or the furniture of their apartments, which savors of the spirit of the world, but they must be formed to all virtue and modesty such as should reign in convents and among religious women, whose minds should be wholly turned away from secular vanity."[67] While the rule was specific to the Dominicans, it nonetheless could inform and, from the sisters' perspective, should permeate the values and culture of the school. Ultimately, although uniforms certainly disciplined the bodies of Catholic school girls and supported the view that girls had a weakness for vanity, the sisters nevertheless distinguished their students and offered the girls a sense of exclusiveness and even shared status with their religious educators.

EARLY UNIFORMS: THE PETER THOMPSON
AND THE MIDDY BLOUSE

The model of the Catholic convent schools offered both a problem and a solution for pastors who needed to both exert control over their parishioners and establish parochial schools. Father Carroll, a member of the Holy Cross Fathers from South Bend, Indiana, complained in his article "Equalizing of Parishioners" that "our convent-educated girls who return to their parish after four or five years' absence at a fashionable Sisters' boarding school, will be found among those who prefer to be alone and therefore of the select. It will be hard work to break down the snobbery of caste, this pride of position, this unmannered aristocracy of wealth."[68] A class of elite young women in a patriarchal organization, the parish, could certainly present a challenge to the pastor, but if one segment of Catholic students could be presented as "select," could borrowing some of the sisters' exclusive strategies render the same effect for Catholics students more broadly?

Rather than being discouraged at the girls' elitist behavior, another pastor adopted their "select" approach. An anonymous pastor wrote an article for the *Ecclesiastical Review* in 1919 explaining his parish's "come back." Transferred from a thriving suburban parish, this pastor found himself in a city parish he called St. Clotille's for anonymity. It was a run-down parish with few organizations, little lay participation, and a failing school. Parishioners frequently tried to avoid going to mass there and attended other nearby Catholic churches instead. The unnamed pastor successfully turned the parish around, however. He started various guilds for men, women, boys, and girls of various age groups in the parish. He assigned the Holy Name Society to look out for the delinquent boys and recruited the best seamstresses to make beautiful Gothic vestments and "exact dalmatics" to beautify the liturgy. This pastor, like Father Carroll of South Bend, identified girls as the challenge to parish identity. He explained, "No matter what the parish there is sure to be foolish social distinctions, based sometimes on a mere formality, but, at that, it must be recognized. . . . A number of girls of the parish of St. Clotille had been doing social work outside the parish and within the parish, in non-Catholic organizations." [69] "Doing social work" was likely code for working with non-Catholic organizations, such as settlement houses, that offered women opportunities to work outside the home. Assessing his obstacles and resources, the pastor of St. Clotille's decided to address the presumable class and educational distinctions among the girls and also form an organization for them. Rather than a sodality, which was a popular devotional organization in many Catholic parishes, he preferred the medieval system of guilds. He assigned the young women "visitation of the sick, the making of clothing for children . . . securing of positions for the unemployed, and in short . . . doling out of counsel and need." [70] After finding an especially well-trained and active young woman, he decided to pay her as a social worker for his parish. [71]

The achievement the pastor was most proud of, however, was his school. He acquired an unused public school building, doubled the number of sisters to teach, and put the students in uniforms. Shifting to the nickname "Miracle Parish," he wrote,

> Now the novelty of the Miracle Parish begins in the school. It was evident that in a parish where children come from the poor and the rich, there would always be the problem of competition in dress. Uniforms are bad for certain institutions because great uniformity in life already exists. But for other institutions, like a parish school, they are exceedingly good, because they give a needed uniformity which is helpful for the general unity that ought to be in every school. So the boys went into military uniforms and the girls in attractive, simple dresses which are called Peter Thompsons. The children manifested great pride in their uniforms both on account of

the novelty of the departure and its attractiveness. Besides, it gave a fine sense of democracy to the youngsters to find that they were all dressed alike, and that no one knew who was poor or who was rich.[72]

In addition, he found that the uniform curtailed misbehavior. He noted that "boys . . . from the Fifth Grade up, form a Junior Holy Name Society. They are, of course, a military organization and, fortunately, they always have had, as their director, a priest who had been a soldier or who, at least, had received a military training. The sense of discipline brought about by a uniform and the natural respect that goes with it has almost put out of use the word discipline. The pride in the school, as typified in the uniform, has often stayed the impulse toward roughness and lawlessness." The pastor went on to claim that in three years there had only been two "serious infractions of discipline that had to be dealt with."[73] In 1919 the pastor of St. Clotille's identified the existence of uniforms for students as a novel innovation. In a way it was. The Peter Thompson suit he adopted for girls had been popular as a "children's wear" style for well over a decade, but the idea of requiring it and exerting control over family clothing prerogatives was new, and so was the interpretation the pastor placed on the uniform. A century earlier, those whose freedom was curtailed wore uniforms. In 1919, uniforms had come to represent freedom.

Belle Case La Follette, wife of Senator Robert M. La Follette, championed the Peter Thompson suit, among other simple styles for women. A suffragist and an attorney, La Follette saw the benefits utilitarian dress would bring to women as they ventured into newly open occupations. In a 1911 article, La Follette explained,

Tight fitting clothes call attention to form and sex, make corsets "indespensible" and maternity dreaded. . . . Today women's occupations, no less than men's, call for dress that gives free use of the body. It has always seemed to me that a modification of the dress of young girls might be adapted to the use of all womankind. It would not require any radical change nor conflict with conventional ideas. The middy blouse and skirt, the Peter Thompson suit, the one-piece waist with skirt, allow variety and give good line with freedom of action for all usual employment. . . . Girls permitted to adapt their dress to their work and their play will grow up stronger in body, contented with their sex, and better balanced emotionally. And though they fall into conventional faults as they reach young ladydom, certain ideas will stay by them in selecting their own and their daughters' clothes. This will have cumulative effect on succeeding generations. Progress in dress, as in politics is slow. We must have faith.[74]

While La Follette was more concerned with functionality of dress for work than with modesty, she clearly overlapped with Catholics in associating women with "conventional faults" and voicing support for limiting women's attire.

A 1919 article in the *Lewiston Daily* of Maine identified regional support for adopting the Peter Thompson as the standard girls' uniform. "Practically all the girls' preparatory schools in Maine are backing a movement to curb school girls' needless extravagance in dress, by the adoption of a uniform costume, the so-called 'Peter Thompson' suit being most favored. The plan was first advocated by President C. P. Quimby of Westbrook Seminary and is gaining favor everywhere. Eventually, Maine school heads believe, some such dress as the 'Peter Thompson' will be worn uniformly by all the school girls of New England." Uniforms on women and certainly on men had become a common sight during World War I, and women's contributions to the war effort conveyed their interest in civic engagement as Congress debated the suffrage amendment. Once World War I was over, as well as the battle for women's voting rights, women did not need uniformish clothing to be taken seriously or to assuage fears of liberation, and the trend dissipated. Catholics, however, were ambivalent about the "New Woman," her unchecked freedom, and her voting rights. Therefore, while reserved fashions such as the Peter Thompson faded in interest among the general populace, Catholic school administrators saw a trend worth retaining. As the pastor at St. Clotille's suggested, uniforms symbolized the limits of democracy, as in a prison or workhouse, but uniforms promoted beneficial outcomes as well, such as strengthening collective identity. In the coming years, uniforms would catch on quickly in Catholic schools as a way to mute class differences as well as to unify, elevate, and control Catholic girls in particular.

The Peter Thompson suit was a type of sailor suit for girls. A 1915 article in the *Honolulu Star-Bulletin* described the outfit in detail. "As you know, the 'Peter Thompson' suits have been the synonym for good taste in dress for girls from 14–18 years old for many years," the author explained. "Most of the schools in the States for girls of this age who use a uniform, use this style or a variation of it. It is simple, comfortable and gives a well-dressed appearance. It is a one-piece sailor-suit, waist and skirt united by a common belt, wide sailor collar and cuffs of contrasting color with several rows of narrow tape. Simple skirts which may be gathered, plaited or plain, but never tight or skimpy."[75] Interestingly, the Punahou mothers contemplated a uniform for the school, but in the end, they did not adopt it—the mothers only discussed the merits of this simple style. They did note, however, that a related style, the middy blouse and skirt, was less appealing to teenage girls because the waist was not gathered at all. This middy blouse and skirt, which dropped straight and loosely over the waist, was another style adopted by the Catholic schools.

Children's clothing designers based the middy (sometimes spelled "middie") on the midshipman's blouse worn by American sailors during the Spanish-American War and the Philippine-American War. This foray into expansionism, with the help of the U.S. Navy, popularized ready-made sailor or "middy" blouses. Easy to manufacture because of its simple and boxy design, what once had been a garment reserved for men or girls' physical education classes, the middy blouse, became a standard feature in both required and optional school clothing for girls.

Girl Scouts continued to advance the popularity of the middy blouse. A carryover from Great Britain, the Girl Scouts organization came to the United States in 1912 and quickly became known for its wholesome all-female activities and service work. What made the Scouts identifiable, however, was their uniform, which was originally a hand-sewn blue middy blouse. Later, in 1914, the blue blouse was replaced by a manufactured khaki middy blouse.[76] Despite the Scouts' lack of direct association with Catholicism, the church surprisingly embraced the organization. In a mass celebrated for the Catholic Girl Scouts at St. Patrick's Cathedral, Cardinal Hayes extolled the virtues of modesty found among the Girl Scouts. "There is a modern tendency to be bold and forward," he lamented, "but you will not find that among the Girl Scouts who follow the code of their organization."[77] The Girl Scouts organization may have disagreed with Cardinal Hayes; nevertheless, by the 1920s the functionality of the basic middy blouse had caught on and served as the "first phase" of Catholic uniforms for little girls.

THE RISE OF PAROCHIAL AND DIOCESAN SCHOOLS

Holy Child Jesus, a parochial grade school in Richmond Hills, New York, had all first-grade girls in middy blouses and ties by 1924. A few years later, parishes in Philadelphia began to adopt the middy blouses for girls as well. St. Peter's Church informed its parishioners in July 1927 that it had "come to the conclusion that uniformity of dress is a *desideratum* in our school. This obtains in many schools of the diocese. Your hearty co-operation is needed to bring about this desired effect."[78] The next month's issue of the *Parish Calendar* once again returned to the issue of school uniforms. Under the title "The School Girls," the author wrote, "As stated last month, we wish our school girls to be dressed uniformly. When school reopens, we shall make known what kind of 'uniform' is desired. Mothers and Fathers, we are deeply interested in the proper training of your children. Will you not co-operate with us in a measure which looks to the best interest of your children, and which, by the way, will save you money?"[79] Parents might have been wary of the new requirement, but the author attempted to satisfy any doubts by pointing out the financial benefits.

St. Edward's Parish Monthly Calendar published a similar announcement, but in the form of a directive. The pastor stated, "Following a custom inaugurated several years ago, all girls from the fourth to the eighth grade, will be attired in the regulation middy blouse and skirt. Absolutely no exception will be made to this ruling. The uniform will be found far more economical than any other form of dress. The uniform may be purchased at the school at wholesale cost."[80] The pastor of St. Peter's felt the need to remind parishioners again in September that his goal was to adopt a uniform. He wrote, "We again wish to inform parents not to purchase any extra clothes for their girls who are to attend our school. We intend to do what so many others in different cities are doing and which has everywhere met with approval of both parents and pupils, namely, we intend to have our children uniformly dressed in white middy blouses and blue skirt (Each class will have its own color tie). We know that the plan will meet your approval and cut down clothing expenses."[81] There would not be any dialogue about this decision. The pastor contended that the uniform had "everywhere met with approval," and therefore it did not need to be debated.

The accessibility of ready-made clothing reduced the price of clothes, but it also increased the variety. Girls from fourth through eighth grade would likely be on their way to developing an attraction to the assortment of affordable styles. Thus the pastor at St. Edward's had concerns about "extra clothes" or all those new clothes he could not control. Nevertheless, he offered a less damning rationale for the uniform, which was that it would ultimately be less expensive for the parents. Catholic educators drew children closer to the world of the clergy and religious who likewise sacrificed consumer pleasure for the greater goal of expressing spiritual values and religious affiliation. Just like the religious habits and clericals, uniforms would be material aids to control the students while they ideally inspired respect and admiration from onlookers.

The contention that uniforms were a money-saving proposition was not universally accepted, however. While Catholic schools used budgeting as an argument for uniform adoption, the dioceses recognized that for some families it could be an added expense. The superintendent of Catholic schools in Philadelphia, Father Edward M. Reilly, forbade the policy of "forcing children

Figure 10. *Children entering parochial school, 1944. Courtesy of Special Collections Research Center, Temple University Libraries, Philadelphia, Pa.*

to abide by a uniform dress code when it proved an additional expense for parents."[82] George Bendinger, founder of Bendinger Brothers, a Philadelphia-based uniform company, estimated that at the end of World War II only about 40 percent of Catholic grade-school girls in Philadelphia dressed in uniforms, while all private and diocesan high school girls wore them.[83] The students pictured in figure 10 are entering their parochial school on 2 September 1944. None of the children, even the girls farther back in the line, are wearing uniforms. In the distance, however, one can make out the faint image of three high-school-age girls walking side by side. These girls appear to be uniformly dressed. Diocesan high schools were controlled by the bishop or cardinal and his superintendent of schools, but pastors oversaw grade schools. These priests, along with the order of sisters who taught in the schools, decided whether uniforms would be required, and they were not supposed to mandate uniforms if expense was an issue. However, in all likelihood, a uniform could be "found" for a needy girl if the pastor and principal were inclined to adopt a dress code.

Parochial schools had begun to be the primary feeders of diocesan or central high schools by the end of the 1920s. Before the turn toward diocesan schools, attempts at establishing high schools in individual parishes had suffered from fluctuating numbers of students, changing pastor assignments, and a lack of funds. The church hierarchy saw their best hope for Catholic high schools in a central school system. Removing the burden of a high school from single parishes and placing it with the diocese would allow parishes to pool their resources and provide a high school education for families who could not afford the tuition required at convent schools. Additionally, the impressive centralizing structures built to accommodate Catholic students added to the presence of Catholicism in large cities and especially the prestige of the bishop or cardinal, after whom many diocesan schools were named.

Based on a model similar to the public high school, a central or diocesan high school was a school established by the bishop or cardinal and whose administration remained with the diocese. These schools educated students from two or more parishes at a nominal cost.[84] For instance, Little Flower High School for Girls, which opened in Philadelphia in 1941, accepted girls from seventy-two parishes. By 1945 approximately 75 percent of parochial school students went on to Catholic high school in the Archdiocese of Chicago.[85] This was made possible by the development of diocesan high schools.[86] Diocesan high schools educated more than one-fifth of all Catholic secondary students in the United States by 1949.[87] In that same year, 83 percent of Catholic teenagers who attended high school in Philadelphia did so at a diocesan high school.[88] According to a questionnaire circulated among diocesan school superintendents by educational researcher Edward Spiers, 45 percent stated that they had a policy of establishing central schools whenever possible.[89] In addition to addressing parish costs and numbers, centralizing the high schools reflected efficiency trends, which permeated industry as well. Left to individual pastors, Catholic youth could enter adulthood with a great variety of behaviors and religious beliefs. Centralized, Catholic youth would ideally adopt a standard Catholicism determined and regulated by the bishops and the superintendent of Catholic schools.[90]

The first free Catholic diocesan high school in the United States opened in Philadelphia in 1890.[91] Boys from around the city could attend the Roman Catholic High School of Philadelphia if they earned qualifying marks on the entrance examination.[92] At the same time, there was discussion among city clerics of opening a similar school for girls, but hesitancy over secondary education for girls and a lack of funds kept this project on hold for several years.[93] A gift of $100,000 and energetic fundraising on the part of high-school-age girls and many others ensured the opening of Catholic Girls' High School

(CGHS) in 1912. In that year, young women from five different parish centers joined for the first time under one roof to start their high school education.[94] Administrators eventually changed the name of the school to the John W. Hallahan Catholic Girls' High School, in honor of the brother of its primary benefactor, Mrs. Mary E. Hallahan McMichan.[95] It took another four years for the Philadelphia clergy to open their third diocesan high school, West Philadelphia Catholic High School for Boys. And in 1927 the fourth diocesan school was finished, West Philadelphia Catholic Girls' High School (WPCGHS).

As in the public schools, diocesan high school administrators and teachers used a Progressive educational model.[96] This curriculum attempted to meet the practical needs of the students as they developed into adult citizens. Home economics, student government, science labs, and extracurricular activities provided experiential learning opportunities that would equip young women for their future lives.[97] Graduates of a diocesan Catholic high school would therefore be educated to compete on the same level for jobs and acceptance into institutions of higher learning as students from convent and public schools.[98] One significant difference between the public and diocesan schools, however, was that after 1924, at least in Philadelphia, all diocesan high school girls wore a distinctive uniform.

CGHS students traveled around Philadelphia by foot and rode trolley cars in a "modified" modern dress. The uniform included a blue jumper, which ideally fell three inches below the knee, worn over a white blouse or half-blouse. Stockings and modest shoes completed the ensemble. The school administrators forbade makeup, excessive jewelry, or high-heeled shoes. And although the dress was reserved, it was not entirely outmoded. Both the hemline and drop-waist cut were recognizable styles. In that way young Catholic women appeared to have accepted contemporary fashion standards. Nevertheless, the dark hue and accessory restrictions kept the girls from appearing too fashionable.

For the twelve years prior to the adoption of the uniform, the young women from CGHS dressed like girls in public high school. They wore blouses and skirts with accessories such as ties and necklaces. Students put on uniforms for athletic events such as gym class or membership on the basketball team or the cheerleading squad in both public and Catholic schools. With the impressive appearance of uniforms on select schoolgirls and the positive reviews standardized dresses received from Girl Scouts, priests, and even Belle Case La Follette, uniforms had become an uncontroversial and even valuable addition to a young girl's wardrobe. Therefore the decision to adopt uniforms probably was not very difficult for the diocesan high schools.

The 1920s was an era of youthful adventure and rebellion, especially for young women. In her groundbreaking work on American youth in the 1920s, Paula Fass argues that in the 1920s, "the tension between modern and traditional modes of thought and behavior, was finally played out."[99] Feminine behavior was no longer predictable as young women tested their independence in school, employment, and social relations. The new fashions that young women wore also bespoke their eagerness to renegotiate the values and behaviors society assigned to women a generation earlier. Girls wanted to create their own social order, one that did not restrict their opportunities but instead would allow them to mix work, leisure, and often marriage. Ultimately, young women attempted to redefine the boundaries of respectable womanhood.[100] Catholic girls did not remain outside the youth culture. As the class photograph from 1922 (fig. 11) indicates, Catholic girls dressed in a variety of styles, employing collars, necklaces, and even a man's tie (see back row) to accessorize their different dresses and jumpers. The girls in the front row sit casually on the floor with crossed legs, and the two girls in the center defiantly cross their arms for the photographer. These girls exude a sense of independence and confidence characterized by the new youth culture. Despite the church's best efforts, Catholic girls likewise often learned the new dances, saw the same moving pictures, and read the same magazines as non-Catholic youth.

Catholic social commentators were keenly aware of the "New Woman," and they feared her potential to corrupt the morals of young Catholic girls. In a 1922 commencement-day speech offered at a convent school, Bishop Dunne of Peoria complained: "Some girls act as if they owed neither obedience, nor respect, nor submission to parents. . . . A brief period of so-called female independence may exact a lifelong penalty. The jazzing, cigarette-smoking, turkey-trotting flapper with her vanity box of powder puff and war paint, lipstick, and cosmetics may think that she is having an uproarious time, but generally it terminates in a roar of grief. Why, the women who wear out their lives in wretchedness because they had their fling in youth are beyond counting. . . . Many a silly girl, preferring the insipid compliments and dangerous familiarities of strangers to parental prohibitions, has spent middle and old age repining."[101] While Bishop Dunne offered a full list of vices young women experimented with, the pastor of St. Edward's Parish narrowed in on the problem of fashion. He grieved,

It needs no acute observer to-day to note that women are becoming less womanly, there are fashions that shock even the worldly men that make no pretense of virtue. The girl with a tender love for the Blessed Virgin does

Figure 11. John W. Hallahan Catholic Girls' High School, Section 3 B.C., 1922. Courtesy of the John W. Hallahan Catholic Girls' High School, Philadelphia, Pa.

Figure 12. John W. Hallahan Catholic Girls' High School, Section 7, B-C, 1926. Courtesy of the John W. Hallahan Catholic Girls' High School, Philadelphia, Pa.

not slavishly submit to fashion when fashion outrages decency. . . . She does not fear being called old fashion. . . . What a world it would be if all aspired to the womanly dignity of the handmaid of the Lord! . . . It is impossible to avoid noticing the pitiful vulgarity and immodesty of the modern dress. . . . If the women who wear them could hear the comments made upon their appearance—much more, if they could realize the sin of which they make themselves the occasion—no doubt they would not allow themselves to be carried away by the craze for fashion.

It is enough to sadden one's heart to see the attire of some of our young girls, even those who come from good Christian homes. How often is such dressing only one step to a loss of all sense of shame! In most cases it is the parents of these girls who are to blame. They may be pious and most are themselves, but if they permit their daughters to sacrifice modesty at the altar of pagan fashion, the sin is at their door.[102]

Young women, church leaders concluded, had to be taught to resist the new social, sartorial, and sexual adventures open to them. Otherwise, their future on earth and in heaven was in jeopardy. With children not listening to parents and parents not asserting themselves with their children, Catholic clergy and religious stepped into what they saw as the parenting void.[103] Taking control of clothing was a clear assertion of the church's parenting role. As the class photograph from 1926 (fig. 12) indicates, there was nothing jaunty in the stance of the girls once the sisters and clergy put them in uniform. They all stood in order with hands uniformly at their sides.

A writer for the *Catholic Mind* recognized the possible harm that came from women's new opportunities but felt there was a hopeful side that should not be overlooked. She explained that women's opportunities in American society had vastly changed due to young women's achievements in higher education, and some of these "new women," in order to prove their intelligence, "wore mannish clothes, became wage-earners and demanded the vote." By competing with men, the author complained, these "feminists" made both men and religion their enemy.[104] Higher education did not have to masculinize women or turn them against religion and men, however. On the contrary, female graduates from Catholic schools could "vindicate the superiority of Catholic education. . . . It is their task to permeate the world with this new feminism." Catholic girls, using Jesus' mother, Mary, as their model, could practice "courageous modesty of dress . . . balanced sanity of their attitudes toward books and plays and pleasure" and recognize "the dignity of poverty and the responsibilities of wealth." The writer concluded that many educated

Catholic women would choose careers, but unfortunately those women would not be able to hear that career pray or "tuck it into bed at night."[105] Despite his long diatribe against the young girls' new apparel, the pastor at St. Edward's likewise recognized the promise of Catholic leadership in the area of fashion. He noted "that in a number of our larger cities and towns Catholic women are sufficiently numerous and influential to exercise not light control over the setting of fashions: and the very least that may be expected from them is a downright refusal to accept any style that savors of indecency—as too many styles at present unmistakably do." With the proper mentorship, a kind of "apostolate of dress" was possible, but it would have to be cultivated by religious who recognized and rejected the potential sinfulness of fashion.

Even teenage Catholic writers noted the challenge facing modern young women. Anna McArdle, a graduate of the class of 1917 from CGHS, wrote an essay for her school yearbook titled "The Catholic Woman in the Business World." In her essay McArdle explained, "Years ago the idea of woman's leaving her sheltered home life to seek a place in the constant turmoil of business life would have been not only frowned upon, but strongly discouraged. Today conditions have so changed that the number of women workers is almost past belief and in that vast army the Catholic woman like her sister must take her place."[106] McArdle went on to comment, "The question of dress will afford her means of influencing those around her to the practice of that modesty and reserve demanded by self reverence." The Catholic woman's appearance, however, may draw negative comments or "criticism so severe as to tempt her to wonder if the struggle is really worth the sacrifice of the popularity that results from doing like others." Nevertheless, McArdle continued, "working girls should not lose heart because under that criticism lay admiration for one who can so thoroughly make religion the guide and inspiration of everyday life." Even without a school uniform, McArdle suggested that Catholic women dressed differently. Notably, all of these Catholic essayists acknowledged clothing as a vehicle for women's public leadership. Catholic women, like the saints who inspired them, may have to suffer. But ultimately, their resistance against contemporary values had the potential to influence others and to protect traditional feminine values.

Although convent schools predated diocesan schools in their adoption of uniforms, it was nonetheless the volume of diocesan schoolgirls, traveling on public transportation and walking to school, that would make Catholic girls' negotiations with this new female youth culture a recognizable look. As Catholic girls moved beyond the confines of their parishes, boarding trolley cars, window-shopping, or participating in athletic events, sometimes against public school girls, Catholic leaders looked for ways to reinforce traditional feminine values and Catholic religiosity. Uniform clothing off-set what the church saw as the corrupting influences of vanity and competition considered so prevalent in modern society and subdued young women's tendencies toward competition. Ideally, by being similarly attired, students would not waste time thinking about what to wear to school and how others would appreciate, envy, or emulate their appearance. Moreover, a functional uniform implied that being preoccupied with clothing was not a worthwhile expenditure of thought and energy.[107] Uniformed high school girls offered an alternative to secular feminism; the Catholic version was a religion-inspired femininity—girded by submission, simplicity, and Catholic identity.[108]

Just as the uniform would instruct the individual wearer, its significance would be felt in the larger Catholic community. The ultramontane bishops and cardinals oversaw the "Triumphal Years" in American Catholicism. They discontinued the formation of ethnic parishes, established seminaries in their dioceses to provide similar training for all ordinary priests, and encouraged local sodalities, fraternities, and clubs to affiliate with a single clearing-house for Catholic organizations, the National Catholic Welfare Conference. These bishops sought centralization and standardization of Catholic education, organizations, and in some cases (such as priests), attire. Until the late nineteenth century, Catholic dioceses were virtually independent of one another, and depending on the diocese, individual parishes might also act independently. This behavior was a liability for a church that wanted to appear confident in the face of Protestant cultural dominance. Standardization would ideally provide more predictable behavior on the part of clergy and laypeople alike, and uniforms, like Roman collars, supported that goal.

Not only did the uniforms promote standard dress and behavior; they also allowed the church to claim allegiance to American values in a unique way. They presented Catholic schoolgirls as a symbol of lost American ideals. According to the church, American women had valued modesty and respectable dress in the past. It was only in the first quarter of the twentieth century that ordinary women applied makeup and wore dresses with hems well above the ankle. School administrators wanted Catholic girls to wear uniforms to control them but also to offer the girls up as symbols of Catholic moral authority and democratic ideals. Although the church assumed it held "authority" over the visual church, it had nevertheless transferred a certain amount of power to the girls themselves. As a student from the CGHS class of 1924 explained, "In the revolution against conventionalities waged by the modern girl there seems to be an absolute disregard of the necessities of wearing clothes suited to the time, the place and occasion. A girl, arrayed in a ball gown ready for work, is to most, and surely to businessmen, a disagreeable sight. The adoption of uniforms has brought before us a true realization of the pleasure of seeing and being dressed appropriately. The individualistic maidens will have to cultivate temperamental fitness in regard to dress."[109] Although the student acknowledged that the school imposed the uniform, it was the Catholic girls themselves who could be examples to wayward Americans of traditional feminine values. As sociologist Nathan Joseph explains, children are often used as "demonstrators of cultural values."[110] Uniforms could help secure a place of cultural legitimacy for the outsider church, as exemplary behaving and efficiently dressed youth traveled around the cities for all Americans to admire.[111]

Finally, the uniform was a way to encourage an identity of desexualized youthfulness. Prior to the high school movement, most working-class girls went on to at least temporary employment before marriage and children. There was no significant liminal space before they acquired the responsibilities of an adult. High school provided a new stage in the life cycle of American youth. High school gave students an extended youth. As historian Paula Fass explained, "Youth is not simply a physical or biological fact. It is a cultural expression of social relationships and a product of a specific set of historical conditions."[112] The uniform, which played down the independence associated with adulthood, reinforced childhood strictures.[113] It also squelched the sexual allure promoted by the new fashions, thus negating the sexual maturity of the students.

Catholic women beyond high school age took up modest dressing along with the girls. In July 1924, the National Council of Catholic Women, "actuated by the expressed sentiments of Pope Pius XI," sent 700,000 "Modest in Dress" pledge cards to its members. The pledge read in part, "The National Council of Catholic Women calls upon its members and their friends to enlist in a great crusade which has for its object the spread of Catholic truth, the defense of Catholic faith and the observance of Catholic standards. . . . Resolve that I will observe in private and public life the standards of Catholic teaching particularly with regard to dress, reading and entertainment."[114] The next year, the International Federation of Catholic Alumnae joined the National Council of Catholic Women and urged members to set an example of modest dress for the younger generation.[115]

To require uniforms, especially on such a large scale, the Archdiocese of Philadelphia had to encourage school uniform manufacturing. Until the late 1920s, uniforms had been a small segment of a department store's or an independent dress shop's offerings. It was through an archdiocesan connection that a distinctive business around girls' uniforms in Philadelphia, for instance, became established. In the 1920s, generally the mother superior of a convent school, where uniforms were already required, would contract with an individual dress shop, tailor, or seamstress. Among the shop choices in Philadelphia, for instance, there were Millards, Steckers, McCarthy & Simon Inc., Brown Sisters, Mary M. Armstrong, Buxbaums, and John Wanamaker's Department Store. The "College Girls' Tailors" was the "Official Outfitter of the Pupils of St. Mary's Academy" in the Logan section of Philadelphia.[116] Along with uniforms, the College Girls' Tailors carried a "very exclusive line of knitted sport dresses and ensembles." Millard's Junior Department also specialized in high school uniforms among its collection of "the smartest wearing . . . Exclusive and Correct" clothing for young and teenage girls. Uniforms were one line of clothing offered among other young women's apparel. In the late 1920s, with two diocesan schools for girls open and uniforms required, the superintendent for Catholic schools in Philadelphia, Monsignor Bonner, sought out a company that could accommodate a large order at the lowest price. Bonner, along with other priests, bought his own mufti or clerical wear at Colby's, a men's shop at Seventy-seventh and Market Streets in West Philadelphia. There, priests could get a good deal on a black suit with two pairs of trousers.[117] Monsignor Bonner was friendly with Edward O'Hara, one of the salesmen, and O'Hara was the brother of a Catholic bishop. In center city Philadelphia, Bishop O'Hara had other connections in the clothing business beyond his brother. Bishop O'Hara knew Victor Eisenberg, an industrious employee at John Wanamaker's. Born to Russian Jewish immigrants in 1905, Eisenberg took a job in the women's garment business like his father and held a position as a cutter at John Wanamaker's.[118] The cutter's job was skilled work. It required cutting through piles of fabric along the lines of printed patterns in the most precise and economically efficient way possible. Cutting piles of fabric was a necessary step in the ready-made production line.

Bonner bid out the contract for his two diocesan schools, and it came down to Mary M. Armstrong and Victor Eisenberg, who by this time had opened a shop separate from John Wanamaker's. In the end Eisenberg won the coveted contract. More comfortable behind the scenes and knowledgeable about fabric and garment construction, Eisenberg sought out a "partner," and he made an offer to the church-connected, outgoing Irish Catholic salesman Edward O'Hara from Colby's. The name of the company was Eisenberg and O'Hara, but O'Hara was a salaried employee rather than a full partner.[119]

Eisenberg and O'Hara had three basic styles and eight colors for their serge jumpers. They would service the diocesan schools or the private academies but made sure that each type of school had a distinctive look. For the diocesan schools, the jumpers were all the same design, but the color was different. For the private academies, committees made up of sisters and mothers would determine a style, and if they wanted Eisenberg and O'Hara, they would have to sign a two- to five-year contract to warrant the investment in inventory. The business of outfitting the convent schools remained open-ended; small shops, therefore, still had a chance to obtain uniform contracts. Clothing diocesan schoolgirls, however, was a business-making contract, and Eisenberg and O'Hara positioned themselves specifically to fill that order.[120] The cut of the uniforms reflected the Catholic leadership's interest in standardization for the diocesan girls; the hierarchy "bagged" the girls in duplicate plain jumpers differentiated only by the color assigned to each school. In the private schools, however, women continued to make the decisions about their more exclusive uniforms. Catholic educators met on the same page requiring uniforms, but they worked at odds by highlighting class differences.

MAINTAINING EXCLUSIVITY

The private academies, not to be outdone, were determined to remain select and stepped up their attention to student dress even more. The sisters, having consistently required simplicity, were already well positioned to argue that they rejected the immodest fashions of the age. They were less inclined, however, to join with the pastors and priests who complained about the sisters' promotion of elitism. While the sisters did not publicly theorize as W. E. B. DuBois did about a "talented tenth" or an intellectually gifted group of Catholic women who would take the reins of political and social leadership, they nevertheless felt they were providing an important service to a unique population. According to historian Mary Oates, sisters "argued that tuition academies served an important social function in that they forged 'a connecting link between all classes, elevating the social position of the Catholics in the town.'"[121] Rather than close convent schools and allow the parochial and diocesan schools to replace them, the sisters positioned themselves for survival. The convent boarding school became attractive to families who sought an education imbued with Catholic values but who did not want to completely hide their class or repress their daughters' sense of social and educational entitlement. A pastor recounted a discussion he had with a superior of a girls' academy in which she said, "We are obliged to mitigate our discipline if we want to keep the children. The Sisters must put up with all sorts of self assertion, not to say impudence . . . because the parents are disposed to back up the pupil instead of reproving them when we are obliged to correct faults in their daughters. Formerly we had absolute control of the children while they were at school. Now the parents demand many exemptions."[122] The pastor recounted this story as an example of how girls were gaining a "spirit of independence—I mean an unbecoming mannish independence which breeds suffragettism."[123] If these were the girls they could get, the sisters would figure out a way to keep, control, and continue to distinguish them from other Catholic school students.

Between 1915 and 1925, the brochure of the Academy of Mount St. Vincent on-the-Hudson continued to indicate general guidelines for dress. Suggestions, however, about cultivating a particular look began to surface. "Tasteful simplicity," the brochure explained, "is greatly to be desired in the dress of a convent school-girl. . . . Her wardrobe should be ample without being extravagant. Elaborate gowns and jewelry not being permitted should not be brought to the school, which will not be responsible for them."[124] The sisters' requirements no longer included "dark" dresses. Instead they required "3 black dresses of Merino, flannel, cloth, serge [or] cashmere." New, too, was that girls could see "sample suits" at the school if they desired.

The Ursuline Academy in Dallas, Texas, also provided more specific guidelines for the student's wardrobe in its 1923–24 catalog. Under the subheading "Daily Uniform," the school administrators instructed both boarding and day students to acquire the following: "Summer Uniform—Two dark blue Serge Skirts, side-plaited. Six white waists or white Middies (no colored cuffs and collars). Winter Uniform—Dark Blue Serge Skirt. Dark Blue Woolen Blouse or Middie trimmed in Narrow White Braid. Black Ties and Hair Ribbons for both Summer and Winter. Winter Uniform purchased at the Academy. In addition to the regulation dress the following is required: Juniors—Six long-sleeved aprons, blue and white checked gingham. Common sense shoes. No silk hose."[125] Presumably the uniforms were not sold at the academy at any great profit, but requiring that the uniform be purchased at their school also meant no savings could be had by sewing it at home or going to a less expensive shop. Likewise, these girls wore a new waist or "middie" each day, which was not a savings. The requirements, however, guaranteed uniformity.

Mount St. Joseph, consistently specific, instructed students in 1917 about the required dress.

> The uniform for pupils over twelve is black Peter Thompson suit; those under twelve, girl's regulation sailor dress. For spring and early autumn, the Peter Thompson suit may be made of blue linen. No color braids or emblems should be used. With the Peter Thompson dresses, a shield reaching to the neckline must be worn, this should match the dress or else be of heavy white linen.

> The uniform regulations must be followed in each detail. No concessions will be granted, and for the sake of uniformity we insist on the adoption of same by our Day Pupils.

> If our patrons desire the firm of John B. Simpson, 914 Walnut Street, Philadelphia, will furnish the regulation uniforms and gymnasium suits at nominal prices. Each pupil at the beginning of school should be furnished with at least one uniform.

> Two blue linen dresses — Peter Thompson
> Two black uniform dresses (for young ladies)
> Two blue uniform dresses (for little girls)
> Two white aprons (for little girls)
> One black gymnasium suit
> Young ladies as well as children may bring whatever white dress they may have suitable for parties and evening wear. In evening dress the neck should reach the neckline, and the sleeves should be at least three-quarter length.[126]

Students were buying more than one uniform according to the season, shifting from serge to linen, changing uniforms as they moved on to higher grades, and attending school equipped with evening wear. The school wardrobe was certainly expanding.

Mount St. Joseph's uniform remained the same in 1920, with the addition of four sets of collars and cuffs. Under the tutelage of the Ursulines in Dallas and the Sisters of St. Joseph in Philadelphia, no distinctions would be made among day and boarding students. Even if the majority of Catholic high school girls eventually found themselves in uniform, the select schools still found ways to indicate exclusivity. Students from St. Mary's Academy in Philadelphia photographed in 1929 and 1931, respectively (figs. 13 and 14), wore dark blouses with removable collars, cuffs hidden from view, and plaited skirts. These dresses were a step up from the jumpers and half-blouses

Figure 13. St. Mary's Academy Primary Department, 1929. Courtesy of
the Sisters of St. Joseph Archive, Philadelphia, Pa.

Figure 14. St. Mary's Academy Class Officers, 1931. Courtesy of
the Sisters of St. Joseph Archive, Philadelphia, Pa.

worn in diocesan schools. Surely Catholics could tell the difference between a female student from a private Catholic high school and a female student from a diocesan Catholic high school. And that was how the parents and sisters wanted it.

NEGOTIATING THE UNIFORM

While the young women's uniform appearance functioned as an anchor for what the church perceived as American insider legitimacy through more virtuous femininity, young Catholic women did not always comply with the church's agenda. Despite the pride they took in displaying their religious and school membership, girls, as we witnessed in the 1922 class photo, also associated with the values conveyed by the new fashions. Freedom from convention and independence were the inspirations of a new generation of young American women who were earning an education to become part of the modern world. Despite the power clerical leaders imbued in the girls' uniforms, they could not control all the significance the uniforms held. The students, too, participated in creating meaning with their uniforms and bodies. Just like the church, they used them to communicate with fellow students and the world beyond the church.

At CGHS the simple dark-blue uniform gave students plenty of room to adjust their look. In the "Fashion Notes" from the class of 1924, a writer sarcastically concluded, "Undoubtedly the most popular shade of the season is dark blue, which attractive color may be seen SHINING forth from all quarters of the school." Not every student wore the uniform daily, however. The article went on to explain that "in their effort to vary the monotony some few girls occasionally detract from this GLOWING splendor by appearing in their 'glad rags.'" Peg Sheridan and Clare Belcher wore a lighter shade of blue, and Jean Brown wore "black, gray, green, everything else but blue."[127] An anonymous bard registered her protest in verse over the uniform's color:

Ode to a Spring Uniform

> O believe me if all the flagrant bright blue,
> Which to many an eye has brought hurt,
> Were to fade in the wash to some delicate hue,
> Both the blouse and the unplaited skirt
>
> Though wouldst then be more fit for the pupils to wear,
> Though thy advocates boost thee sky high,

For this loud awful color is more than we'll bear
If thy shade can be changed by a dye

For 'twas on't while thy brightness the dark closet hid
Or when dulled by the night shadows' length
That the brilliance and glare of thy marvelous shade
Shine forth in their boldness and strength
'Tis when the eye sees them, the head starts to hum —
This is caused by thy color so wild —
So we hope that the dresses in school days to come
Will be made of a chromo more mild.[128]

The poet seemed resigned to the fact that uniforms would remain a requirement, but students might, nevertheless, retain some diversification options. An observer of Marie Chester, class of 1924, from CGHS noted that "Marie believes that 'variety is the spice of life,' and every morning we wait with bated breath for her to remove her hat to see what color her bow is that morning."[129] A bow in the hair was one simple way of spicing up the otherwise uniform look.

Hair accessories or styles could indicate individualization or group membership, depending on the context and viewer. Bobbing one's hair was the mark of a risk taker as well as an entrée into certain high school cliques. Anna Devlin, class of 1924, experienced this. A classmate wrote of her, "Anna surprised us all one day when she walked in with her 'crown and glory' shorn. We other bobbed-hair misses breathed more freely when our 'Rock of Common Sense' so clearly showed her approval."[130] Margaret Finely did the same. According to her classmates, "Margaret's favorite indoor sport used to be to pull out each hairpin, separately . . . arrange it to her satisfaction, and . . . replace it. But one morning this changed. . . . She created a sensation by appearing with it bobbed."[131] Elizabeth (Evangeline) Quigley, also class of 1924, was queried by one of the writers about why it was taking her so long to bob her hair. After all, she had promised.[132] Restricted by the uniform dress, Catholic girls looked for other areas of their appearance in which to express themselves.

Beyond hairstyles, ties were a popular way to break up uniformity. One student recalls wearing her father's ties, at least until 1928. After that the school administrators raised the neckline of the uniforms at Hallahan, leaving little room on the new uniform for innovative neckwear.[133] Girls at WPCGHS were still displaying colorful neckwear in 1929, however. Classmates suggested to Sarah Lawler that her brother might want her to wear a bib — that way his ties would be protected during Sarah's lunch period.[134]

The drawings of a student in the 1930 John W. Hallahan "Silver Suds" section of the yearbook show the older-style uniform that seniors likely wore since they began school in 1926 (see fig. 15). The illustration provides a sense of how the girls saw themselves. They wore attachable hair "nots" in their hair. They drew on their book covers to make them look distinct. Sporty ties, a clearly masculine style, communicated their desire for equality. Since the artist emphasized earrings on a page marking youthful rebellion, the jewelry was likely not allowed. The shifting hemline indicates the way girls wanted to present themselves—vampy and modish after 2:45 P.M. Finally, the illustration of the disheveled girl after her game shows that the girls were playful, physical, and aggressive. The "Silver Suds" showed a picture of a girl very different from what the staid photographs of girls with their hands at their sides conveyed.

Stockings and shoes, likewise, provided a playful canvas on which to display the latest fashions and individuality. Students wore multicolored and horizontally striped stockings. Ballet shoes with no heel at all as well as higher-heeled pumps were popular. Although the schools forbade high heels, the stylish shoes made their way into the school halls on occasion.[135] A yearbook contributor complimented her classmate Zoila Esperanza Cifre on her taste in shoes. She wrote, "We need never send for a footwear catalogue when we have Zoila for she sports a stunning pair of the latest style each week."[136] Photographed walking down the hall in 1937, the high school girls from Little Flower in figure 16 are displaying a variety of shoe wear. It was the shoes, after all, that stood out when the uniform was masked by a coat.

Students groomed themselves not only for one another, but for the public and special friends as well. A student writer asked Genevieve Smith, class of '24, "How long do you and Cele spend every afternoon getting fixed up to go home?"[137] Another student had observed that "Cele may be seen on the same car every Monday with . . . ."[138] Both Genevieve and Cele, or "Che-Che," challenged the erasure of fashion the uniform aimed to promote.

Student illustrations (see fig. 17) suggest that girls could virtually disguise that they were Catholic school students with their coats and a little help from their belts. Fur-trimmed coats and cloche hats that students pulled snugly over their heads were popular. Accessories such as earrings and makeup could also be donned for the trips between school and home. And a belt cinched around the waist could temporarily raise the hem of the dress to hide it under a coat. Raising the hem would also expose the knees.

Sabina Marie Pidgeon of WPCGHS, immortalized by an artist friend, was fond of raising her hem until she was caught. A fellow student suggested

Figure 15. C.G.H.S. Fashions, 1930. Courtesy of the John W. Hallahan
Catholic Girls' High School, Philadelphia, Pa.

Figure 16. Little Flower High School girls in uniforms and rebel shoes, 1937.
Courtesy of the YGS Group, Philadelphia, Pa.

that "perhaps the songwriter had Sabina in mind when he wrote 'Have Her Ups and Downs' for one day her uniform would be unusually short, and, on the next, noticeably shorter." The writer went on to explain that Sabina's hem continued to change until "someone possessing authority somewhat superior to Sabina's stepped in the breech, and now that much altered hemline is a good three inches longer."[139] The drawing of Sabina (see fig. 18) suggests she not only raised her hem but donned makeup and spruced up her coif after 2:30 P.M. when school let out.

Ultimately, students used their clothing to both comply with and defy the womanly ideal designated by the church. Even if they could not disguise the uniform, they nonetheless did not relinquish their individualism. A 1930 illustration from WPCGHS had the girls lined up to sing, but the illustrator exaggerated the differences among the girls (see fig. 19). They are tall, short, wide, and thin. Some jumpers come up to the neck, while others dip down and allow for a tie. Shoes, stockings, hair, and voices (the different lettering

Figure 17. Student illustration in the "Silver Suds," 1929. Courtesy of the John W. Hallahan Catholic Girls' High School, Philadelphia, Pa.

Figure 18. Yearbook illustration, 1929. Courtesy of West Philadelphia
Catholic Girls' High School, Philadelphia, Pa.

Figure 19. Yearbook illustration, 1930. Courtesy of West Philadelphia
Catholic Girls' High School, Philadelphia, Pa.

and punctuation indicate intonation and inflection) are likewise varied. The
girls saw themselves as unique regardless of the uniformity of their dress.[140]

Despite all the sartorial transgressions young Catholic girls committed,
they embraced their alterity. An anonymous poet from WPCGHS penned the
following verse in 1929:

My Uniform

> The prettiest dress I ever knew
> Is a simple one of navy blue
> A sleeveless jumper with emblem bright
> And under this a blouse of white
>
> The blue is for strength and loyalty
> And the white for sweetest purity
> While the monogram of blue and gold
> Shines forth, excellence, our virtue of old.[141]

■ Uniforms took hold among Catholic girls for a variety of reasons. Initially they were not a sign of exclusivity but, rather, prescription and restriction. Children in Catholic asylums and industrial schools wore uniforms as a mark of undesirable distinction—they were students who belonged to the institutions. The sisters who taught in the select schools, instead, employed dress codes. These guidelines were also meant to restrain students and their families, but they did not set the students off as being limited by class, ethnicity, or a combination of both.

The trend toward greater uniformization of girls in Catholic schools loosely followed the decision of the Third Plenary Council to require pastors to build Catholic schools in all of their parishes. As a result of this directive, women religious were no longer the primary initiators of Catholic education for young girls. In response to the new mandate, women religious sought to convey a greater sense of exclusivity in their academies to attract families. One distinguishing feature of the convent education became the neat and respectable uniform. Although elitism was not an attribute "promoted" by the church, it was nonetheless accepted in order to acknowledge the wealthier class of Catholics and retain their necessary contributions. These same sisters who opened private academies also staffed parish schools, and pastors, along with the sisters, saw the benefit of uniforms on Catholics of ordinary means as well. Nevertheless, uniforms for select schools were distinct from uniforms for parish schools. For Catholic children generally, the uniform would ideally diminish class differences in the same school, and for girls, thought to be more susceptible to the sins of materialism and vanity, it would restrict their so-called fondness for display.

Finally, uniforms drew children and teenagers closer to the religious and the bureaucratic structuring of the church. Uniforms gave female students, in particular, a taste of the routine and sacrifice that came with religious life. Regardless of the notable increase in regimentation, Catholic schoolgirls were unpredictable models of Catholic femininity. While they seemingly supported the church's interest in encouraging modesty, religiosity, and discipline, they also displayed a willingness to challenge the church. Diocesan girls, and likely convent schoolgirls, too, who traveled on public transportation and walked around the cities, altered their uniforms to display their individuality and interest in consumer culture and coquetry. Sartorial rebellion indicated that Catholic girls had their own ideas about womanhood and Catholic identity. Despite the best efforts of Catholic schoolgirls at personalizing their appearances, the requirements surrounding uniforms would only increase for these girls in the years to come.

CHAPTER 4

OUTFITTING THE MYSTICAL

BODY OF CHRIST

APPAREL AND ACTIVISM

As American Catholics approached the middle of the twentieth century, identifiable dress, particularly among students, could be observed more and more frequently. Catholic leaders fully expected priests, sisters, and female students, especially, to dress in church- or school-regulated ways. Nevertheless, society viewed almost all Catholic clothing locally, congregationally, or regionally until the 1930s. For instance, Catholics and other Americans would see distinctive attire such as chasubles, cassocks, habits, and school uniforms in places such as churches and parish processions, on the dais of important dedications, or even perhaps just walking down the street. But a variety of factors converged between the 1930s and the 1960s to render the unique and burgeoning Catholic wardrobe a national icon. Among the most significant promoters of Catholicism's visibility were the rise of an image-rich mass media as well as niche media, the inclusive and activist "Mystical Body of Christ" theology, and the large-scale expansion of the Catholic education system into the American suburbs. In the wartime context, both hot and cold, America's critique of totalitarianism and desire to build national unity found useful symbols in the Catholic cultural system. The unique parareligious attire of Catholics exuded military-style discipline, religious freedom, and patriotism—what Americans believed was the antithesis of fascist and communist nations. While clothing seemed to signify Catholicism's triumph in America, the promotion of clothing or a specific form of materialism raised questions as well. Due to the GI Bill of Rights, American Catholics enjoyed greater access to education and became better educated in traditional subjects, social sciences, and theology. This training provided Catholics with new resources to examine received teachings and practices more closely. Catholic dress, even while it expanded and diversified, would invite inquiries and amendments from multiple constituencies, but mostly from those within the church.

In 1941 an article appeared in the *Chicago Daily Tribune* titled "Immaculata Joins 'Citizens' Parade." While not garnering the front page of Section A, the feature nevertheless commanded top billing in Section N and was accompanied by no fewer than ten pictures of students from Immaculata High School. Collectively the *Tribune* included the uniformed bodies of thirty-seven students in the photographs. "The Immaculata," as locals referred to it, opened in 1921 under the auspices of the Sisters of Charity of the Blessed Virgin Mary in the Uptown neighborhood on the northeast side of Chicago. Similar to the John W. Hallahan Catholic Girls' High School and West Philadelphia Catholic Girls' High School, Immaculata was a central high school built to educate hundreds of students coming from multiple parishes. The number of Catholic schools had grown exponentially since the bishops' decision to require the establishment of parochial schools in 1884 and then construct central diocesan high schools to further educate Catholic students beyond grade school. By 1930, 2.5 million students received some Catholic education, and by 1965, one in eight American students was being educated at a parochial school.[1] And although Immaculata was a city school, much of the Catholic school growth occurred in postwar suburbs.

The occasion that landed the Immaculatans in the paper was an upcoming radio broadcast of "Citizens of Tomorrow" sponsored by station WGN, which for the first time would feature a Catholic school on its show. Reporter Juanita Daly explained to readers that "as the first Catholic school to appear on the program sponsored by *The Tribune*, the Immaculata girls, looking alike in their dark dresses and demure white collars, will set the standard in their program for future Catholic groups."[2] Whether that "standard" was in dress or performance was unclear, but the description of Catholic girls as demure lookalikes provided a mental picture reinforced by multiple images.

Newspapers and radio stations such as WGN were two popular media outlets that conveyed information about Catholics and by Catholics, and the print sources often included detailed descriptions of what Catholics wore in processions and ceremonies. A 1935 story about the final service for the National Eucharistic Congress, for instance, vividly recounted the attire of the various participants. "Thirty-five archbishops and bishops, wearing white mitres and the rich robes of formal ritual . . . Scores of girls garbed in papal white and gold . . . Monsignori in purple edged cassocks, monks in austere habits of their orders, learned Jesuits in solemn black, clerics of the oriental rite in sparkling vestments, abbots in the garb of their rank—these con-

Figure 20. First day of school, Little Flower, 1939. Courtesy of the YGS Group, Philadelphia, Pa.

tributed to elevate the procession to one of awesome dignity," explained the writer. In addition to print media, radio became a popular conveyor of news and information in the 1920s, and Catholics were again included as both subjects and distributors. Priests such as Father Charles Coughlin and Bishop Fulton Sheen occupied the airwaves in the 1930s. CBS gave Father Coughlin a short-lived national outlet in 1930, and that same year the National Council of Catholic Men offered the Reverend Fulton Sheen a spot on the NBC-carried program *The Catholic Hour*.[3] Despite the roles Catholics enjoyed in the media, readers and listeners had to rely on their personal experiences and their imaginations to picture Catholics. This inventiveness for readers and listeners, however, was ripe for change as innovations such as the 33mm camera simplified photography by reducing camera setup and introducing quick, candid shots. These 1939 "flower pots" (as local Philadelphians called the students of Little Flower High School photographed by a staff photographer at the *Philadelphia Inquirer*) captured the throngs of students on the first day of school (see fig. 20)—a photograph unlike the staged class pictures that conveyed control and order. Although some communities of women religious did not even allow themselves to be photographed, both the popular and Catholic media found Catholics in Catholic dress ideal subjects for the photographic medium.

The photos that accompanied the article "Immaculata Joins 'Citizens' Parade" were instructive in who and what the photographer chose to capture. The images narrated a "day in the life" of the typical Immaculata student. The story began with four girls, three members of the school sodality along with the senior class president, arriving at school before classes began at 8:45 A.M. The next photo showed six students in a biology class "studying plant life" and "mounted specimens." The next two photos addressed the girls' training for domesticity: millinery class in the household arts department and a cooking class. The fifth picture captured girls grabbing a quick lunch, and the sixth image pictured members of the band in marching attire. In the seventh photo, students sketched and dressed a miniature mannequin, while the next two shots highlighted the sodality and the girls at prayer. The final picture showed two happy girls boarding the bus to go home. Outside the band uniforms and jacketed girls boarding the bus, the girls were always dressed in their school uniforms, and sisters and priests did not appear in any of the photographs.

Daly's description of the girls and their school was nothing short of promotional. Immaculata High School appeared to espouse a religious culture that was fully assimilated into American society, steeped in lay rather than hierarchical leadership, and guided by internally derived discipline. It was a clear example of what historian Anthony Burke Smith described as the resignification of American Catholicism. No longer an immigrant church or solely a top-down structure where bishops expected congregants to "pray, pay, and obey," these Immaculatans were models of the wartime American values of self-direction, purposefulness, and religiosity. And in the tension-filled days of 1941 with the United States attentive to the entrenched war in Europe and preparations for the possibility of America's involvement, the sartorial distinction of these uniformed girls became a symbol that carried more than Catholic affiliation and traditional modesty. In that increasingly militarized context, the uniformed girls foreshadowed the fusion of patriotism and religion and the central role Catholics would play in representing that union.

In the case of Daly's coverage of the Immaculata students, both the image and the prose worked together to situate Catholics as exemplary Americans. This may seem rather remarkable considering that American Catholics were just over a decade removed from the unabashedly anti-Catholic sentiment mobilized to defeat Democratic presidential candidate Al Smith and to promote Ku Klux Klan membership throughout the country. However, the Depression era served to unify Americans through shared economic concerns and not only assisted in pulling Catholics into the American mainstream but allowed Catholics to contribute to America's understanding of economic justice. Monsignor John A. Ryan, a well-known scholar and activist, was a champion of Franklin Delano Roosevelt's New Deal, even "advising the president on labor and social security legislation."[4] Despite Father Coughlin's vociferous criticism of Roosevelt, with Monsignor Ryan's support, the Catholic vote went to FDR.

By 1940, however, Roosevelt had shifted his attention away from economic issues and toward the war effort. Daly's article illustrates Catholicism's corresponding transition away from the Depression mentality and toward military readiness and patriotism. In her piece, Daly quickly validated Immaculata's academic credentials, citing its "affiliation with the North Central Association of Secondary Schools and the State Department of Education." While Catholic schools had waged battles over curriculum in the past, accreditation was clearly not a concern. Graduates would find themselves eligible for acceptance in "college, universities, nurses' training, and normal schools all over the country." The sisters told Daly that while the school could boast that "from 35 to 50 percent of the graduates attend college," the past year's graduates had over "50 percent enrolled in advanced schools." As the image of the science class suggested, Catholics did not shy away from teaching biological sciences. Although the article did not specify that students learned about the theory of evolution—a controversy that never quite found Catholics—the "mounted specimens" certainly led readers to the conclusion that Catholic schools did not have any qualms about science in the way that fundamentalist denominations did.[5] Much of the rest of the curriculum encouraged traditional feminine training. Girls sewed, cooked, played music, drew, draped, and prayed. Teachers claimed that at the end of the day, "we give them enough work to keep them at home in the evening and the parents approve of that arrangement." Staying at home was code for not spending the evening socializing with boys. Immaculata came near to meeting what historian Barbara Welter described as the nineteenth-century "Cult of True Womanhood" with its standards of purity, piety, and domesticity. The last feminine attribute, however, "submission"—a problematic association for Catholics in that critics claimed that Catholicism's requirement of submission rendered Catholics incapable of independent decision making—was not taught. Catholicism was unlike totalitarian regimes that dictated beliefs and behaviors to their followers. Both Juanita Daly and the teachers characterized the girls as perfectly behaved young women who were active and independent leaders. In fact, the article described the girls as the sole guides of their religious activity within the school. "The religious phase of the school life," Daly recorded, "is left primarily in the hands of the students to be carried out through the Sodality of Mary, an organization open to every girl. Meetings are held in the auditorium with the prefect presiding from the stage." Commonly known features of Catholicism such as a church, mass, sacraments, and priests were not mentioned in the article. The school had a "small chapel where students may go for devotion," but there appeared to be no religious requirements. Curiously, Daly did not define the sodality for readers. Catholics perusing the article would have understood that the sodality nurtured deeper faith and reverence for Mary through devotional practices and activities such as preparation of altar linens and flower arranging along with group attendance at mass and regular reception of communion. Non-Catholic readers, however, would not have gleaned typical sodality activities from the article, nor would they have likely brought any previous knowledge of sodalities to their interpretation. Daly, instead, depicted the Immaculata sodality as a feeder organization for the alumni association. "In the sodality the sisters foster leadership which will function beyond the span of high school," Daly explained. "The natural successor to the sodality is the alumnae organization," which had over 2,000 members and took on as "its main project . . . a scholarship fund to help the girls in high school." The article concluded by highlighting a unique characteristic of Immaculata High School—it had "no organization corresponding to a student council in the public high schools." Why? There were no discipline problems or concerns that needed attention, and so the group dissolved. These girls appeared to be uniquely mature. "Perhaps," Sister Emilita reflected, "this is because the teachers work closely with the students and anticipate the problems. The homeroom plan with a limited number of students for each teacher fosters this personal friendship and understanding." Daly quoted Sister Emilita: "We have 43 teachers here and only a few of them are secular. The teachers have no other life outside of their teaching. They can give it their undivided attention and the girls benefit from this concentrated effort on their behalf." The sisters educated the girls in academic subjects as well as domestic arts, while the girls espoused loyalty, religiosity, and hard work. The Immaculatans offered a model for female citizenship in a country on the brink of war. Nothing in the behavior of these students raised concerns about their religious affiliation. Even if they chose to enter the convent, which the article noted a minority had done over the years, this "maternal careerism" would not challenge traditional gender roles.

Six months later, in "South Side Catholic Seniors Elected Spokesmen for Their Classes," the *Chicago Daily Tribune*, covering eight Catholic high schools, interviewed and photographed the senior voted by his or her classmates as the most outstanding. The newspaper writer also provided a general summary of each selectee's views and activities. According to the article, "The girls unanimously believe that marriage is more important than a career and are interested in dancing, dramatics, reading and writing. These girls also like boys who exhibit personality. The boys prefer to talk about higher education, sports, and girls rather than the war. All the students said they were sorry to leave high school."[6] Once again the *Tribune* offered readers typical American teenagers, some in distinctive uniforms, many members of sodalities, and all Catholics. Laudatory prose accompanied by a spate of photographs portrayed these Catholics, and by extension their co-religious, as ordinary if not ideal Americans. Catholics were not a preoccupation of print media or photojournalism in midcentury, but when they did appear, their attire conveyed a sense of American pluralism rather than the religious outsiderism that encouraged disguises a century earlier. Films, too, as will be discussed later in this chapter, portrayed Catholics positively, and once again their clothing figured importantly in their depictions.

MEMBER OF THE MYSTICAL BODY OF CHRIST ON DISPLAY

While journalist Juanita Daly may have misled readers somewhat about the absences of priests and sisters in overseeing religious practice at Immaculata High School, she was nonetheless accurate in noting a spirit of greater activism and independence on the part of youth when it came to rituals, prayers, and Catholic organizations in the early 1940s. This lay initiative was, in part, an outgrowth of the Liturgical movement discussed in Chapter 1.[7] It sought to educate the laity about the church and include them more closely in its practices. The movement ultimately gained critical support from the Vatican in the early 1940s. Pope Pius XII also issued his encyclical *Mystici Corporis Christi* (On the Mystical Body of Christ) in June 1943. In the encyclical he specified a more inclusive interpretation of the church and the role of everyday Catholics in it. First, he argued that righteous pagans, by their godly behavior, express an "implicit desire" to be part of the Catholic Church, opening up the possibility of salvation outside Catholicism.[8] This was a significant step toward the ecumenism that was more fully embraced by the church as a result of the Second Vatican Council twenty years later. Second, *Mystici Corporis Christi* drew attention to the significance of Christ's mystical body. According to Pius XII, Jesus became flesh and had an earthly body, but upon his death, he became the head of a new body, a social body, whose limbs were united in baptism. This "mystical body" was visible through the clergy, religious, and laity. All "limbs" were intrinsically valuable. He elaborated, "Christ has need of his members. . . . As our Savior does not rule the Church directly in a visible manner, He wills to be helped by the members of His Body in carrying out the work of redemption."[9] Pius XII went on to explain that "as the nerves extend from the head to all parts of the human body and give power to feel and move, in like manner Our Savior communicates strength and power to His Church so that the things of God are understood more clearly and are more eagerly desired by the faithful. From Him streams into the body of the Church all the light with which those who believe are divinely illuminated and all the grace by which they are made holy as He is holy."[10] The pope identified a more expansive role for the laity than had hitherto been expressed by the Vatican. Rather than mere followers, all Catholics would be essential actors in "carrying out the work of redemption," and their duties in all different areas of life on behalf of the church, from then on, would be considered vital to its success.[11]

Many advocates of the Liturgical movement wanted Catholics, but especially the youth, to see themselves as necessary members of the Mystical Body of Christ. Rather than simply watch the priest say the mass, the youth could participate in mass, incorporate prayer and devotion into their private lives much the way religious did, and recognize opportunities to be Christlike in all their daily activities through Catholic Action. The sodality that the Immaculatans and other high school students were members of was one such organization, which in this case aimed to promote a more active and devotional Catholicism among the youth. Historian Joseph P. Chinnici identified this trend as the "pedagogy of participation." "Threads of learning," Chinnici explained, "that had been separated before, segmented somewhat like the Catholic body into which they were woven, now began to appear in their public unity."[12] Clothing figured into this theological milieu in two unique ways. First, young Catholic girls became activists in regard to their clothing choices. Drawing on Catholic standards of modesty, sodalists throughout the country encouraged their peers to dress more modestly and demanded that stores offer less-revealing fashions or lose Catholic girls' business. Second, Catholic schools ushered in a clothing revolution by expanding clothing prescriptions or uniforms beyond a smattering of schools and dioceses. In the years after World War II, Catholic girls and boys, grade school to high school, private and parochial, found themselves in uniform attire or at the very least restricted by a dress code. The regulation of the attire of Catholic students linked them, however subtly, with the clergy and religious who led their religious culture and conveyed to American society the willingness of Catholic youth to submit to authority and wear their religious priorities proudly.

Sodalities played a prominent role in exhibiting Catholic attire and Catholic-inspired dress for teenagers, again especially for adolescent girls.

In 1925 Father Daniel Lord, SJ, took over direction of the sodality magazine *The Queen's Work* and turned it into a popular magazine for Catholic teens. Lord brought a unique set of skills to his publication endeavor. He was a theologian, playwright, and technical advisor to film director Cecil B. DeMille for *The King of Kings*.[13] And it was Lord who produced the initially ignored but ultimately persuasive Production Code for films in the late 1920s. Lord appreciated the power of visual media and cultivated the material dimension of Catholicism through his emphasis on photography and popular culture. Before Lord's tenure the magazine was titled *The Queen's Work: A Magazine of Catholic Activities*. In an effort to narrow the magazine's focus to teenagers, Lord and his staff changed the title to *The Queen's Work: The Sodality Magazine* beginning in January 1926.[14] The next month, Lord introduced a photo contest to the publication. The notice explained, "Each month we are giving a five-dollar prize for the best play picture submitted by a sodality, parish school, or Catholic club. We offer the same prize for the best Sodality picture and three dollars for the picture thought to be second best. The best picture need not, and by preference should not, be a formal group. Send pictures of your processions, receptions, picnics, teams, officers. Interest for our readers is the chief consideration."[15] Whether it was the lure of prize money or the invitation to see themselves informally on the pages of a national Catholic magazine, the students submitted pictures that piled up. Year after year they could see their local sodality or Catholic group looking back at them from the journal. The images showed teenagers for the most part, and often girls, in various forms of Catholic dress: school uniforms, "religious habit costumes" for vocations week, wedding gowns on young women entering the convent, formal wear for processions, and religious habits. Young men were typically in jacket and tie or cassocks. Perhaps students submitted more pictures with rather than without identifiable dress, but *The Queen's Work* regularly reconfirmed the significance of clothing to Catholic identity. Catholic youth across the nation saw their co-religious and recognized them as such, frequently because of their clothing or costume.

Although Catholic priests traditionally organized sodalities by age and sex, and focused primarily on devotion, Lord saw sodalities as having potential beyond encouraging a more prayerful life. Sodalities could become involved in a variety of activities. For instance, Lord believed that sodalities could combat the attraction of fascism in Europe and unthinking conformity in the United States. In particular, he wanted to help youth learn to apply a Catholic approach to their engagement with the modern world.

Female fashion was one area where the editors of the sodalist journal saw a need for attention. The February 1947 edition of *The Queen's Work* provided an explanation of the theory of supply and demand for apostolic consideration. Certain clothing manufacturers, the author explained, sell "long-sleeved undergarments and black cotton hose to postulants and nuns. . . . Arrow shirt people get out Roman collars for the clergy." The point is that where there was *demand*, smart companies *supplied* the desired wares. In the case of Catholic girls, the author extended the example of specifically Catholic attire to include fashions for young women. Teenagers would not be able to purchase decent clothing unless they *demanded* modest designs. "No money for indecent clothing," it was suggested, "could be the rallying cry."[16] Distinctly modest clothing, like Roman collars, and special undergarments for women religious, could become part of the Catholic wardrobe.

Coeditors and sodalists wrote in with their support. Patricia Ann Powers of St. Walburga's Academy in New York City wrote, "'Dare to be different,' and Mr. Manufacturer will pay heed. We Catholic girls intend to have our summer wardrobes express the character that our religious training and common sense dictate. So let's band together, girls, to demand decent, sensible, and yet good-looking apparel for our summer's fun." Cecilia Wellborn from Blessed Sacrament Parish in Houston, Texas, wrote her comments in verse. "They call it daring, but it causes staring, aside from embarrassment to the one wearing it—that's two bits of scrap called a 'bathing suit.'" And Phyllis Collins of St. Joseph's Academy in Stevens Point, Wisconsin, added, "Not only is it a Sodalist duty to refuse to wear clothing that is indecent but she must dress in a manner in which Mary would if she were a young girl of today."[17] Sodalists from Seton High School in Cincinnati, Ohio, responded promptly. Calling their campaign Supply the Demand for the Supply, or SDS, they set out to inform clothing stores that they would only buy clothing that "a Catholic girl could consciously wear."[18] Beyond visiting stores, sodalists organized fashion shows to display appropriate attire.[19] By October 1948, *The Queen's Work* reported that SDS had 4,000 members.[20] And by 1950, SDS, through *The Queen's Work*, offered other sodalists a program kit to start their own SDS chapter. The publishers of *The Queen's Work* also provided a constitution that members could recite and promise to uphold. One group in Bartelso, Illinois, identifying themselves as "Marylike Crusaders," took the following pledge: "While I am determined always to dress with Marylike modesty, both at home and in public, I intend to be specially careful to do so when visiting any place dedicated to God."[21] In addition to starter kits, sodalists could obtain instructions on how to approach store managers and set up "a sample fashion-show program" in their own school or parish.[22] SDS was a gender-appropriate channel for girls' leadership and activism, and it enlisted girls to endorse and maintain a Catholic visual presentation based on respectability, modesty, and restraint.

A popular way to convey the sodalities' fashion priorities was through fashion shows, parades, and floats. These public programs gave Catholic girls an opportunity to display their modest approach to clothing in all-American ways. Although teens across the United States participated in pageants, Catholics tended to join in those that were sponsored by Catholic associations and conveyed religious themes.[23] The May Procession and Mary's Court (the queen's attendants were either from the high school or sometimes from the grade school) were annual functions put on by Catholic schools and organizations to feature girls dressed in modest formal wear. Students from Notre Dame Academy in 1942 and Cecilian Academy in 1951 completed their May Processions with a devotion to Mary (see figs. 21 and 22).

Pope Pius XI issued clothing guidelines for young girls in 1928, but it was not until midcentury that they seemed to gain significant attention in the United States. The pope's instructions clarified that "a dress cannot be called decent which is cut deeper than two fingers breadth under the pit of the throat, which does not cover the arms at least to the elbow, and scarce reaches a bit below the knee. Furthermore, dresses made of transparent material are improper, as are flesh colored stockings which suggest the legs being bare."[24] While the girls did not keep to all of the requirements, especially in the area of sleeves, they tended to exhibit relatively conservative attire for onlookers. Vocation week sometimes included a fashion show to display the apparel of various Catholic "vocations," such as nun, priest, brother, nurse, mother, and businessman. SDS inspired a new kind of Catholic fashion show. At Canisius High School in Buffalo, New York, the Western New York High School Sodality Union sponsored a Miss Modesty Fashion Show for an audience of 2,500 in which high school girls competed for the most modest dress.[25] Other SDS-inspired fashion shows were held in Syracuse, New York; Milwaukee, Wisconsin; St. Catharine's High School in Racine, Wisconsin; and All Saints High School in Flint, Michigan.[26] Students at Marywood High School in Evanston, Illinois, created a cardboard model of a teenager holding a placard displaying a new SDS slogan each week, such as "S.D.S. Says: 'It's Smart To Be Modest.'"[27] Similar to uniforms, organizing on behalf of modesty reinforced Catholicism as an alternative to feminism and allowed girls to be activists for a religiously inspired cause.

By the mid-1950s "Marylike" tags, placed on dresses determined to be modest, could be found in dress shops in cities such as Pittsburgh, Syracuse,

Figure 21. May Procession, Notre Dame Academy, 1942. Courtesy of the YGS Group, Philadelphia, Pa.

Figure 22. May queen and her brother, Cecilian Academy, 1951. Courtesy of the Sisters of St. Joseph Archive, Philadelphia, Pa.

and Baltimore.[28] And *The Queen's Work* provided "A Blessing for Your Clothes" that could be offered as a prayer.[29] Sodalists had created an apostolate that encouraged the promotion of modesty while allowing girls to engage with modern society. Historian Kathryn Jay argued that for "SDS members, urban commercial culture served as the key mediating space between the concomitant pressures of participating in urban youth culture and remaining a spiritually devout Catholic. Modesty crusades were spiritually motivated, but they also need to be understood as part of a burgeoning youth culture obsessed with fashion and style and centered on prosperity and the possibilities of consumerism."[30] The Mystical Body of Christ theology gave every activity, even shopping and dressing, the potential to express Catholic ideology and, as with uniforms, placed teenage girls in a position to interpret and convey Catholic ideals through their dress.

Marylike modesty in clothing also gave Catholic girls an opportunity to express their patriotism as well. According to the stories of Mary's 1917 appearance at Fatima, Portugal, Mary specifically linked immodesty with the degradation that would come from communism. Marylike fashion symbolically rejected communism by promoting overtly modest femininity. A 1949 sodality pageant, which was part of a Holy Name parade and rally in St. John, New Brunswick, included girls from St. Vincent's High School marching "three abreast, the flankers in their school uniforms and those in the center in beautiful white formals. They carried a large rosary, composed of eighteen-inch, rose-colored beads, connected by silver chains; the joining medal was a small shrine of Our Lady of Fatima."[31] The parade combined the precision of a military march, the display of Catholic identity through uniforms, and modest femininity modeled in formal wear. In one carefully orchestrated procession, Catholic girls demonstrated religiosity, patriotism, and traditional gender roles in opposition to what they perceived to be godless, desexing, communist values.

A 1952 advertisement in *The Queen's Work* made a direct connection between the role of religious symbols and the fight against communism. Our Lady's Sodality promoted a new pin that members could wear. The promotion explained, "Pins are important in our modern society: They are the external sign of an inward loyalty. . . . They say: This is the organization I belong to. By any chance are you a member of the same club?" The author contended that the political environment called for a public affirmation of Catholicism and explained, "These days, when there is a world-wide attack on Jesus Christ, an external expression of your faith is well worth making. . . . When Stalin outlaws the Mass and the Chinese Communists make Holy Communion almost impossible for the Christians of the Orient, we should be making strong public professions of our belief that Christ dwells among us. . . . The times call for a loud and vigorous protestation of our faith." In addition to making a public statement, a pin would also invite non-Catholics to ask Catholics about their faith.[32] The pin was in the shape of a cross with the host at the center. Readers were reminded that "the first Red peril" was the Mohammedans, and the Crusaders carried the cross. The rise of the Soviet Union necessitated another kind of crusade, and for this one, the pin could display the wearer's allegiance and her freedom to wear it.[33]

The devotion to Our Lady of Fatima was most visible in the Blue Army of Our Lady, a rosary crusade established by Father Harold V. Colgan at his parish in Plainfield, New Jersey.[34] The church drafted students like the girl pictured in figure 23 into Mary's war on communism. As with sodalities and other devotions to Mary, there was a wearable symbol to communicate membership. For the Blue Army, members were originally encouraged to "wear a blue ribbon or a blue string by which you will be recognized as a member of the Blue Army, fighting by prayer and penance the Red Army of Communism." Later, the organization offered a pin that varied according to country: "the Miraculous Medal in the USA, a blue cross in France, a blue star in Portugal and a blue heart in Britain."[35] Shortly after founding the Blue Army, Colgan joined forces with a member of the brown scapular movement and the founder of the Scapular Press, John Mattias Haffert, and the brown scapular of the Carmelites was adopted.[36] While scapulars and medals had been in use in some form for centuries, a new emphasis on wearing one's affiliation and devotion became apparent in the 1950s. In the Cold War climate, Catholicism offered welcome symbols of religiosity and deference to American values.

The link between God and country is revealed in the record of a sodality installation ceremony in Milwaukee, Wisconsin, during the war years. On 26 May 1944, the Gesu School Sodality installed 150 sixth-through-eighth-grade girls and boys in the National Sodality of the Blessed Virgin Mary. The chronicler recounted, "The beautiful ceremony opened with a solemn procession of white-veiled girls and neatly dressed boys" entering the Gesu church. After listening to the sermon of their pastor, Father Cahill, the students proceeded to the altar and knelt at the rail. "Father Cahill presented the beautiful gold medal to each boy who reverently kissed it before receiving it. He was assisted by Father Grace who slipped the blue ribbon over each white-veiled head."[37] Each sodalist received the Miraculous Medal.

According to the story of the medal, the Virgin Mary appeared to Sister Catherine Labouré, a novice preparing to join the Daughters of Charity, on 18

Figure 23. Student photographer, Blue Army of Our Lady of Fatima, Cecilian Academy, 1951. Courtesy of the Sisters of St. Joseph Archive, Philadelphia, Pa.

July 1830, the 200th anniversary feast of St. Vincent de Paul, the founder of her order. The Virgin Mary spoke to Sister Labouré and told her to have a specific medal made. "All who wear it after it has been blessed will receive great graces, especially if they wear it around their neck. Graces will abound for those who wear it with confidence."[38] The wording on the front of the medal announced Mary's immaculate conception: "O MARY, CONCEIVED WITH-OUT SIN, PRAY FOR US WHO HAVE RECOURSE TO THEE."[39] Displaying

Mary's medal championed religiosity, purity, and the types of government that allowed people to express their religion freely.

In both the appearance to Sister Catherine and the 1917 Fatima apparition to the three children, Mary tells her audience what to wear and what not to wear. Mary's actions conform to female stereotypes in that she concerns herself with apparel. Regarding the Miraculous Medal, Mary challenges men in particular, because of their secularism, to wear the medal. Central to the tale is the significance of displaying faith. According to the story of Sister Catherine, "A few old men . . . did not want to wear the medal about their necks. They preferred to carry it in a pocket, or have it pinned to their clothing. In this way they would not be advertising their piety. . . . For many years the Church had been cruelly persecuted in France. Even now the godless ones in charge of the government were doing their best to banish it from the land. . . . As a result, there was little public interest in religion, and only a few people were to be found praying in the churches."[40] Therefore, Mary demanded a public display, and those who wore the medal would receive "greater graces." Sister Catherine's next great challenge was convincing reluctant men to wear the medal around their necks.[41]

Eventually Sister Catherine was able to win over the men. According to the legend, the Virgin Mother, however, was still not satisfied. In 1836 Sister Catherine heard from Mary again; this time she wanted a chapel and a new organization formed called the Children of Mary. It would include girls cared for by the Daughters of Charity, and the students and orphans would wear the Miraculous Medal both night and day.[42] Not long after, the sisters invited young boys to join as well. According to the stories, Mary's concern centered around wearing the medal. Mary did not have to be concerned with Sister Catherine wearing a symbol, since she was joining the Daughters of Charity. But other Catholics—men, girls, and boys—needed to demonstrate their faith and to do it with a visible sign.

At the Gesu School installation, after the procession, the ceremony began with the "Prayer for our Country and Flag." The congregation and inductees recited, "Almighty God, Judge over men and nations, we stand before Thee today as loyal sons of our country, grateful for its splendid heritage. . . . O God, by whose word all things are sanctified, pour forth Thy blessing upon our Flag, and grant that whosoever shall live under it with thanksgiving according to Thy law and will, may receive from Thee, through the invocation of Thy Holy Name, health of body and peace of soul. Through Christ our Lord. We pray for Thy blessing upon the emblem of our Republic. May it float forever over our free land. May our ancient watchword, 'In God we trust' sustain and guide our people. Amen."[43] Once the prayer was complete, Father Cahill recited the Act of Consecration to Mary, and he questioned the children on their intentions to keep up their devotion to the Blessed Mother. By the end of the day, "the girls in white dresses and white veils and boys in good clothes, had all received a blessed medal. In addition, the girls have received a blessed badge."[44] The badges, similar to scapulars, provided a symbol of the wearer's commitment to Mary, but also a girl's commitment to the purity and modesty that Mary both represented and requested in her message at Fatima. High school students devoting their yearbooks to Mary are shown in figure 24 as if they are seeing an apparition of Mary rather than looking at a statue, while in figure 25 students read from a Catholic publication, Our Lady of Fatima. As Mariology became more popular in the post–World War II years, religious accessorizing served the dual purpose of expressing a commitment to Marian devotion and to anticommunism.[45]

A UNIFORM EXPLOSION

Former uniform company owners, such as George Bendinger and Ned O'Hara, agreed that the school uniform business was a promising venture in the post–World War II era as more and more Catholic schools seemed to be adopting uniform dress for girls and now boys. Ned O'Hara explained that sisters who entered religious life in schools that required uniforms took the clothing model with them as they moved to new suburban parishes or other dioceses.[46] Ned O'Hara worked with his father, Edward O'Hara, at Eisenberg and O'Hara's and then took a job with George Bendinger. At Bendinger's Ned met Edward Flynn. Eventually Ed Flynn and Ned O'Hara formed Flynn and O'Hara's. As more Catholic schools opened, more Catholic children found their school wardrobe dramatically reduced to specific items such as school-designated jumpers, blouses, gym suits, beanies, ties, and trousers. In other words, the schools outfitted their students in uniforms.

Beyond signifying membership in the Catholic community, uniforms arguably allowed Catholics to demonstrate their engagement with the era's consumer-oriented economy, albeit through virtuous and overtly Catholic-inspired purchases.[47] On the surface, Catholic school students, in particular those clad in uniforms, may have appeared to be taking up a position against mainstream consumer culture. Catholic school uniforms, almost exclusively worn by girls until the postwar period, distinguished Catholic students from public school students, partially diminished class differences, and reduced students' ability to display new and potentially immodest fashions. Neverthe-

Figure 24. Cecilian girls dedicate yearbooks to an apparition of Mary, 1951. Courtesy of the Sisters of St. Joseph Archive, Philadelphia, Pa.

Figure 25. Cecilian girls read Our Lady of Fatima, 1951. Courtesy of the Sisters of St. Joseph Archive, Philadelphia, Pa.

less, the 1940s and 1950s witnessed a dramatic expansion and diversification of uniforms for Catholic students. Cathedral High School in Springfield, Massachusetts, adopted its first uniform in 1959. Rather than a simple jumper or serge dress with detachable collar and cuffs, Cathedralite girls wore "a green wool blazer, plaid wool skirt, tailored white blouse, white socks, and saddle shoes." The boys dressed in a "grey wool blazer, white dress shirt, tie, and pants." Blazers for both girls and boys "displayed the Cathedral seal on the left breast pocket."[48] Bishop Hughes Memorial High School in New York City was a parish high school established in 1905 that eventually became a diocesan high school. While Bishop Hughes High did not adopt uniforms in the early wave, it did so in the years after World War II. Overall, where Catholic uniforms had not been adopted, they came into greater use, and when specific clothing for school was already in place, it became more varied and accessorized.

As noted in the previous chapter, several Catholic schools for girls, particularly the convent schools, required uniforms before the onset of World War II as a way of promoting both simplicity and exclusivity. When the parochial and diocesan schools adopted uniforms, they seemed to care more about respectability and "classlessness." After World War II, however, both the select and the diocesan schools moved in the direction of greater Catholic consumerism. Where uniforms had been employed strategically in the past, their presence became almost a foregone conclusion. What that uniform would look like and how it would be accessorized became the question. Yearbook photos from 1945 of students at Cecilian Academy, a private coed elementary and all-girls high school run by the Sisters of St. Joseph in Philadelphia, reveal the changes under way. In that year Cecilian Academy adopted a new uniform. Freshman and sophomore students debuted jumpers with blouses and ties, and the junior class was split between those with the old dark serge dresses and detachable collars and cuffs and those with the new jumper, blouse, and tie. Although the shoes were not standardized in the 1940s, by the middle of the 1950s Cecilian girls were wearing regulation saddle shoes. And while boys had been exempt from the various uniform regulations at Cecilian Academy prior to 1945, by 1950, as figure 26 illustrates, they were all in matching blazers with insignia and regulation ties.[49] Finally, book bags for high school girls eventually became part of the standard ensemble. As a picture from the 1966 Cecilian yearbook (fig. 27) indicates, the school regulated blazers, school bags, uniforms, socks, and shoes. Only the girls' purses remained individualized.

Figure 26. Third and fourth grades with boys in uniform, Cecilian Academy, 1950. Courtesy of the Sisters of St. Joseph Archive, Philadelphia, Pa.

Figure 27. Girls walking with blazers, uniforms, book bags, and saddle shoes, Cecilian Academy, 1966. Courtesy of the Sisters of St. Joseph Archive, Philadelphia, Pa.

Although school uniforms had been touted as economical in the 1920s, the new era of consumption gradually strayed from that impulse. A diocesan school jumper made from three-fourths of a yard of dark serge would cost a family $16.00. If purchased with three half-blouses (a blouse that did not extend to the waist) and a gym suit, the total would come to $19.00.[50] The requirement for one jumper, however, did not last long. Diocesan high schools, the less expensive option among Catholic high schools, were not immune to the consumer-oriented uniform overhaul. Girls attending West Philadelphia Catholic Girls' High School were required to wear a hunter-green serge jumper with a tan blouse in the early 1940s. By the early 1950s, this dress was accompanied by a regulation green beanie with a tan peak. For 50 cents, girls also purchased a different colored emblem that they sewed on their uniforms each year to indicate their class. By the 1960s, diocesan schools had moved to seasonal uniforms, adopting "summer uniforms" made of pink, green, or blue seersucker for warmer months.[51] Families then purchased not one but two uniforms and mandatory and voluntary accessories such as hats, badges, class rings, and regulation shoes.

Several select or private Catholic schools instituted completely different uniforms for seniors. In 1941, Chicago Catholic girls attending Alvernia High School joined St. Scholastica Academy and the Convent of the Sacred Heart Academy, also in the Chicago area, in adopting tailored suits or businesswomen's attire for the last year of high school. Alvernia seniors wore a "midnight blue, wool gabardine suit."[52] The ensemble included a "long cardigan jacket with two handy patch pockets and a softly curved neckline, cut to allow a soft shirt collar to peep over the top."[53] A gored skirt completed the outfit. Another "senior-specific uniform" was initiated in the early 1960s at Our Lady of Lourdes in Poughkeepsie, New York.[54] Ideally, a money-conscious family could dress their daughter in the same uniform for all four years of high school. But changing styles and senior-year-specific attire undermined attempts at savings and created a "one-year" uniform.

In the fall of 1944 Monsignor Bonner, superintendent of schools in the Archdiocese of Philadelphia, prepared an address for the beginning of the school year to give the Sisters of Notre Dame de Namur who taught at Notre Dame High School in Drexel Hill, Pennsylvania. Reflecting on the girls' uniforms, Bonner wrote,

> We feel that some of them are engaged in an endurance contest. They make up their minds as Freshman that they are going to make their uniform last through their senior year. I don't think they should be allowed to do that

now [that] the economic situation has improved. Perhaps you should have daily inspection. Soiled spots should be noticed. Don't humiliate them, but take them aside and tell them that no respectable person appears in clothes subject to criticism. I noticed a Wave on my way here and that brought up the subject of wearing hats. We have given up the battle, and just forgotten to emphasize the fact that a lady wears a hat every day. Evidently the Navy thinks so because these young ladies are obliged to wear hats in public. I believe they also insist upon gloves. We couldn't go that far, but that might be a selling argument. Many of these children lack proper supervision at home. Both parents are working, and the children more or less do as they like so that it sometimes happens that they started out to school in the morning without having combed their hair or washed.[55]

Despite Bonner's criticism of home life, it was likely the dual-income family that provided the financial resources to replace an ill-fitting or poorly maintained uniform as well as pay the tuition. Bonner seemed well aware of the consumer culture drawing teenagers in, but he wanted at least some of their purchases to promote Catholic identity and values. Mothers working away from home, Bonner implied, made the need for the uniform that much greater. Less supervision at home necessitated more supervision on the part of the church, and young Catholics were all the more in need of institutional guidance. The message Bonner wanted to communicate through attention to uniforms, to both the students and observers of the students, was that Catholicism valued military-style order and social respectability.

Students agreed with Bonner's sentiments, and they became uniform watchdogs in the spirit of lay activism, school spirit, and Catholic respectability. The 1943 student council at Mount St. Joseph Academy stayed on the lookout for uniform transgressions and resolved to fine girls who wore "offensive make-up, such as heavy powder and dark rouge."[56] Along the lines of Monsignor Bonner's concerns, Mounties charged fellow students 10 cents for "untidy shoes and uniforms" during the 1945 school year. The next year, holes in uniforms also became fine-worthy. Other sartorial violations included stockingless legs on the bus or while playing tennis, as well as wearing rings or wide hair bands.[57] The John W. Hallahan Catholic Girls' High School was notable for its dress regulations, and a staff photographer at the *Philadelphia Inquirer* staged a picture of senior and president of the student government Elizabeth Hastings explaining the rules to two younger students in 1942. Among the rules was "Freshmen must learn to wear hats to scho[ol]." (See fig. 28.) Peer regulating and financial pressure protected the

Catholic school image and indicated that Catholic girls also had an investment in maintaining their look.[58]

Children attending parish school experienced the uniform revolution as well. In 1965, girls attending St. Rafael's in Long Island City, New York, wore a green wool plaid jumper with pleats that overlaid a white blouse. While solid colors had been the mainstay of Catholic uniforms through the 1950s, the introduction of plaid made Catholic school students stand out all the more and imprinted a kind of Celtic Catholicism on students, regardless of their nationality.[59] Writer Maureen Corrigan remembered wearing "snap-on green bow ties, 'flesh'-colored leotards, green kneesocks, and . . . green oxfords," along with a "green-and-gold Robin Hood–style felt hat."[60] For boys, the uniform consisted of green wool trousers along with a crisp white shirt and a green plaid tie. During that same period, New Yorker Dan Barry attended St. Cyril and St. Methodius Parish School in the Deer Park section of Long Island, New York. His uniform included "dark green pants with a black stripe down the sides. Green socks. Green belt with gold trim. Black loafers sold exclusively by the shoe store near Ha-Cha Stationers. . . . A gold shirt with the circular icon of the Holy Spirit stitched into the breast pocket" and "A green tie emblazoned with the initials SCSM."[61] Uniforms, while not restricted to use during school hours, nevertheless were sometimes so "distinct" in color and style that they took on a style of their own—never to be confused with clothes worn out of school.

Just like the high school uniforms, Catholic uniform ensembles on young children were meant to draw attention and convey Catholic ideals. Mother Madonna Maria's lead article in the 1966 St. Agatha's School newspaper, *The News Leaf*, took up the topic of appearance for the parent readers. In her piece, Mother Madonna Maria thanked parents for their cooperation, especially in getting the children to school in time to assemble before the bell and having the children dressed appropriately. The assembly was part of what Mother Madonna Maria considered the students' citizenship education. Punctuality and presentation were important ingredients in "becoming a worthwhile citizen." She noted that "the majority of children have taken such pride in this assembly that they are in line and ready to begin long before actual starting time." The result was an orderly presentation of 600 students, "standing in perfect formation offering allegiance to God and Country." Mother Madonna Maria offered a further remark of appreciation for those "parents who are so careful about the cleanliness and appearance of their children. It is such a pleasure to look at children who are dressed in a special way for the very special work of 'going to school.' To help you reach 100% in good grooming we will continue with navy blue uniforms and white blouses for the girls. To this we have added navy blue knee socks and 'beanies.' Beanies are part of the school uniform and must be worn everyday. For your convenience all of these items may be purchased through the school. The boys are expected to wear white shirts and ties and regular school trousers. Suit jackets are to be worn by all boys in grades 6, 7, and 8."[62] The value of uniformly, respectably, and gender appropriately dressed children needed no explanation in Mother Madonna Maria's view—the meaning was obvious. "We hope every parent will see the wisdom behind our efforts," she concluded, "and that all will join us in leading the children safely along the road to tomorrow's citizens." The school's concept of citizenry had to do with demonstrating order, the ability to follow directions, maintenance of proper gender roles, and respectability. All boys wore ties and older boys wore both ties and jackets, and all girls wore dresses. School administrators even required the girls to wear hats—a contested accessory by this time both inside the church (post–Vatican II) and outside in public schools. High school students were just beginning to let their "freak flags" flow and challenging the perceived authoritarianism they found regarding school hair and dress codes.

The next year, 1967, parents at St. Agatha's found another front-page address on the topic of attire. "It is with a certain amount of pride," Mother Madonna Maria wrote,

> to tell you how pleased we are with the splendid cooperation of the majority of you. However, there is always room for improvement in all that we do this side of heaven. Therefore, we ask you, the parents, to continue in your efforts to make ladies and gentlemen of our boys and girls. To those of you who are still not aware of our requirements, we repeat the following rules:
>
> Dress: Girls must wear uniform, long-sleeved white blouse, navy blue knee socks, and school "beany."
>
> Boys must wear white shirt and tie with school suit. Jackets are worn in Grades 6, 7, and 8.
>
> (Jewelry and sneakers are forbidden at all times.)[63]

Catholic youth had become unquestionably "visible" from the 1940s on. As Monsignor Bonner had indicated, the "economic situation has improved," and school administrators and pastors required parents to use their financial resources to outfit their children in more varied and accessorized school clothes and religious accessories. According to Barry's account of his uniform, his family noted the greater demand for Catholic purchases, and his father identified it as "a Catholic shakedown." [64]

CLERGY

Virtuous consumption extended beyond Catholic schools as well. In the post–World War II years, through the new advertising adopted by priestly journals, priests too could learn about the best styles of liturgical garments as well as where to buy these vestments. The Mystical Body theology, however, operated in reverse with priests' clothing. Unlike the students who gained a stronger connection to the religious and clergy by appearing in uniforms, many priests diversified their wardrobe and dressed in nonclerical attire. Laymen's clothing enabled priests to be more approachable as they engaged in active apostolates along with Catholic youth.

Before World War II, there was little to no advertising in priestly journals. After the war, however, advertising made its way in, and priests could shop around for vestments. The *Homiletic and Pastoral Review* began with "aditorials" that ostensibly educated the priestly readership about proper vestments while advertising the clothing manufacturer that could supply these garments. The E. M. Lohmann Company in St. Paul, Minnesota, used a series of full-page aditorials to provide background on and advertise items such as the Medieval Chasuble, the Gothic Chasuble, the Chasuble in the Liturgical Revival of the Twentieth Century, Christian Symbolism, the Stole, the Maniple, the Dalmatics and Tunics, the Humeral Veil, the Cope and Hood, Ornamentation in Vestments, and the Surplice and Rochet. Through 1944, the advertisements maintained the aditorial status — seemingly hesitant to overtly market their religious wares. However, by 1945, the E. M. Lohmann Company no longer identified their promotions as aditorials and instead let them stand as pure advertising. The sacerdotal garments, previously marketed by word of mouth, entered the mainstream marketplace through overt advertising. Other vestment companies such as Thomas A. Blake on Fifth Avenue and Wildermann Company, Inc., on Barclay Street, both in New York City, joined E. M. Lohmann's and purchased advertising space as well. Handmade liturgical wear crafted by nuns or independent tailors could still be purchased, but advertising demonstrated Catholicism's comfort with the free market and modern business techniques for sacramental wares.

While clerical garments, both mufti and vesture, had become more widely marketed, they were not the only attire that adorned the clergy. Priests were clearly purchasing nonclerical wear at midcentury as well. In 1954 an anonymous priest, "Fr. Y," reflected on his distaste with what he saw as a new type of clerical visibility. In his essay "I Love My Cassock," published in the *Homiletic and Pastoral Review*, Fr. Y explained to his ordained readers that he was writing his article on a warm evening in his Mississippi rectory while "a rotating fan" blew the hem of his cassock. Fr. Y loved the cassock despite the heat. He felt that wearing clerical dress provided "a powerful check on any act unbecoming a cleric." Fr. Y went on to ruminate on the ease with which many priests seemed to put the cassock aside. He recounted a few stories of clergy in street dress: a man who he thought was stopping for directions dressed in a T-shirt and white trousers turned out to be the priest who was scheduled to visit and take up a mission collection. In another episode, he remembered a priest who could not get permission to say mass on any of the unoccupied side altars at a church in Brussels. This priest had presented himself in a T-shirt and, despite a second request, was still refused. Fr. Y's own father had an unpleasant encounter with a monsignor in lay clothes. The cleric, dressed "as a successful businessman," had lost control of his car and inadvertently taken down a segment of wire fence that bordered Fr. Y's father's farm. During his confrontation with this driver, Fr. Y's father found out the man's identity. Not only was the offending driver a monsignor but a former classmate of his son's. The revelation of the monsignor's identity disappointed Fr. Y's father, since the monsignor was "disguised" in business attire.

Fr. Y confessed that he, too, was not as strict with his dress as he might be. Referring to the growing popularity of the "vernacular movement," he acknowledged that he no longer recited or even remembered the Latin prayer he had said in the past while vesting. Likewise, he admitted to feeling a little guilty with his "black tropical suit and straw hat in the presence of European brethren sweltering in cassocks of real heavy material." Although his focus was on clothing, Fr. Y suggested that the informal attitude toward dress was simply one aspect of the general atmosphere of casualness among priests. Not only did the journal he was writing for neglect the topic of T-shirts, but so too did retreat masters. Few American Catholic leaders were reminding or disciplining priests who appeared in nonclerical attire. Fr. Y concluded that while there was no shortage of jovial priests, properly dressed priests were in short supply.[65]

A decade before Fr. Y's article, filmmaker Leo McCarey and actor Bing Crosby gave tacit support to the casual priest with character Father O'Malley in films such as *Going My Way* and *The Bells of St. Mary's*. The 1944 film *Going My Way*, winner of seven Academy Awards, including for best picture, offered a Hollywood version of the type of priest Fr. Y was concerned about. Father O'Malley, played by Bing Crosby, was an accessible "everyone's man." Director Leo McCarey depicted Father O'Malley as an accomplished pianist, notably athletic—having "worked out with the St. Louis Browns"—and unmistakably heterosexual. Father O'Malley chose the priesthood over a relationship with an attractive and successful opera singer. Finally, Father O'Malley was simple and indistinct in his dress. According to historian Anthony Burke Smith, "Audiences encountered a powerful new image that overturned long-standing stereotypes of Catholic authority. Father O'Malley, more than any depiction of the celibate Catholic cleric up until then, created a new icon . . . the priest as American hero."[66] In the Mystical Body, beyond the head, all parts were equally essential. Just as the students gained membership status with their uniformed visibility, clerics with their varied wardrobe sometimes purposefully lost their religious identification. They came off the pedestal to join young people as one of several essential parts in the Mystical Body.

Non-Catholics watching Father O'Malley could identify him as being of Irish descent by his name, but he was not an immigrant—he did not have a brogue like Father Fitzgibbon, the cassock-donning elderly prelate in the film, or the nosy and overly devoted Mrs. Quimp. Father O'Malley, pictured in figure 29 wearing a neat black suit and straw boater, indicates his professionalism and easy accessibility, unlike Mrs. Quimp, who is suspicious and unworldly. In one scene, Father O'Malley is filmed from behind as he walks down a busy neighborhood sidewalk. Within the shot composition, the eye is drawn to the men in dark uniforms—men of service, patriotic men, Father O'Malley and the sailors. Throughout the film, Father O'Malley wears baseball caps and golf clothes; he owns a fishing rod and a tennis racket. In figure 30 he is showing Father Fitzgibbon how to golf. Non-Catholics, including the young mortgage salesman in the film, had nothing to fear or complain about with this Catholic.[67] Father O'Malley's clothes and behavior represent a more democratized and American brand of Catholicism, while his easy exchanges in the world—the non-Catholic world specifically—point to his welcoming approach to well-intentioned pagans. One pagan O'Malley clearly converts is the young real estate man who marries the wayward Catholic girl and joins the military. The real estate agent cannot join the priesthood (he's not Catholic yet), but he can have the next-best-uniformed profession in this film; he becomes a soldier.

The *Homiletic and Pastoral Review* approved of the film. In an answer to a query asking how the *Review* accounted for the fact that "priests here and there bitterly censure this film as if it were positively harmful," the editor dismissed the criticism, arguing that he had read or heard complaints from only three sources and that it was therefore only a "minority opinion."[68] In the December issue, a fourth critic surfaced, although he had not seen the film. Once again, the writer dismissed these few complaints about *Going My Way*, contending it was a "mirthful introduction" to Catholicism.

Another Hollywood film, *I Confess* (1953), directed by Alfred Hitchcock, a Catholic, offers a close look at French Canadian Catholic culture and clerical life. Set in Quebec City, the film employs thoughtful costuming to communicate the unique characteristics of Hitchcock's cast of Catholic characters. In the film, Father Logan, played by Montgomery Clift, hears the confession of the church caretaker, who has just murdered a wealthy town lawyer, Mr. Villette. Although the murderer, Mr. Keller, receives Father Logan's word that his confession will be safely kept, Keller becomes paranoid and attempts to frame Father Logan for the murder. Keller is almost successful, as Father Logan also has a secret from his past that is perhaps worth hiding. The dead lawyer had

Figure 29. Mrs. Quimp and Father O'Malley, Going My Way. Courtesy of Photofest.

Figure 30. Father
O'Malley golfing,
Going My Way.
Courtesy of Photofest.

been blackmailing Father Logan's former girlfriend, Ruth, which gives Father Logan a motive for murdering the lawyer.

Father Logan, like other priests in the film, almost always appears in a cassock. In Canada, the cassock was common attire for a priest. A priest is suspected of the murder because the killer used a cassock as a disguise when he retreated from the murder scene. Nevertheless, Hitchcock takes a few opportunities to show Father Logan in ordinary clothes. In one scene, Father Logan is painting the rectory wearing a casual, button-up shirt with rolled-up sleeves and dark trousers. In another scene, Father Logan meets Ruth on a ferry, and although Logan wears his cassock, Hitchcock juxtaposes the handsome priest with costumed friars who are also traveling on the ferry. Father Logan wears a cassock, close fitting in the torso, which shows off his manly physique, while the friars, representing an antiquated church, appear round and oddly tonsured. Finally, Hitchcock uses flashbacks to show Father Logan as an attentive and amorous suitor as well as a brave soldier in World War II before he selflessly decided to become a priest. Once again, Hollywood offered an honest, brave, and even sexy priest for audiences to admire.

In the 1954 Academy Award–winning film *On the Waterfront*, Karl Malden (who plays the detective in *I Confess*) took on the role of Father Barry, a socially conscious priest concerned about labor conditions on the docks in New York. Dressed in a black suit with a "turned around collar" in most scenes, Father Barry also wore a raincoat and a black fedora hat. In addition to his clothing he had behavioral accessories that coded him as a regular guy, one whose behavior was not always "checked." He smoked and drank in the bar with the dockworkers whom he was trying to organize to stand up to the union or mob that controlled them.[69] It was because he let his behavior stray and he ministered on the docks—in a familiar and public space—that Father Barry was successful in his ministry. (See fig. 31.) He was able to convince Marlon Brando's character, Terry Malloy, to quit the dirty union and bring justice to the docks.

Catholic clothing for both students and priests responded to the flexibility of the Mystical Body of Christ theology. Adolescent Catholic girls could participate in consumer culture as activists and could wear "civilian" or uniform attire that communicated Catholic values. Priests could also participate in consumer culture, learning about their vestmentary options through advertising. Real-life clothing and the costuming for movie priests assisted the clergy in appearing both charismatic and inviting. Women religious, as we will see, had to wait, or chose to wait, a little longer for a new approach to clothing.

Figure 31. *Father Barry with collar and fedora,* On the Waterfront. *Courtesy of Photofest.*

WOMEN RELIGIOUS

While the presentation of priests in both real and film life shifted toward a more casual and accessible American persona, the appearance of women religious remained relatively static. In the film *On the Waterfront*, an exchange takes place between Pop Doyle, a dejected dockworker, and his daughter Edie, played by Eva Marie Saint, that provides a sense of sisters in the 1950s. Trouble has been brewing between the mob union and the dockworkers, and Pop Doyle tells his daughter that she has to go back to school—to the sisters at St. Ann's in Tarrytown, New York, where she'll be safe. The sisters are away, both physically and metaphorically, "in the country," while Father Barry is reestablishing his ministry with the longshoremen on the docks. Although *On the Waterfront* came out in 1954, a time when convents were seeing record-size novice classes, the film seems to dismiss women religious as both out of touch and rigid. Pop Doyle wants to send his daughter back to St. Ann's, where the sisters can look out for her; Father Barry, surprisingly concerned with Edie's view of him, notes that while Edie wants to deny that she thinks he is a coward, her training under the sisters has taught her "not to lie." And Terry Malloy, Edie's love interest, shares his story of being "whacked" by the sisters. The off-screen sisters offered shelter, told the truth, and punished children, but they did not contribute to bringing justice to the docks. Edie would not go back to her school after the brutal treatment of workers she had seen on the docks. Sisters were safe and apolitical, but the real work of redeeming the world according to Christ's message, the film suggests, was happening outside the convent. The unchanging appearance of the sisters' dresses in real life seemed to suggest an aversion to social and political risk.

The bookends of moral certitude in *On the Waterfront* are Father Barry and Edie, both dressed in black and white (see fig. 32). Like Father Barry, Edie has a limited wardrobe in the film. With the exception of one scene in a white slip, she wears a black dress with white-trimmed collar and cuffs, not unlike Catholic school uniforms of the late 1920s and early 1930s (see fig. 33). Edie represents the possibility of giving Catholic witness without taking religious vows. She is brave, modestly sexy, and religious.

Pope Pius XII also seemed to be looking toward another model of Catholic womanhood when he announced his endorsement of a "new" kind of apostolate for Catholic women in 1947, the secular institute.[70] Pius XII "spoke of a world that needed more than priests and religious to get Christ's work done. He pointed out that there are, particularly in the modern world, areas which only the laity can effectively penetrate. He called for . . . generous laymen and laywomen to dedicate their lives to a special vocation which would have an identity all its own. They would take private vows and have a central house, but no special manner of dress." One of the main features of the secular institute was "its flexibility."[71] In the following years, secular institutes such as Caritas Christi, Oblate Missionaries of Mary Immaculate, and Rural Parish Workers of Christ the King welcomed non-habit-wearing recruits to participate in more active and public apostolates.[72]

If Pope Pius XII had been concerned about the appearance and visual message of the religious habit in his promotion of secular institutes, the message was subtle enough to miss. In 1952, however, he spoke of his concerns regarding habits more explicitly. Pius XII addressed the International Congress of Mothers General and cited a "crisis of vocations" and called for sisters to be "attentive lest the custom, the manner of life or of spirituality be an obstacle and a cause of loss. We mean certain usages which, if they had a meaning in the past in another cultural environment, no longer have it today and would only be an obstacle to the vocation of sincerely good and courageous girls."[73] He further explained, "The religious habit should always express the consecration of Christ; that is expected and desired by all. By other respects the habit should be appropriate in keeping with the demands of hy-

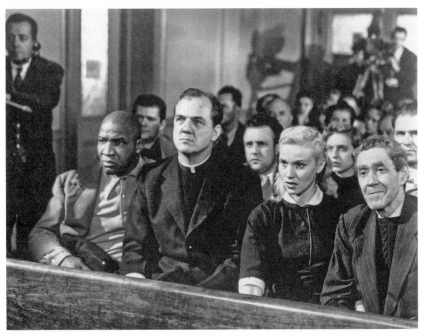

Figure 32. Father Barry and Edie in pew, On the Waterfront. Courtesy of Photofest.

Figure 33. Edie and Terry,
On the Waterfront.
Courtesy of Photofest.

giene. We could not refrain from expressing our satisfaction at the fact that during the course of a year a few congregations had already taken some practical steps in this matter. To sum up: in things that are not essential make adaptations counseled by reason and well-ordered society."[74] Although the number of religious women had not declined as the Vatican claimed, the demand for their services had increased. In particular, the success of Catholic schools necessitated more sisters to teach in them.[75] As for habits, the pope's address did not offer any specific directives, and so sisters, for the most part, continued with their work in their same habits.

Two religious orders established in the United States after World War II, however, selected more modern habits. The Home Visitors of Mary in the Diocese of Detroit (1949) and the Sisters of the Divine Spirit in the Diocese of Greensburg, Pennsylvania (1954), chose contemporary fashions. The former wore "a simple navy dress and a hat and coat in modern style" with a large Miraculous Medal. The latter donned "an oxford gray skirt and jacket with white blouse and a small black hat."[76] According to coverage by the *New York Times*, the Sisters of the Divine Spirit credited Pope Pius's appeal for their departure from "old fashion long skirts and close fitting headdress."[77] But beyond those two orders, there was little indication that the pope's recommendation had altered the thinking of the mothers general regarding the habits.

The invisibility of sisters in *On the Waterfront* and the new papal endorsement of secular institutes aside, American sisters were perhaps more visible and active, in habit, than ever in the post–World War II years. Galvanized by presentations at the National Catholic Education Association Conferences in the late 1940s and early 1950s and worried about the effects of their lack of educational training, women religious, cutting across congregations, organized what would become the Sister Formation Conference (SFC) in 1954. One of the founders and the first editor of the *Sister Formation Bulletin*, Sister Ritamary Bradley, laid out a carefully crafted rationale for the group's establishment. She explained that if teachers in the Catholic schools were not adequately educated and did not have the same credentials as public school teachers, Catholic schools would be easy targets for criticism. According to chronicler Kenneth A. Briggs, "By 1952, a total of thirty-three states required or would soon require teaching candidates to have a bachelor's degree."[78] The SFC members worried that by 1965 all states would require a bachelor's degree for public school teachers. The sisters were concerned that "this could easily result in agitation to legislate the Catholic schools out of existence."[79] Additionally, the demand for Catholic school teachers had increased along with the building success of Catholic institutions, but it had happened so rapidly that the sisters had been called to the classroom before they had, in some cases, begun or, in other cases, completed their undergraduate degrees. For instance, in 1925 over thirty sisters enrolled in summer session classes at Columbia University, but by going through degree programs piecemeal, the sisters sometimes required up to twenty years to finish their degrees.[80] According to Sisters Annette Walters and Ritamary Bradley of SFC, habits had substituted for credentials, since to many children the dresses conveyed authority.[81] Sister Ritamary arrived at the opinion that to enter the classroom without adequate training was a disservice to sisters and students and ultimately jeopardized the future of Catholic education.

Sister Ritamary never mentioned, in 1954, that the sisters should acquire an education because they were Catholic leaders, professional women, or simply promising individuals who deserved an opportunity to expand their skills. And they did not question whether educating students in Catholic schools was the best use of their talents or whether the habit could be an obstacle to their work—that would come later. In 1954, the National Catholic Educational Association, sympathetic clergy, and mothers superior accepted the rationale of women like Sisters Ritamary Bradley, Mary Emil Penet, Bertrand Meyers, and Madeleva Wolff that more education for the sisters was a worthwhile investment and good for Catholic education. An assortment of Catholic leaders gave their endorsement to the SFC, and the project got under way.[82]

Thinking cooperatively as the new SFC while retaining congregationality, and refraining from seeking authority while communicating the need for credentials and college courses at cost, presented interesting challenges to the habit-wearing sisters. The habit, for sisters, had represented a badge of distinction and was a source of community pride. To a non-Catholic, women religious might not seem too different, since they all wore unusual garments; but within the Catholic world, co-religious knew the different orders, and it was the habit that provided the mark of distinction. In "bird books," named so for their similarity to nature books that described the different kinds of birds, each page provided a picture of a sister modeling the habit of her community. Like the distinctive coloration and arrangement of feathers on a bird, in the "bird book" of sisters, what appeared to be most important about the order or the woman was the clothing.[83] Therefore, establishing an organization that sought to think across congregations without diminishing distinctiveness, which was gained through a habit, was potentially a Pandora's box.

Although the focus of the SFC was on professional and religious training, the habit nonetheless did gradually become an object of attention. A vocational survey conducted by the SFC and concluded in 1956 reported on "deterrents to the acceptance of religious vocations on the part of students."[84] The survey revealed that "the greatest complaint . . . is that the Sisters have so withdrawn themselves from contact with life that they do not know the world in which the students are living. Students do not want the Sisters to be worldly; but they think that, as teachers, Sisters lose their efficacy for good when they isolate themselves from contact with the world in which their students are living."[85] Students compared sisters to priests and stated, "Priests are better equipped because they are in contact with people all their lives and seem to have a better understanding of problems because of it." Another asked, "Why can't Sisters be as modern as priests? They would attract more vocations."[86] According to the survey, "Only 25 percent of our students believe that Sisters think for themselves," while "a fourth of the students affirmed that they would advise someone who has ideas of her own not to try to enter a religious community. Why? Evidently something makes the students believe that Sisters do not think for themselves."[87] Other comments indicated that the sisters did not seem "human" and that they did not smile. "Some Orders," a student wrote, "keep their members too strict. They lose their own individuality and become a carbon copy."[88] Students internalized a deep respect for the habit and seemed hesitant to criticize it directly, but they certainly hinted that the habit was problematic.

The survey emphasized that students saw a lack of academic preparation for teaching, an antiquated life, general unhappiness, and conformity. Sister Judith, the author of the report, saw the elusive remedy to all of these problems as "time." With thinly veiled annoyance she remarked, "If the Sisters are to maintain equable dispositions—not to mention sunshiny ones—keep up on current events, read the latest periodicals, prepare interesting enough lessons to overcome student ennui, be friendly and sociable, take time to converse with students after school, participate in student activities, and avoid looking rushed, irritable, cranky, inhuman, stone-faced, preoccupied, cold, then they are desperately in need of time."[89] Prayers, chores, teaching, grading, and now studying all filled the sisters' days and then some. The habit, especially, required special attention. The headpiece in many orders had to be pinned on daily, and the intricate plaits required regular ironing. The sisterhood was not a carefree life.

Curiously, although the survey was initiated in part by the comments of Pius XII, who noted that "custom, the manner of life or of spirituality" could become an obstacle to vocations, the habit did not emerge as a specific obstacle in Sister Judith's report. The sisters accepted the gendered significance of attention to apparel and did not see their clothing as a significant issue.

Fashion discussions of any sort were, they believed, one of the weaknesses of the female sex and a problem that religious life dispelled. Sisters were beyond "clothes talk," and superiors practiced "selective obedience" and ignored the pope's directives.[90]

A year later, the *Sister Formation Bulletin* reported on obstacles sisters faced in the field of social work. In studying to be a social worker, the author explained, a student in the late 1950s was "forced to look at his own thinking and feelings. He cannot but make some unpleasant discoveries about his own past behavior, as the new knowledge . . . seems to bring into the sunlight of full consciousness personal weaknesses that previously remained comfortably obscured in shadowy recesses." For a sister who was expected to maintain the "ideal of what a religious should be," the self-reflection was particularly disturbing. A priest member of a religious order observed, "To me the biggest . . . obstacle has been about helping them develop insight into their own personality and behavior. They are under a very strong cultural impress to see themselves as they are supposed to be, and religious orders to some extent foster this with their tacit idea that religious formation is something like putting a bunch of differently shaped stones into a bag, shaking them around for a few years to wear off the rough edges, and then emptying the bag to show the same shaped marbles it now contains. This often makes it very, very hard for the Sister to see the individual human being under the habit, a being with strengths and weaknesses and with all the complex motivations that characterize the human being."[91] The sisters, whether teachers or social workers, received criticism from within and without—they should have more knowledge or better skills, be more modern, act like "humans," and be individuals. At the same time, they should not be too "individualistic" on the community level, seeing their community as essentially different from other religious communities.

Despite the enhanced roles for the laity offered by the emphasis on the Mystical Body, in the late 1950s sisters could still look at themselves as an elite apostolate, and the habit contributed to that designation. As the Jesuit editor of *Spiritus* magazine explained, despite the need for sisters to be in greater dialogue with the laity, "the situation which places the Sister side by side with lay collaborators in the Church's apostolate can never dim the truth which intensifies the mystery within her: between a religious and a lay person, there can never be pure and simple equality, as if the only point of comparison were the degree of charity attained by each. In virtue of her vocation the Sister has entered into a higher state of life than that lived by the lay worker."[92] Sisters received conflicting messages from the church about the significance of their position. The emphasis on the laity seemed to suggest sisters did not carry greater value in the church; however, certain church spokespersons still considered the sisters' role to be privileged.

Father Daniel A. Lord, the well-loved master of the sodality movement, argued for sisters' special status, and the habit, he believed, symbolized that achievement. In a book he wrote for young women in 1947 titled *Letters to a Nun*, Lord endorsed the traditional habit. He explained: "In recent years there has been a great deal of talk about religious habits. There has been a strong movement—entirely outside of religious orders—to modify them and make them very simple. Something like that probably took place during the French Revolution, when the perils of the times and the attacks made upon men and women religious prompted some religious orders to wear the ordinary dress of the period, so that the women religious might be indistinguishable from the lay women around them. A similar movement has had its origin in our times, and many young women like the idea. They prefer to serve God without a distinctive dress." Lord went on to remark, "Yet it is significant that the movements to abolish religious dress invariably come from those who are not nuns. The liking for the religious life without the conventional habit is strongest in those who have never worn a habit."[93] He compared the habit to a military uniform: "It marks you as a person set aside for something distinctive. You are on guard before the throne of God. You are a nurse in the army of Christ. You are a citizen consecrated to special work in the kingdom of heaven."[94] Although Lord was writing for young women, the message was nonetheless available to American sisters regardless of age. Was the habit "His uniform," or was it an obstacle to vocations, as the pope suggested? The importance of the habit for sisters' religious witness and work had become slightly less certain.

While a segment of the sisters felt drawn to accommodate American standards, many—even the forward-thinking SFC—continued to maintain separatist practices. For instance, in the mid-1950s the SFC members determined that the sisters would need a significant influx of money to support higher education for sisters. Some sisters, however, did not participate directly in fundraising, nor did the Vatican approve of close connections to nonvowed Catholic women. A compromise was struck in Milwaukee. Two laywomen could be representatives who communicated with the sisters and turned over money to them. The two women would organize a Sisters' Day, with the slogan "Say it with dollars." The sisters would not appear to raise funds, nor would they have much contact with the laywomen. A suggestion was made that two laywomen, Mrs. E. R. Duncan, president of the Council of Catholic

Women in Superior, Wisconsin, and Mrs. John Reidl, president of the Home and School Association of the Gesu Parish in Milwaukee, both of whom expressed an interest in helping the sisters, could be put in contact with one another, and they could raise the money without the sisters' involvement. In the minutes for the January 1956 meeting of the SFC, there is no evidence that Sisters' Day happened, but the chairmen were still trying to organize the fundraiser. Rather than leave it to two laywomen without any involvement on the part of the sisters, they proposed a "Committee on 'Discreet Cooperation' to address Sisters' Day." The fundraiser finally took place on 9 November 1956 under the leadership of a Catholic women's sorority, Kappa Gamma Pi. The sisters could not be directly involved, but they did lend their "encouragement."[95] Fundraising was an absolute necessity, but rules restricted the interaction between religious women and laywomen that was vital to making fundraising successful. The SFC came up against community and ecclesial restrictions that hamstrung the advancement of their goal. In 1956, however, the sisters did not "rebel," but they "discreetly" worked around their rule until they could acquire what they needed.

■ The church, with its new goal of bringing Catholics closer to non-Catholics and imbuing American society with Catholic influence, achieved its goals, partially through attention to dress. Sodalists took their place in consumer culture with pins and badges while attempting to bring teen fashions more in line with Catholic values. School administrators required parents to become active consumers of Catholic attire with new, more stylish, and seasonal uniforms; school-specific ties; saddle shoes; blazers with insignias; and band and athletic clothing. Clerical journals advertised the variety of "correct" clothing for each ceremony and invited priests to shop around for their ceremonial garments. And priests used casual and professional clothing to diminish the difference between themselves and ordinary men. Capitalism, consumerism, patriotism, and visual Catholicism all seemed to function well together, especially in the militarized environment of the Cold War. However, the sisters' role in this burgeoning visual culture was unclear. Perhaps one of the reasons the priests and girls could make the transition to modern Catholicism was because sisters acted as place markers in the past. According to cultural studies scholar Rebecca Sullivan, in the post–World War II years, especially in film, the sisters became "a crucial icon in ongoing debates about women's roles in society that claimed progressivism and modernism as its hallmarks while seeking to maintain a place for tradition in ways that perpetuated an unequal distribution of power and access across the sexes."[96]

Women religious became a trope utilized by the media to negotiate this tension in women's roles until the feminist movement became fully realized. Habits, too, supported women's dualism. Women religious were active in their professions and religious culture, but all the while denying individualism and ambition. As a result, when the sisters did alter their clothes, as other members of the Mystical Body had, and gave up their role as the keepers of tradition, they would find that the symbol of their dress, as confirmation that they were obedient daughters, was more important than the church initially revealed. The habit communicated submission to the patriarchally structured organization. Sisters, as a symbol of discipline and traditional gender roles, allowed the church to make forays into modern society without jeopardizing its outward presentation of timeless continuity. A vestmentary makeover for Catholic sisters, however, changed that equation and ultimately opened the church for a public battle over corporate and gender ideology and how specific dress represents those ideologies.

CHAPTER 5

TEARING AT THE SEAMS

THE CLOTHES NO

LONGER FIT

There was not one single event or influence, but several clustered in the long decade of the 1960s that shifted the discussion of distinctive Catholic clothing to national attention and kept it there for years. By the beginning of the decade, women religious had more than a half-dozen years of experience at promoting "professional reform" aimed at gaining more academic and spiritual training for sisters throughout the United States. A new pontiff, John XXIII, initiated the Second Vatican Council, a churchwide effort to bring Catholicism into the modern age with, among other goals, a renewal of religious life and a greater emphasis on "the people of God" as the church, rather than simply the hierarchy. And the civil rights, feminist, and antiwar movements pressed all Americans to consider personal, corporate, and national complicity in instances of oppression and inequality. Catholics had to decide whether they would be activists, observers, or opponents of these social and political revolutions. While only one of these movements, Vatican II, specifically addressed religious clothing, the other movements, Sister Formation Conference (SFC), civil rights, feminist, and antiwar, nevertheless contributed new perspectives on identifiable dress and the obedience required for maintaining that attire. Although most clergy and religious changed their unique attire to some extent in the 1960s, it was the experience of women religious that shook the church and laid bare the tension between a truly participatory Mystical Body that relied on all parts and a hierarchal body where each limb deferred to the head. Ultimately, although the church leadership had a genuine desire to consider the immediate conditions of the world and to reexamine Catholic teaching, structure, and practice in light of new conditions, the ideology that was not open for reconsideration was gender. Revisions that destabilized the church's firm belief in male headship, at all levels of society, would ultimately be condemned, and debates about clothing revealed that resistance.

In 1962 clergy and religious embarked on sustained transnational discussions on many church-related topics, and among them was the issue of habit reform for women religious. Two figures initiated the discussion: Pope John XXIII and Cardinal Leon Joseph Suenens of Belgium. The Vatican had not held an ecumenical council for almost 100 years, and Pope John XXIII determined that the church was ripe for self-examination and renewal. The world around the church had changed dramatically, and John XXIII encouraged his bishops to fearlessly consider what was truly sacred in church teaching and what could be adjusted to meet the needs of the time. Cardinal Suenens was particularly concerned with the potential women religious could realize if they looked carefully at their own roots and the contemporary needs of the world. Suenens was aware that the Maryknoll Sisters had achieved great success in their missions during the first half of the twentieth century, despite the climate of canonical restrictiveness. If the Maryknoll could go out among the people in a restrictive climate, Suenens questioned, what could all sisters achieve once the church became more open and flexible?[1] In Suenens's estimation, sisters had been misguided over the last century, and they had leaned toward a more monastic style of existence when their true charisms often called for them to be out among the people.[2] To communicate his vision to the sisters and other interested readers, Suenens wrote *The Nun in the World: Religious and the Apostolate*. In his book, Suenens spoke to the sisters directly and explained why change was necessary for them. He communicated a knowledge of and respect for the life of women religious, but also criticism, and he placed renewal in professional, personal, and historic terms. The SFC, in particular, was drawn to Suenens's interpretation and suggestions. Many orders in the United States were invested in professional and spiritual improvements and were eager to listen to a Catholic leader who was keenly focused on the potential of the various sisterhoods.

The Nun in the World began by providing a brief explanation of women's historic oppression and the position of the church regarding women's rights. Suenens contended that Christianity was an early ally of women's rights — historically it liberated women from local subjugation. Unfortunately, he observed, people came to believe that Catholicism discriminated against women and relegated them to second-class citizenship. Despite the "confusion," the church never aimed to subjugate women. Discrimination against women, Suenens insisted, emanated from civil codes rather than church codes.[3] Delicately acknowledging that the church, in the past, may not have encouraged women's leadership as forcefully as it should have, Suenens nevertheless believed it was time to urge women religious toward action in the world. Catholics were embarking on a new age. In this era, "modern woman," Suenens contended, "does not passively accept her fate, she takes charge of it."[4] Suenens believed Catholic women, especially the sisters, would have to do the same—take charge—if they wanted to be relevant in the modern world.

Having corrected "misconceptions" about the church's authentic teaching regarding women, Suenens went on to explain that the religious habit was no longer suitable for women in contemporary society. "Most religious habits," he pointed out, "seem to the layman to be ill adapted to current conditions, to have outlived their purpose, to be archaic and inconvenient. They raise at best an ironic smile when a nun is seen on her way to tend a sick person, flapping through the streets on her scooter with her habit and veil streaming behind her to the imminent danger of herself and other traffic."[5] Not only did the conventional habit dim the sisters' seriousness in the eyes of the laity; the sisters themselves were not choosing to interact with other adults in what Suenens considered to be the most important work of the laity, Catholic Action. Through Catholic Action, the laity brought Catholic understanding to all of their work and interactions in the world. Instead of taking Catholicism out into the streets like the laity, Suenens felt sisters gravitated toward domestic service, working as cooks and housekeepers. To Suenens, it appeared to be the young women the sisters taught, like Edie in *On the Waterfront*, who brought Catholic values into the world through the apostolate of Catholic Action.[6] While most American religious likely raised an eyebrow about being "housekeepers," considering the general level of their education and their leadership in education and health care, Suenens's concerns, nonetheless, resonated with sisters. Suenens valued the contributions of the sisters and thought that for the sisters to lead other Catholic women and represent a relevant church in the modern world, they too must be modern.[7] Suenens stated his position plainly: If the sisters' practices and behaviors were at odds "with the present place of women," then those aspects of the sisters' lives must go.[8] Significantly, Suenens linked sisters to nonvowed Catholic women, restoring them to their sex and therefore rejecting the "interstitial gender" status that had rendered sisters somewhere outside the experience of ordinary women for more than a century.[9] And while sisters might have viewed the linkage with ordinary women as a kind of demotion, from the Catholic mindset, Suenens saved the sisters' status by identifying the church as an advocate of women's rights. The sisters were women, and "sister-women," he believed, should be leaders among women in the church. Rather than pull away from the mundane world, sisters should embrace society and bring it along with them. Finally, Suenens supported his criticism of habits with research. The Ursulines, Suenens recounted, did not have a habit from 1544 to 1566, until they were "obliged to accept enclosure."[10] Likewise, Suenens pointed out, the Daughters of Charity founded by St. Francis de Sales called the sisters a "company," and they wore the blue and grey "dress of common people."[11] Alluding to the origins of the orders, Suenens stated that habits were not always the founder's choice, nor were they distinctive; so why had the habit taken on such a significant role? Suenens encouraged sisters to go back to their founders' ideals and reevaluate the significance of the habit in their lives.

In May 1963, the Conference of Major Superiors of Women placed Suenens's book at the center of discussion for their meeting at Mundelein College in Chicago. Sister Annette of SFC distributed thirty-four preliminary discussion questions, among which were "How can a community fully exercise its influence in the adult world, while at the same time carry on its present work with youth which is a full-time job? Are we to conclude that some communities should abandon their traditional work of educating youth, caring for the sick and aged, etc. and embark on a new mission in the adult world? . . . Explain the meaning of 'the world' is our convent."[12] The discussion questions continued, asking how sisters would remain relevant in the "new 'Springtime' of the lay apostolate" and with the popularity of Catholic Action among the lay.[13] Under "Adaptations" the questions asked what "poverty in facilities" meant in the twentieth century; if the "honorarium" (spiritual practices) should be changed to invigorate the soul; and whether television viewing should be encouraged so as to keep in touch with the students' world. The sisters explored whether their peculiar names were a barrier to laypeople, and they wondered if they had "deified routine."[14] Finally, the last topic of discussion was the "Habit." They noted that European orders "have made much more radical adaptations in their religious habits than have those of the U.S. Has their more modern attire made any appreciable difference in the way they are regarded by new applicants or in the general effectiveness of their work?" They queried, "Do you think that America is ready for it?"[15] The sisters devoured Suenens's book. Not all agreed with his recommendations, and the tone of many of the questions suggested that the sisters took offense at Suenens's suggestions. Nevertheless, many sisters wanted to hear from Suenens, and women's congregations invited him to speak at their gatherings.[16] Audiences of sisters were clearly intrigued by what Suenens had to say.

Other influential prelates spoke out regarding the roles they thought sisters should adopt in the modern world. Archbishop of Cincinnati Karl J. Alter concurred, at least in part, with Suenens that the sisters should make some changes. He "urged nuns 'to review your purposes and methods' and to 'set aside traditions and customs that are out of touch with the world of which we are a part.' "[17] He went on to say, "Undoubtedly you have found there are certain practices which need review. . . . If you find some that are obsolete and no longer being practiced, take them out of your rules. . . . We should be concerned with the building more than with the scaffolding." Alter complained that a form of "individualism" fostered in part by distinct habits and religious rules distracted women from paying attention to the Christian community, which was according to the new Conciliar theology, the church. The individualism Alter saw was congregational. Sisters belonged to individual groups within Catholicism that ultimately isolated sisters from other people (Catholics included) and limited the sisters' potential to contribute to society. He concluded that "nationalism, provincialism, and too much concern for 'my group, or association,' " blinded sisters from working toward Christian unity.[18]

Gradually sisters began to speak up about their lifestyle, behavior, and presentation. An anonymous member of the Franciscan Sisters of Perpetual Adoration in La Crosse, Wisconsin, wrote an open letter published in the *Sister Formation Bulletin* after returning from a summer "Rejuvenation Class" in 1963. Fifty-two other sisters who made their profession between 1943 and 1945 attended.[19] Two-thirds of the rejuvenation program was "an intensive study geared to an understanding of oneself and others in coping with modern culture."[20] This particular attendee came away with a new awareness of the potential for false appearances and disembodiment that could occur in the convent. She wrote,

As the days passed, I became aware of a danger which I didn't realize existed: angelism. Angelism . . . is the attempt to convince oneself that it is possible to live as a disembodied spirit by ignoring, despising, or even denying the existence of natural inclinations of the body. The fact that the body is very much with us and demands its due would surely lead to disillusionment. . . . The trouble is that it cleverly hides behind various masks, sophistications, and studied-behaviors thus producing a false self that deceives not only the observers but the victim herself. The false self does many things that seem irreproachable, but are really lost to the owner because of the fact that the motive stimulating the act is a desire to act like the angel she thinks herself to be. . . . Spirituality becomes merely a veneer which because it is just that, crushes one completely with its burden of falsehood, and/or builds up in the heart a depressing cynicism which accuses everyone else of fakery.[21]

The anonymous writer—a woman who, based on her year of profession, had had close to two decades to live and observe religious life—spoke as an insider, and she recognized the sensitive nature of the topic she was considering. She did not make any specific reference to dress, but the habit certainly conspired with other outward behaviors to denounce the body and project an otherworldly or angelic mask. Ultimately, this sister saw this "fakery" as not only detrimental to the individual sister and the authenticity of her vocation but also a danger to those around her who were duped by her falseness. She offered a radically different way to think about rules and "studied behavior." Rather than piety and precision on the outside representing goodness on the inside, the aloof and perfect behavior might in fact be a disguise for sin.

RENEWAL AND THE "CATHOLIC PRESS"

While Cardinal Suenens can be credited with providing a thorough critique of religious life and making suggestions for sisters to consider, a genuine dialogue about the dress of women religious came about in 1964 on the pages of a new "Catholic" publication, the *National Catholic Reporter* (NCR). The topics covered, the subscribers, and the contributors were overwhelmingly Catholic; however, unlike most Catholic newspapers, the NCR was not the official organ of any one diocese or bishop. The NCR's founder, Robert G. Hoyt, wanted to bring the investigative skills and open-endedness of journalism to a paper that was concerned with Catholic issues. As in any newspaper, certain topics received greater attention than others, and the NCR was eager to promote and cover the new era of reform.

The NCR itself participated in the renewal by its very existence. The editors invited nonvowed lay Catholics, non-Catholics, and religious to contribute articles. Notable writers and scholars such as Gary Wills, Rabbi Arthur Herzberg, and Martin Marty were among the contributors.[22] Likewise, the paper published the documents of the Second Vatican Council to encourage greater awareness and understanding of the church's reforms. As for criticism of church policies on war, materialism, birth control, and "Catholic clothing," everything was fair game.

It did not take long for sisters and their habits to come up in the pages of the NCR, and writers cited Suenens as a "special authority" on the topic. In the article "New Deal for Nuns Urged as Council Discusses Orders," the author quoted Suenens complaining that "too many of the religious orders 'retain ridiculous complications from past centuries which give more of an impression of the Church growing old.' . . . One complication . . . was the robes of some nuns, which he described as a cause of ridicule and as most impractical for the various tasks facing nuns."[23] The article noted Suenens's criticisms of convent life, such as nuns always having to go out in pairs and the excessive maternalism of mothers superior. Suenens argued that nuns are treated like children, and unless they are "allowed to act like adult women," they will not make the contributions necessary to sustain the church. Without offering a counterargument to Suenens's position, the NCR appeared to be an early supporter of habit reform. It seemed that if sisters wanted to make an acceptable and genuine attempt at renewal, they would have to alter their habits.

Experimentation and modification of religious dress began in earnest for several communities in 1964. The Daughters of Charity, affectionately or perhaps amusingly referred to as "God's Geese," laid aside their cornette and replaced it with a "veil-like headkerchief" that reached the shoulders. Ironically, the cornette was considered a sort of bonnet, and the adoption of a veil was a medieval requirement that, depending on one's interpretation, kept women from tempting men or simply marked women as nuns consecrated to God. The dress remained conservative, but it was nevertheless a significant change. The sisters' hair did not show, and rather than a full, ankle-length gown, the sisters wore a simple dress, designed by the House of Dior, with a hemline six inches from the ground.[24] Approval for new habit designs fell to the Sacred Congregation of Religious, a papal committee made up of cardinals and bishops.[25] The Sacred Congregation of Religious accepted the new habit of the Daughters of Charity, and almost 50,000 members worldwide adopted the reform habit beginning in September 1964.

While putting aside the cornette was dramatic from the perspective of losing a French national icon, the Ursulines at McGuinness High School in Oklahoma City provided a different type of drama. Rather than make small changes to the hemline and shoes, they experimented with a modified habit that mirrored 1960s women's professional work attire by having a knee-length skirt, no veil, and medium heels. The NCR covered the habit "pilot study," displaying a full-length photograph of a smiling sister and citing interviews conducted by the *Oklahoma Courier*, the diocesan newspaper. Reaction was positive. Reportedly, a non-Catholic was no longer "afraid of the sisters" when they appeared in modified habit. Sister Immaculata, one of the sisters in the pilot program, explained, "I feel like I've been freed and let out of armor. . . . We feel more genuine. The traditional habit creates a false impression—the habit is regarded rather than the person. The new habit helps us in having [a] . . . personal identity."[26] The sisters involved in the experiment discussed how their founder, St. Angela Merici, would have approved of the change because she would have wanted the sisters to be approachable. Finally, they decided that what they had done, putting on modern and attractive dresses, was also what Pope John XXIII had asked the sisters to do.

The Sisters of Sion, with roughly 2,000 members, had each sister submit "ideas and sketches" throughout 1964. Once they decided on a style, they submitted it to the Sacred Congregation in Rome and received approval. Significantly, as with the Daughters of Charity, the habit was modified but still distinctive. In clerical grey, the sisters' new habit was "a calf-length, straight-lined dress with a box pleat at each side in the back, and a turn-down white collar. A detachable scapular, buttoned at the shoulder and waist is worn in the front. . . . Sisters . . . wear a short veil—black or white—fronted by a white band which allows part of their hair to show."[27] Sisters interviewed liked the new habit but contended that if the modified habit was deemed unsuitable at any time in the future, they would simply change again. Embracing a flexible attitude about the habit became an example of their new approach toward their work and lives. The sisters did not want to be perceived as rigid women. Instead, the sisters wanted to be the generous, spiritual, and professional women they had set out to be before they became waylaid by rules and routines. Opening themselves up to change was not always easy, but they hoped it would be a restorative process.

Despite the habit changes appearing in the press, both Catholic and even popular, several orders moved slowly on clothing reform. The NCR interviewed four mothers superior: Mother Mary Consolatrice of Dubuque, Iowa, of the Sisters of Charity of the Blessed Virgin Mary; Mother M. Denise of the Benedictine Sisters at Tulsa, Oklahoma; Sister M. Luke, superior general of the Sisters of Loretto at Nerinx, Kentucky; and Mother M. Omer, mother general of the Sisters of Charity at Cincinnati, Ohio. Collectively leading over 4,000 women religious, the orders had no single mind on the issue of the habit. Only one order, the Sisters of Loretto, had a "new habit" pilot program in South America, and the other orders were still in a "wait-and-see" stage. None of the orders rejected reform outright, but they varied on issues such as maintaining a veil or how modern the habit should be.[28] Questions about how the older sisters would adjust if change came or concern over sisters speaking negatively in public venues about the habit were mentioned. Tension among the sisters over the issue of habits was already apparent. If certain Catholics were worried about how habits could promote psychological disconnection from humanity, discussion of taking the habit away invited plenty of humanity. A variety of emotions came to the surface: excitement and hope about freedom and contemporary compatibility, pain and disappointment about losing a cherished garment and tradition, and fear of showing hair (or lack of hair if the headpiece had stifled growth), legs, and waists. In addition to personal concerns, sisters now had to worry about what others, especially the laity, were saying about their new attire. Canon law, the hierarchical view of the church, and the elevation of religious above ordinary Catholics, as well as the authoritativeness of the habit, had all worked together to shelter sisters from hearing or caring how ordinary Catholics felt about them. Sisters had in fact embraced their habits toward the end of the nineteenth century in part to assert themselves with the Americanists and the school boards on the topic of dress. Now sisters were hearing about their garments again, and they could read these opinions in the pages of the NCR.

One of the most frequently employed places for expressing feelings about the habit was a new feature in the NCR, "Sisters' Forum." Once a month, the paper devoted a section to topics that were of particular interest to the sisters. Habit reform came up regularly. Articles such as "Principles for Thinking about Sisters' Habits," "The Neutral Nun," and "Sisters and Symbols, Honest to God Prayer" illustrate the centrality of the habit to the column. The openness with which the renewal was discussed and explored, especially surrounding the habit, was controversial, however. Some readers wanted there to be a separate edition for the clergy; having nonreligious comment on religious orders and men and women sharing "insider perspectives" on what went on in religious orders violated the privacy and exclusivity offered by religious life.[29] Readers, too, aired their feelings and concerns. In contrast to the sisters' desire to retreat from public scrutiny during the compromise plans at the turn of the century, sisters submitted to open evaluation of their appearance. For instance, one sister wrote regarding an article on habits, "We do not know the answers yet, barely the questions, in fact. Surely though God is blessing the considerable suffering going on in our communities where Sisters of all ages and positions are wrestling with consciences and trying to assume their own personal responsibilities, usually without guidance and seldom with any comfortable precedence to follow."[30] Father Maynard Kolodziej, OFM, complained that sisters were inappropriately using the NCR for "crying on others' shoulders" and "airing out their problems."[31] Sister M. Henrita Ecker, SSND, from Mankato, Minnesota, took up the response and explained to both Kolodziej and other concerned readers that "secretiveness is unhealthy soil, in which a false theology of the spiritual life and a false philosophy of man can easily take root. Nothing so stultifies the mind and solidifies a false ideology as absence of criticism. . . . *National Catholic Reporter's* Sisters' Forum is one of the few outlets where religious can cut across community lines and the religious-laity screen in sharing their common problems and difficulties. Out of a realization that they do not stand alone in their weakness, they can gain added strength and courage."[32] She closed her response with a reference to Pope John XXIII's analogy of Vatican II with fresh air: "Let's not close the damper upon the fresh, free breeze we feel in its columns."[33] The paper itself, with weekly dialogue about renewal, clearly propelled the sometimes painful renewal forward. At the very least, more hesitant orders could read about and see pictures of what other congregations were doing and find inspiration and support for experimentation of their own.

In addition to Sisters' Forum, Letters to the Editors conveyed opinions about the change in habits, the politics and poverty of clothes, and the future of priests' attire. These letters were frequently lengthy quasi-articles. A laywoman, Mrs. Catharine Krusie from Los Angeles, California, gave an impassioned response to the editors regarding the article "Principles for Thinking about Sisters' Habits." Krusie explained that she couldn't hold back her thoughts on the sisters' habits. "To put it bluntly," she stated, "it [the habit] is a symbol of selfishness—not conscious perhaps—but the 'self' of the nun and her community shows up to be the primary concern. The 'lay person' . . . is second. . . . The question of the habit is for many nuns a question of 'our tradition, distinction, cost, comfort, style' not of how to bring Christ to more people." Krusie went on to discuss how the habit allowed a nun to "hide from herself as well as others behind that formidable wall of attitudes and material." She lamented, "I fail to see how anyone can think of a 'total encounter with Christ in Himself and in His Mystical Body' as *distinct* from 'human encounters.' With this point of view," Krusie continued, "nuns cut themselves off from commitment and responsibility to themselves as well as to others. It is phoney."[34] Krusie focused on the rigidity of the sisters' lives, their aloofness, and the way sisters deliberately distanced themselves from ordinary Catholics, all under the guise of holiness. Most criticisms were not so damning, but they encouraged sisters, male religious, and priests to take a hard look at their unique clothing. The Ursulines in Oklahoma inspired male religious, who applauded the sisters and wrote to the editors asking when men would begin to make changes. One writer suggested getting rid of habits and cassocks altogether.[35]

Circulation of the paper grew from 11,000 to 100,000 within just a few years of its establishment.[36] Superiors, even if they wanted to ignore the press, could hardly keep the news out of the hands of their young sisters. After all, with the assistance of the SFC, sisters were earning degrees at colleges where the NCR would be found in the lounges as well as the libraries. Time away from the convent and greater exposure to an intellectual Catholic environment gave the issue of habits more urgency.

In the summer of 1966, the prefect of the Sacred Congregation of Religious, Cardinal Antoniutti, felt the time had come to address the flurry of newspaper commentary circulating about clothing reforms for women religious. He sought to clarify for the major superiors, in particular, the intentions of Rome regarding habits. Antoniutti observed that "THE NEWSPAPERS busy themselves in a truly extravagant way about the so called ecclesiastical and religious fashions, with new designs for the costumes of Sisters and of Religious. . . . The public might think from the stories in the newspapers that the 'aggiornamento' of Religious should come about by a radical change of Habit, and consider the change of religious Habit as an essential point."[37] Although he felt there were more important events to cover, Antoniutti feared that confusion regarding the Habit, with an upper-case H, had set in, and he provided clarification. "It is necessary to preserve the gravity and dignity of the religious Habit," he explained, "because it is the visible sign of consecration to God. It is necessary to keep the veil when the Constitutions prescribe it. . . . The dress should be designed in a manner becoming to consecrated persons for whom the safeguarding of modesty takes the first place. Reduce, however, the quantity of material, the trimmings and certain useless ornaments, suppress the white wimple, but preserve the sober and austere line, so it may be a sign of penance, of consecration, and of piety always suffused with delicate modesty." In closing he stated plainly, "Therefore, let your Habit be long, simple, sober, so as always to be able 'to present a chaste virgin to Christ.' "[38] Antoniutti wanted to put the brakes on both the press and the renewal by laying out more specifically what was acceptable attire for women religious. Antoniutti retained traditional ideas about the habit. He simply wanted habits to have less fabric. Religious garb for women, in Antoniutti's mind, was an expression of the modesty that he expected to see on a consecrated virgin. Likewise, a distinct habit was also a sign of organizational allegiance. Wearing a uniform, the sisters were more clearly representatives of the bureaucratic church. The sisters were part of the religious administration, although distantly. They assisted the hierarchy in maintaining obedience and order, and without the uniform, the diversely clad sisters would invite questioning and disorder. For those who wanted sisters to make more dramatic changes to the habit, however, adaptation and renewal were about exposing the individual, taking personal responsibility, and becoming truly involved in the world. Critics of the habit did not want sisters to invest in being empty symbols; instead, they wanted sisters to be activists. Although the hierarchy and the sisters seemed to have divergent goals, the facade of cooperation could be held together under cover of the civil rights movement. Ultimately, however, the civil rights movement, too, would invite sisters to reconsider the religious habit and the power of outward appearances.

PROTEST AND HABITS

During the first half of the 1960s, the habits of women religious were important symbols in the Catholic witness for social justice, particularly civil rights. Catholic sisters were forerunners in the movement for civil rights in urban areas. In Chicago in 1963, for instance, sisters picketed the Illinois Club for Catholic Women, which "repeatedly rejected black applicants."[39] Since the club was located on Loyola University's downtown campus, the sisters' public protest won the attention of local television stations, which had cameras on the scene to film.[40] According to writer John J. Fialka, "It was a revolutionary moment for Catholics in the city. . . . They all identified emotionally with the image of women wearing the habit. These were the same women who had taught them the basic principles of morality."[41] The Illinois Club for Catholic Women changed its policy immediately. Priests, too, joined the demonstrations, but their vestmentary statements were restricted to the Roman collar and black suit. Seeing priests in a public setting was a common sight, but seeing the sisters who followed the rules, traveled in pairs, and almost never ate in public participating in a protest—that was radical.

At this early stage in protesting, the sisters and their supporters focused on the positive aspects the habit held as a symbol of moral certainty and a form of protection in potentially dangerous situations. If the retiring sisters in sartorial cloister came out to the streets and made a public statement with their presence, denouncing the unjust treatment of blacks, then everyone watching knew that prejudice and racism were sinful. Sisters also worked in poor, often all-black areas before Vatican II, staying in urban parishes despite the white flight of Catholics to the suburbs. Since there were fewer Catholics and greater poverty, the habit gave sisters a kind of public status and form of protection as neighborhoods changed around them. A Chicago woman, concerned over potentially dramatic alterations to the habit, argued, "The Sisters will have no male escorts, and if they are to fulfill the duties that the famed Belgian Cardinal Suenens urges, they must—and do—go bravely into all kinds of neighborhoods and situations. Those who do this report that their habits are an initial protection, because they [the habits] mean charity to people everywhere. If they are to continue these activities, and extend them, they must wear something that says, unmistakably, as no lapel insignia can, that they come in God's name, to do good."[42]

According to historian Amy Koehlinger, in southern society the habit also allowed women to manipulate the instability of race. If habited sisters worked with blacks, regardless of the color of their habit, they would often be considered, by blacks and whites alike, to be black.[43] The fact that their title was "sister" or "sistah," as well, provided them with an ironic connection to blacks in that the sisters' title of respect was the community's colloquial expression for a woman who belonged. If sisters relied on the traditional teaching about the value of habits disguising individuality so that only God could distinguish their special deeds, then letting the habit do the work as a tool of protest and interracial outreach was absolutely fine.

In a letter to the editors, a sister from Sacred Heart College in Wichita, Kansas, pointed out the power of the habit in protest. Regarding the sisters who participated in the Selma, Alabama, marches in March 1965, the sister wrote, "The point has been well made in connection with the recent Selma march that the obvious presences of the nuns was important—what impact would they have made in a blouse and skirt, medium heels, and a ribbon in their hair. The pages of history remind us that one of the first things a godless and/or anti-clerical society does is forbid the public wearing of religious garbs and symbols. Now should we voluntarily give up our public witness by putting aside our religious habit when we go into the marketplace?"[44] A costume designer and artist reflected on whether sisters should wear distinctive habits at all. One of the factors that persuaded her that the sisters should keep the habit was their presence in the Selma marches. As recently as Selma, she explained, "many people were made conscious of the power for good and the strength . . . symbolized in the easily recognized presence of a nun in the crowd. Many nuns have told me of the people who come up to them for help . . . because they represent a familiar sign of charity and discretion."[45] Observers who supported the civil rights movement welcomed the habited sisters' sartorial statement. Americans in the post–World War II era regarded Catholics as patriots and devoted Americans. Now in the civil rights movements, the most conspicuous Catholics were lining up to protest. Gaining the support of the nuns would indeed make America take notice of the movement.

The sisters at Selma appeared on television and in newspapers, and disc jockeys interviewed them on the radio. Popular culture in the 1950s and

1960s, as Rebecca Sullivan uncovered, recognized the value of women religious and convents as tropes that safely mediated society's new opportunities for women without fully challenging the primacy of domesticity. Movies won sisters a level of familiarity as Hollywood produced "nun films" one after another, such as *Heaven Knows, Mr. Allison* (1957), *The Nun's Story* (1959), *Lilies of the Field* (1963), and *The Sound of Music* (1965). As Sullivan convincingly argues, these nuns were brave, ambitious, and confident, but the nun characters relied on or at least deferred to men. They took action when necessary, but they were not interested in radically changing women's roles in society. The real habited sisters who protested were also risk takers, but their habits, like the habits of the nun characters, conveyed humble submission even as they marched subversively against racial injustice.

The church leaders expected and valued obedience within the organization, and while bishops may or may not have endorsed the long and elaborate habit, it was nevertheless a "symbolic declaration" that sisters who wore it would adhere to church norms and expectations.[46] The civil rights movement, while confirming the value of the habit as symbol of Christian values, nevertheless raised issues about the other values the habit represented, such as obedience. As part of each community's rule, orders required sisters to wear the habit each day and present themselves uniformly. Keeping the requirements of the habit was one aspect of being a "living rule" along with walking, eating, or praying in a precise manner. Therefore, when bishops, as religious authorities who valued obedience, either remained silent on the topic of racism or discouraged religious from participating in the protests, they put sisters in a vexing position. The bishops placed their moral authority over other clergy and religious into question, thereby weakening the sisters' resolve to obey. In the case of Selma, for instance, Archbishop Thomas J. Toolen of Mobile, Alabama, removed Father Maurice Ouellet, pastor of a black Catholic church, for his support of the civil rights marchers. And in a speech to 1,000 Sisters of Notre Dame de Namur for the dedication of Blessed Julie Billiart, Boston's Cardinal Cushing took time out to remark that "a nun's place is in the classroom—not marching in street demonstrations." He went on to say, "I don't think you'll find in the story of Julie Billiart's life where she went out on the highways and byways." He wanted sisters to pray for Julie Billiart's canonization, "but I don't mean by carrying placards."[47] Habits, which acted in part as symbols of charity, were nevertheless symbols of the "inert traditionalism" that kept sisters inside saying their prayers rather than acting out their faith and values in the streets. Therefore, between the time when habit reform fully got under way and the time when the sisters had begun to participate in civil rights demonstrations, the habit endorsed two "contradictory trends," the old church and the new.[48]

While the sisters contributed to the civil rights movement, the movement also gave them something back: It provided sisters with a way to understand a kind of prejudice directed at the sisters. Sister Mary Berchmans Shea, OSU, offered a chapter called "Protest Movements and Convent Life" to the book *The New Nuns*, which compared the habit to a kind of "skin coloring." People see the habit and think that it represents goodness and morality, but they don't give much thought to the person inhabiting the costume. "Even when nuns are called on to participate in public demonstrations," she suggested, "one sometimes gets the feeling that it is the habit, not the person, whose presence is sought." Sisters wanted to be witnesses, but they also wanted to bring Christ's message to black people, both Catholic and non-Catholic. This required creating relationships, not simply presenting an image. Another sister explained, "I'd like to draw a parallel . . . between this habit question and segregation law. You see, the habit effectively segregates us from society. It subordinates us into a category, first of all, and then segregates us. . . . Many of us are refusing this . . . segregation. It strikes at the basic human right of full and unimpeded human communication with one's own contemporaries in one's own time."[49] Habits held ambiguous values. They were symbols of the Catholic institutional church and morality, but the habits could also be seen as prisons that denied personhood.

The missing "personhood" not only constituted a form of prejudice; it was psychologically unhealthy. Robert McAllister, Ph.D., M.D., contributed an article titled "Self Image and Self Acceptance" to the *Sister Formation Bulletin* in the winter of 1966. In it he discussed "The Perils of Anonymity" in religious life. He explained,

> In different ways the religious life seeks to disguise the identity of [a] person and to conceal the uniqueness of the personality under the cloak of community conformity, much as the special appearance of the person is concealed under the common garb of religion. Such a life must truly endanger the self concept for it tends to hide the self from view and from expression. This is a situation peculiar to the religious, for it is only the religious who can never escape from this all en-compassing role. . . . Even a housewife, a mother, can get away from being a housewife or mother for a while and see herself as distinct from either of those roles which she has

assumed. . . . But this is not open to the religious. She is and remains a religious twenty four hours a day, 365 days of the year. She ceases to be anyone other than a religious.[50]

McAllister went on to write, "I would question whether that is healthy. She is something more than a religious; she is first of all a person, and she should not lose that in the religious life, for if she does she may lose herself and suffer the disintegration of personality which follows from such a loss of self, or she may lose her vocation because she refuses to tolerate that loss of identity. . . . Priests can take off their distinctive garb and become a golfer, a vacationer, an average citizen, etc. Even this is not open to sisters. . . . How frustrated a religious must feel if she cannot relax and communicate freely with others within her own home, which is now her convent."[51] Sisters, unlike male religious, did not own other sets of clothes. If a brother needed to visit the doctor, he had an option of wearing something besides his cassock or even clericals.[52] But sisters, as Dr. McAllister explained, were sisters all the time. They had no other clothes that they could change into, except perhaps pajamas, and therefore they never took time away from being sisters.

Another important development feeding the sisters' renewal was the theological popularity of personalism. Recognizing the self and the concerns that motivate individuals to act, personalism emphasizes the role of the individual in constructing an appropriate Christian response within a certain set of conditions rather than following a rote rule. Acknowledgment of self, acting like an adult, and revising one's approach to the vow "obey"—so that it did not simply mean to follow rules and do as one was told but to obey one's own observations and judgments about where there is a need to be met—initially motivated the small group of sisters who participated in protests. Soon enough, the same sentiments galvanized sisters more generally. Mother Mary Consolatrice, BVM, general of the Sisters of Charity in Dubuque, who two years earlier appeared to be on the fence about change, now seemed eager to demonstrate her sisters' renewal activities. She discussed how sisters responded to the War on Poverty and racial injustice. She explained, "The Council decree on adaptation and renewal in religious life makes it quite clear to all of us that the non-contemplative religious is expected to act, not to become a passive spectator or to settle for offering her prayers and sufferings in the name of a cause."[53] The sisters in the Chicago area embraced the challenge. They "cooperated with the Job Training program for teenagers and the Headstart Program" and with Urban Gateways, which exposed children to the arts. They worked with neighborhood organizations to combat gang violence, wrote references for the Illinois Youth Commission, taught adult classes, and participated in the Chicago Area Lay Movement, the Southern Christian Leadership Conference, the Catholic Interracial Council, and the National Catholic Council for Interracial Justice. Mother Consolatrice concluded, "What then is the role of the Sister in race relations and in the war on poverty? I see it as one of involvement, of action, and of educated leadership. I see her role as something which cannot be neatly defined or categorized in advance, but one which will emerge as the generous and alert sister responds with alacrity to human needs where and when she sees them in our rapidly changing society."[54] Rigidity and routine, according to Mother Consolatrice's account, had to be left behind for the sisters who chose the active apostolate; to be open, accessible, flexible, and faithful were the new requirements.

IT'S OFFICIAL—"NORMS MUST BE CHANGED"

On 28 October 1965, the Second Vatican Council promulgated *Perfectae Caritatis* (Of Perfect Charity), which included the "Decree on the Adaption and Renewal of Religious Life." This was the decree referenced by Mother Mary Consolatrice. *Perfectae Caritatis* stated that "the religious habit, an outward mark of consecration to God, should be simple and modest, poor and at the same time becoming. In addition it must meet the requirements of health and be suited to the circumstances of time and place and to the needs of the ministry involved. The habits of both men and women religious which do not conform to these norms must be changed."[55] The renewal, especially for many in the Midwest, was already well under way, and for others it was just beginning. The sartorial picture of religious life for women, with yards of fabric, quickly became a canvas of diversity. A year later, in October 1966, Pope Paul VI issued *Ecclesia Sanctae*, a *motu propio*, or a document of his own, to reinforce the idea of experimentation and to provide guidelines for religious renewal.[56] Paul VI encouraged the sisters to go back to the "original spirit" of their founders and to "purify" religious life of "alien elements" and those practices that were "obsolete." He went on further to explain that "those elements are to be considered obsolete which do not constitute the nature and purpose of the institute and which, having lost their meaning and power, are no longer a real help to religious life. Nevertheless, consideration must be given to the witness, which the religious state has as its role the obligation of giving."[57] The Vatican opened the door for broad interpretation regarding the habit.

Renowned theologian Bernard Haring, CSSR, wrote of the challenges and benefits that would come from putting aside the religious habit. He explained,

Ascetic discipline may never become an end in itself but must always re-
late to the values at stake. . . . Training must be tested constantly on the
battlefield of daily events, not in a secluded chamber where news of the
completed contest has failed to arrive. . . . How are we to practice this ascetic discipline? . . . Let us detach ourselves from habits and forms of life,
irrelevant in the spiritual combat, for example from clothing. This seems
to me to be realistic and true ascetic discipline, perhaps a notably difficult achievement. Possibly a sister entered religion because of an attractive
garb; now after forty years, detaching herself from this garb, she sees the
result in a looking glass. This is merely a quaint example, a symbol. . . . It
is not fitting that we load ourselves down with relics of the past. . . . Each
age has its own spirit. If we carry along items from various centuries which
belong to museums only, we are unable to fight with the Lord against the
spirits of this world.[58]

Haring went on to suggest that sisters needed to become more comfortable
with accepting criticism and listening to recommendations. By 1968 Haring seemed to have lost patience with the slow rate of change on the issue:
"Those who are in an outstanding way signs of the Church," he wrote, "virginal brides of Christ—the religious—must be relevant for the world, and
they will be only to the extent of their watchfulness, never through a me-
chanical external obedience. Why do some of you appear as if you were of the
past? If you look over 70 or 100 congregations, you can see that they constitute a perfect museum of all customs, costumes and clothing of the past centuries. Outlandishness does not make for a relevant witness in the modern
world; it merely represents the collection of past centuries."[59] Sisters found
themselves in a difficult position. Outspoken theologians who appeared to be
liberal condemned women's habits while still identifying sisters as "virginal
brides of Christ." The pope, who was clearly more conservative, wanted modification of the habit and would have agreed with the sisters being thought of
as virginal brides. And then the sisters had many other voices both inside and
outside the convent telling them to be flexible modern women—not quiver-
ing brides or brides at all.

In March 1967 the Sacred Congregation of Religious in Rome hosted a
gathering of the International Union of Superiors General to address the
formation of postulants and novices in light of the *aggiornamento*. Regarding
clothing, the congregation did not reject specific dress for the women entering the convent. Instead, it commented on the attitude and ceremony surrounding clothing. "Too often," Archbishop Paul Philippe, OP, wrote, "for

the families and even for the Sisters, the clothing has a greater importance than the profession. . . . As for 'Clothing,' the Sacred Congregation of Religious is of the opinion that it should be reduced to an internal ceremony in the oratory of the Novitiate or in the Chapel, but without the presence of the family and without the presence of Ecclesiastical Authorities and especially without solemnity." [60] The congregation implied that the habit, per se, was not a problem, but the sacralizing of it through public ceremony, solemnity, and ecclesial imprimatur gave it inappropriate significance. Otherwise the directives were vague. The superiors general left Rome having committed to objectives such as revising their constitutions so that their rule corresponded to the needs of the world and the "charism of the founder"; creating "structures for the exercise of authorities which will encourage active and responsible obedience to bring about a unique service of charity"; and moving forward toward the "Trinitarian life . . . and model of fraternity . . . where each is acknowledged and accepted as a unique and necessary person." [61] This left an open field for habits. Since each order's constitution would be revised, all sisters would take the habit under discussion. Whatever the new constitution of a particular order required regarding the habit was what the sisters of that order would wear. If the constitution did not require a habit, then the sisters did not have to wear one, but they could retain their old habit if they wished.

By the end of 1967, the sisters' sense of excitement about renewal began a gradual shift to frustration and annoyance. The directives on "renewal" and "adaption" were vague and unhelpful. Likewise, despite support for habit reform, the Sacred Congregation of Religious was not easy to please. The Glenmary Sisters and the Sisters of Loretto did not gain approval on their first attempt at habit reform. The Glenmary Sisters wanted to wear a jacket, but the Sacred Congregation thought a cape would be more appropriate. The Sisters of Loretto "proposed to wear a black suit" in which the skirt came below the knees and the jacket was long-sleeved and loose. The Lorettos' suit also came with a short black veil. Nevertheless, the Sacred Congregation thought the outfit was "too feminine" and rejected it.[62] Outside the company of priests, sisters winced at the willingness of religious men to take up the topic of women's clothes and even undergarments.[63] Celibate men approving the clothing of professional religious women seemed, at the very least, inappropriate and bordered on the ridiculous. The church was calling on sisters to be active and bring Catholic values out into the world, but sisters could not make decisions about what clothes to put on without the help of the clergy.

According to canon law, the endorsement of the Sacred Congregation of Religious was necessary for habit approval, but other influential and well-regarded prelates disagreed. Cardinal Suenens, author of *The Nun in the World*, the book that launched the discussion among women religious about their lives, activities, and appearance, gave an address at St. Mary's College in Notre Dame, Indiana, in June 1969 that denounced the legalistic process of approval. In his speech, he set himself in opposition to the Sacred Congregation of Religious, and he emphasized that "unity does not mean uniformity." The sisters, he contended, required freedom to do their apostolate. Beyond freedom, the sisters must be treated as adults and be respected. Regarding religious habit, he commented that "it is very abnormal that you should send to a Roman Congregation the folds of your new dress and obtain sanction for all of this. . . . We are not competent; we have no charism in that matter. We are speaking about the competencies of women, not only religious. You have to consult women, lay people . . . because they are more competent than you, because they can give you very wise advice. I think perhaps we would make some mistakes if we ignored the reactions of the people." [64] Suenens's position was controversial. He denounced the role of the Sacred Congregation of Religious; he exposed the disrespect with which the Vatican treated women, and he once again encouraged sisters to look to the company and advice of other women.

The discussion of religious clothing began to feel demeaning for some sisters. For centuries the church expected women religious to be deferential to authority, even while the sisters wielded considerable power in their own institutions. The pope, superior, bishop, and often a pastor had power over the sisters. Likewise, authority or privilege was based on seniority in the convent. Moving toward collaborative decision making and "maximum feasible participation," as Sargent Shriver called for in the War on Poverty's Community Action Programs, was difficult, and clothing and the topic of appearance could be disproportionately time consuming and attention getting. Finally, those making comments about the sisters' renewal seemed more concerned with the sisters' dress than with their genuine efforts to apply the teachings of the Second Vatican Council and to be intelligent and caring apostles. Sister Emil of the SFC remarked, "I have often thought that if the Post-Conciliar Commission, or the Sacred Congregation for Religious, had ordered us to embroider pink strawberries on the front of our new habits (or non-habits as the case might be), that news would have made every medium of communication in the country from the *New York Times* to *Playboy* magazine. But when the plan of education is suggested which would clearly make the sisters the best equipped professionals in the nation, we have silence, deep silence." [65] Perhaps it was their own fault, she mused. "And so I wonder whether we may not be spending too much time on the question of whether we will part our

Figure 34. Alejandro Rey and Sally Field in The Flying Nun. *Courtesy of Photofest.*

hair . . . or on whether the sisters should be watching the late late movie." [66] Instead, the sisters should plan their contribution. She went on: "In the decentralized post-conciliar church . . . our bishops will listen to us if we have something to say. The hammering out . . . and winning group support for what we have to say about Catholic education should be high on the agenda of our chapters." [67] Decision makers as well as media observers focused on insignificant topics, such as appearance, and Sister Emil wanted to redirect the conversation back to more substantial concerns.

Worth noting is that the process of renewal and the "new nun," while energetically covered in print media, was fodder for television and film as well. Debates and messages about appearance were custom-made for a visual culture. For instance, four sisters appeared on the David Susskind Show in 1966 to explain the goals and hopes for renewal. One of the key messages the sisters conveyed to Susskind was that they wanted to be taken seriously. Complicating the goal of seriousness was the television show *The Flying Nun*, which began airing in 1967. (See fig. 34.) The comedy featured a petite novice, Sister Bertrille, played by Sally Field, whose wind-filled cornette allowed her to fly. Close observers would have recognized Sister Bertrille as a "new nun" inspired by Vatican II. In the first episode she arrived late to Convento San Tanco because she had been delayed at a free-speech rally. Viewers learned that Sister Bertrille clothed orphans, taught them music, painted the convent car Lenten purple, played cards with go-go dancers, and frequently met with a handsome gambler and womanizer in order to save the convent and per-haps his soul. Sister Bertrille was clearly interested in human rights and social justice, but her clothing communicated comedy; her headpiece sent her fly-ing and landing on military installations, ships, beaches, and assorted places where she was unexpected. *The Flying Nun*, produced in cooperation with the National Catholic Office for Radio and Television, suggested that both the church and viewers saw sisters as amusing entertainment.[68]

The film *Change of Habit*, with Mary Tyler Moore and Elvis Presley, treated the challenges facing the new nuns more directly, but it relied on the possi-bility of a romance for one sister with none other than Elvis to capture viewers' attention. In figure 35, Sister Michelle in her Notre Dame sweatshirt comes back from playing football with Elvis, dressed appropriately in his University of Memphis sweatshirt. In the film, Sisters Michelle, Barbara, and Irene—in somewhat burlesque fashion—change into stylish secular clothes and move to a poor and potentially dangerous neighborhood to work in the commu-nity. (See fig. 36.) Without their habits, no one defers to the sisters, and they are not safe from the leering eyes of the men on the street. The pastor of the local Catholic church, Father Gibbons, does not approve of the sisters' experi-ment. He criticizes the sisters for putting "flapper skirts on a Bride of Christ" or acting as "underground nuns." Despite its status as a B-film, *Change of Habit* delved into the possibilities and complications brought about by wearing or discarding the habit. Did the habit diminish racial awareness and identity? How would young nuns in plain clothes negotiate intimate communication with men? What did women in habits know about the everyday oppression and objectification of nonvowed women? America was entranced by the de-bate and amused by the Hollywood entertainment.

TAKING CHARGE OF RENEWAL

The Los Angeles–based Sisters of the Immaculate Heart of Mary (IHM) de-cided to reframe the renewal and move away from appearance concerns and instead concentrate on raising their professional standard and investigating new work opportunities. Considering all the statements from the bishops, the

Figure 35. Sister Michelle and Elvis, Change of Habit. Courtesy of Photofest.

Figure 36. Three sisters in lay clothes, Change of Habit. Courtesy of Photofest.

Sacred Congregation of Religious, and Pope Paul VI, the IHM sisters, under the leadership of their superior Mother Mary Humiliata Caspary, came up with a plan they believed met the aims of the church. Included in their experiment were several changes. In October 1967 the sisters announced their plan to dispense with one habit and instead allow sisters to wear clothing that was "suitable for their work."[69] Sisters could return to their baptismal names, and "Mother" Mary Humiliata would now answer to "Sister." Regarding work, the sisters had new options. Although the IHMs would continue their traditional occupations in education and nursing, other possibilities were available, too. In an interview, Mother Mary Humiliata explained that "diversity in works is not to be discouraged, but encouraged. Thus we may assume social service, or work with economic opportunity projects, or such specialized tasks as with the mentally retarded, or with young people."[70] Sisters with special talents such as art or journalism could also pursue those fields. Within education, the order decided to withdraw sixty to seventy teachers from the parochial schools so that the sisters could complete their education. Likewise they proposed that the class size of the parochial schools be reduced from forty students to thirty-five in order to improve the quality of education the sisters offered.[71] Finally, decisions for each house would be made by the sisters living within the house.

Not unexpectedly, Cardinal James McIntyre rejected the proposal and suggested revisions, among which were a reduction in the number of sisters who would leave the schools and that the sisters would continue wearing the habit. The sisters maintained their original plan, however, and Cardinal McIntyre interpreted the sisters' unwillingness to negotiate as an ultimatum. Both the cardinal and the IHMs turned to the Vatican to reinforce their respective positions.

According to historian Mark Massa, the stakes were particularly high in this situation. The media quickly picked up the story and publicly presented a private debate where people who had committed their lives to the church were "taking sides."[72] Likewise, with approximately 180,000 religious women in the United States, "women were far more visible as 'official representatives' of the Roman Church than ordained clergy. . . . What the sisters said, how they acted, and even (or perhaps, especially) the clothes they wore—these were the 'visible signs' of the true church."[73] The Sacred Congregation of Religious ruled in favor of Cardinal McIntyre, determining that the sisters must wear a "uniform habit"; that teaching would be retained as the sisters' primary apostolate; that "they must retain at least some daily prayer in common, including Mass; and that, even though they were subject to the Roman Congregation for

Religious, they were still 'subject to the local bishop.'"[74] The male leadership had closed rank.

Despite the official ruling against the sisters, which became public in March 1968, the sisters won resounding and diverse support from concerned observers. In addition to the sympathy of the *Los Angeles Times* and the *National Catholic Reporter*, thirteen Jesuit seminary professors from Alma College in California praised the sisters in a published letter for making "a notable contribution to a restored understanding of authority in religious life."[75] Between February and March 1968, 3,000 sisters signed a petition indicating their support of the IHM renewal plan, and in April another "194 prominent educators, artists, writers, and clergymen had signed a letter to Pope Paul VI, urging freedom for the nuns to 'experiment.'"[76] By May 1968, 25,556 concerned southern Californians had signed a petition requesting more time for the sisters to consider their renewal plan. The public support for the sisters aside, those holding the most church authority on the matter voted against the sisters. Pope Paul VI, the Sacred Congregation of Religious, and the four-bishop committee assigned by the pope all rejected the sisters' renewal plan. It appeared that Suenens's interpretation of the church's teaching on the leadership role of women had some qualifications.

In the spirit of shared decision making, the sisters voted on their next step. In June 1968, 50 sisters chose to comply with Cardinal McIntyre, and these sisters retained the title of California Institute of the Sisters of the Most Holy and Immaculate Heart of Mary; 315 sisters sought release from their vows and "organized themselves into the 'Immaculate Heart Community.'"[77] Both sides gave each other time to reconsider, but neither could accept the other's position. For the sisters, the issue was about making a genuine renewal, which ultimately included rethinking their right to make decisions. President of Immaculate Heart College Sister Helen Kelley, in what came to be known as the "hairdryer speech," explained:

> I attach no importance to the fact that I didn't get up at 5:20 this morning, or that I made what I think was a pretty good meditation under a hair drier, or that I flew from Washington to Pittsburgh yesterday, alone. . . . None of this is worth burning at the stake for. . . . The significant thing is that the sisters look at themselves, at their lives, at their work . . . at their times and what their times are doing to people, and the way they live, and they say: not only our lives but the lives of almost everyone are very much in need of fundamental change. . . . What is worth burning at the stake for is not letting anyone else's conscience (individual or corporate) rob me of

the responsibility for my life, no matter how tempting an alternative that may continue to be.[78]

To lay aside the habit, to experience real poverty, and to make decisions were all much more difficult than following along when someone in "authority" told sisters what to wear and do. What the IHM sisters viewed as taking responsibility, however, the Sacred Congregation of Religious as well as Pope Paul VI saw as insurrection.

The California IHMs were not alone in their efforts and the reactions they drew. The School Sisters of St. Francis decided to withdraw from East Chicago Catholic School at the end of the 1969 school year due to conflicts with the pastor, Father Zubak. The sisters argued that the pastor was critical of their decision to modernize. The sisters wore street clothes, visited people in their homes, attended the theater, taught evolution, and encouraged their pupils to consider the significance of "conscience" regarding religious activities. Father Zubak lamented to one newspaper writer, "As far as their modernization is concerned, it is the talk of the parish. People of the parish were taken aback. You can't tell they are nuns."[79] Daily mass was another point of contention. Father Zubak argued that the sisters were not promoting the "formation of the right conscious" by neglecting to attend daily mass or not requiring it of the schoolchildren.

Rebels appeared in the pews as well, as Catholic women considered sexual discrimination in the church. An early convert to feminism with a doctorate in theology, Elizabeth Farians formed the Ecumenical Task Force on Women and Religion in 1966 and, with some convincing from Betty Friedan, linked sexism in the church to the National Organization for Women in 1967. Together with Mary Daly, Farians set out to "change the culture of the church and educate women as to the roots of sexism in religious tradition."[80] According to historian Mary J. Henold, apparel requirements were the first "catholic feminist" protest action. Farians launched an action to confront oppression within the church. In 1969 she organized the "Easter Bonnet Rebellion," or "The National Unveiling," at an Easter Sunday service in Milwaukee where the "pastor . . . recently castigated women for appearing bareheaded."[81] He threatened the women of the congregation with denial of communion, a punishment employed for various transgressions, such as sending a child to public school or approaching the altar wearing too much makeup. Fifteen women wore elaborate Easter hats to church that Sunday, but when it came time to receive communion, they knelt at the altar rail, removed their hats, and placed them on the rail. Despite the demonstration, the pastor gave them the sacrament.

The women had won. Considering that all changes brought about by Vatican II were "leaked" prior to their announcement, Farians and the other participants may have gotten wind that the Vatican's requirement for women to cover their heads would be changed in just a month, but a statement, nevertheless, had been made. Gender-specific mandates, such as women covering their heads in church, should also be included on the agenda for reform.

In February 1970, a *Time* magazine correspondent interviewed Anita Caspary, formerly Mother Mary Humiliata, a member of the Immaculate Heart Community. Caspary contended, "I am convinced that if tomorrow permission came to do everything we're doing, I would not want to go back. The old structure simply is not geared to the 20th century woman." [82] Within two years the number of noncanonical communities, such as the Immaculate Heart Community, reached fifty.[83] Despite the attrition of sisters, or perhaps because of it, Pope Paul VI chose to rein in what he viewed as excessive renewal. In February 1972 he "forbade nuns to discard 'distinctive religious garb' for secular dress." [84] While many religious women had simply moved beyond even the discussion of specific clothing, for the Vatican the appearance of women religious remained crucial. The message was clear: Vatican II did not alter the lines of authority, and the appearance of corporate unity was still a valued priority. Sisters did not, however, dust off their habits and return to uniforms. Instead, sisters quietly continued their renewals, and most orders decided to wear clothing deemed appropriate for their work and ministry.

MEN AND RENEWAL

Consideration of clothing for priests and male religious garb came out of the Second Vatican Council, although it did not garner the same attention as clothing reform among women religious. A priest's distinctive black apparel, without the Roman collar, was, after all, contemporary clothing. Priests and male religious also had nonclerical attire for relaxation and recreation. Finally, vestments, which also underwent experimentation, were primarily for Catholic viewing and therefore were not the type of garment to draw sustained popular attention.

Ceremonial clothing was part of the early reform. In 1965 Pope Paul VI discontinued certain ceremonial garments, such as the nine-foot scarlet cappa magna, or cape made from distinctive watered silks. Reviving Roulins's concerns from earlier in the century, Paul VI explained that to leave aside the use of the silks and capes would be a "sign of humility and poverty on the part of the cardinals." [85] For distinction of office, therefore, the pope left cardinals with the pectoral cross, emerald ring, and a small scarlet tab that sat "just below the square cutout at the throat of the Roman collar."[86] Cardinal Suenens went further than Pope Paul VI in his recommendations for bishops. He argued that "the bishop also must take a fresh look at his position among the people of God under his care; he must come closer to his clergy and faithful; he must live as they do—even down to the kind of clothes he wears—while yet preserving in its totality the authority he receives from God by virtue of his consecration."[87] This was a potentially provocative suggestion, but similar to other proclamations emanating from Vatican II, it was all in the reading. Dressing similarly to their clergy and the faithful while retaining their air of authority was a confounding recommendation for the bishops and one that produced little effect.

Priests took the initiative to make changes and laid their Roman collars aside, but without any consistency. A Dutch theologian, the Reverend Leo G. M. Alting Von Geusau, who ran an information and documentation service in Rome during the Second Vatican Council, intrigued a Los Angeles Times reporter by wearing a dark suit and ordinary tie during an interview. He explained to her that in countries such as "Holland, Austria, and Spain," clerical garb was less popular. He went on: "Priests who wear the tie 'feel they should not be classed apart from the laymen and not distinguish themselves.' Such separation . . . inhibits true dialogue between the church and its people."[88] In addition to forgoing the Roman collar, priests also grew longer sideburns and hair to fit in with contemporary styles and to make themselves appear more approachable. A survey conducted of the Association of Chicago Area Priests by the Reverend Richard W. Bell found that 65 percent of its members younger than fifty "believed that parish priests should be able to decide where they live and what they wear."[89] The majority of Chicago priests over fifty, however, did not support these changes. As with the sisters, the topic of changing clothes was not an easy one.

The Holy Cross Brothers in Chicago and the Jesuits at Fordham University in the Bronx took up sartorial experimentation in 1967. The Reverend John McLaughlin, SJ, an assistant editor at the Jesuit magazine America, advocated change for all priests. He, like several other dress reformers, pointed to Europe: French, German, and Swiss priests have vestmentary choices, and it should be the same in the United States, he argued. "I am bored and angered by stereotyped reaction—stared at by some people, cultivated by others, gratuitously, because of the collar. I don't want people to respond to my clothes. I want them to respond to me. I wasn't able to be myself."[90] Similar to the sisters, the Holy Cross Brothers and Jesuits, as members of religious orders, adhered to constitutions, but also like the sisters, they wanted people to respond to the individual inside the distinctive dress rather than the symbol of the clothing. To achieve this authentic connection with the people, priests sought more flexibility regarding their attire.

Other orders of men made changes as well. Members of the Society of the Divine Word, an order distinctive for its 1920s efforts to support seminary training of African Americans, had members who experimented with lay attire throughout the 1960s. The *Chicago Tribune* featured an article about the Reverend Harrie A. Vanderstappen, a professor in the art department at the University of Chicago, for his lack of clerical garb. Vanderstappen believed that dressing in ordinary attire enabled both religious and priests to get closer to everyday people. In addition to choosing their clothing, some priests lived independent of other priests or brothers. In Vanderstappen's case, he lived close to the University of Chicago campus in order to attend to parish life and meet the demands of his job.[91] When brothers lived in community, the habit or clerical dress assisted in reinforcing that sense of brotherhood. However, when a brother lived alone, habits and clerical attire appeared to be peculiar dress on one individual.

Although priests sometimes put the Roman collar aside, they also recognized its symbolic importance in witnessing for a cause. Just as sisters marched in their habits, priests wore their collars when they attended the march in Selma and continued to wear their collars at other civil rights demonstrations. Likewise, when the Chicago Fifteen went on trial for breaking into and vandalizing a draft office in May 1969 as a protest against the war in Vietnam, Judge Edwin A. Robson ordered priest attorney Father William Cunningham not to wear his clerical collar during the trial because of its symbolic importance.[92] Robson told the lawyers that "they should be aware of the irreparable damage wrought to our legal system and to the dispassionate rule of law which occurs when counsel and parties engage in a strategy designed to inflame public passion and prejudice."[93] Judge Robson also required that Cunningham be referred to as "Mr. Cunningham" rather than "Father." Despite the outrage of the American Civil Liberties Union of Chicago at the order, the judge thwarted Cunningham's collar "strategy."[94] The judge determined that the clerical title and attire were merely props designed to manipulate the sympathies of the jurors.

Vestments, too, became more experimental in the 1960s. A study of chasubles sewn by the Sisters of St. Francis Vestment Department in Hankinson, North Dakota, between the 1950s and 1970s reveals "greater diversity in percent of embellishment, number of motifs used per garment, and design organization" in the 1960s than in either the 1950s or the 1970s.[95] These findings substantiate sociological arguments which maintain that if either the institution for which the clothing is designed or the roles of individuals who work for an institution are in flux, the instability will come through in the clothing.[96] According to Mary Ann Littrell, chasubles in the 1950s were highly embellished and projected a "king" role for the priest, while the 1970s offered more simple designs, which for Littrell suggests a "shepherd" role. In the 1960s, however, the designs were much more diverse, suggesting a lack of role clarity altogether.[97]

Just as the hierarchy reined in the sisters, the priests, too, experienced a limit to their experimentation. In 1975 Archbishop of St. Louis John Carberry ordered the diocese's more than 1,000 priests to "get a haircut and shave." He also demanded that they desist with the "secular dress" and get back into the "Roman collar and the customary black."[98] Long hair made a statement: It suggested that the owner rejected authority, and the church did not want priests to express antiauthoritarianism. Not all dioceses issued pronouncements on priestly attire, but after the tumultuous era of protest, debate, and exodus for religious and clergy, the church wanted to restore discipline, and clothing and appearance had been one of the most effective mechanisms to achieve that goal in the past.

■ For most sisters, however, there was no turning back. Amending habits or laying them aside was not completed without careful thought, research, and discussion. And when sisters did change their clothes, it seemed like the most Christian and, ultimately, the least significant action, despite the attention it gained in the press and among everyday Catholics. The change was based on humanity-centered theology. For some sisters, the adoption of distinctive clothing by the church had been one of many ways that it began to distance itself from the people of God. "The introduction of celibacy and special costumes in the fifth century," wrote one contributor to the *Sister Formation Bulletin*, "increased more the social distance of the hierarchy from the rest of the Christian community. Pope Celestine I upbraided Honoratus, Abbot of Lerins, for introducing a special dress: a tunic and belt, to the Pope. This first monastic habit appeared a divisive innovation." The chronicler went on: "Writing to the bishops of Narbonne province, Pope Celestine said: 'We should be distinguished from others not by our dress but by our knowledge; by our conversation, not by our way of life.'"[99] Another contributor explained, "Our old image of being docile daughters in quaint long skirts gathered passively around our matriarchal mother superiors must be laid away with the tintypes of another age. We must know our own identity: professional women, women of God, members of *ecclesia*, a Christian community where all have the right and the responsibility of contributing to the common good according to the needs of all and the talents or charismatic gifts of each. Anything less is unfitting."[100]

Although amending religious dress was canonically approved, the Vatican ultimately felt it had gone far enough, and in many cases too far. The church was still an organization that demanded submission and a certain degree of separateness for its leaders and representatives. Priests and male religious, after a period of experimentation, for the most part continued to set themselves apart with Roman collars in public. As nineteenth-century seminary reformers suggested, priests were expected to be respectable, professional, and masculine. They could convey these attributes with their contemporary clerical suits and relax their appearance when they wanted with recreational clothing. The habitless sisters, however, presented a challenge to the Catholic leaders. The habit, particularly in the twentieth century, had been a dramatic statement of the church against the modern world, individualism, and women's sexuality. The "new nuns" chose to define themselves individually and as women in the modern world, and they rejected the church's negative assessment of women. Habits that confined and hid women had reproduced Catholic ideas about women's dangerous sexuality and the need to control women. By renouncing not just the habit but rules in general surrounding dress, the sister-women took back their humanness and their personal authority. In the minds of many reform-oriented sisters, they did not need to be dressed as brides of Christ, because Christ was never looking for wives; he wanted followers and apostles. Likewise, Jesus never required a uniform; corporations might place clothing demands on their employees, but sisters did not see the purpose in taking directions from the corporate church about their clothes when they could decide for themselves. Ultimately, sisters wanted to respond to the concerns of the people around them and join the discussion about how to make the world a better place, and most decided that they could do that best without a uniform.

BEYOND THE 1970S

Clothing has remained a symbolic and sacred aspect of the Catholic tradition beyond the 1970s. Catholics of varying stripes continue to intentionally manipulate their appearance to communicate their values, negotiate relations, draw people in, or hold them at a distance. While Vatican II may have unsettled the "triumphant language" of Catholic clothing, the subsequent years have nonetheless invited contentious and even creative expressions of Catholic materiality.

The sisters who garnered so much attention for the clothing segment of their renewal undertook in many ways what this study attempts to do—they went back to examine the history. That simple act of looking at their past and writing and talking about it among themselves shattered their sense of the Catholic "untime capsule." Uncovering their origins, communities came to see the consequences of making specific clothing the central feature of their religious expression. Dressing in strikingly antiquated garb each day, performing "studied behaviors," and separating themselves from ordinary Catholic women conveyed a sense of inviolability.

As sisterhoods reflected on their stories, they came to see that the habit occupied too great a place in the way they saw themselves and the way others saw them. Most communities' initial goals had been living in poverty, serving those in need, and sharing resources in common, not adopting habits. Sisters did not discount the benefits of habits in the past, but as they looked toward the future, most communities saw little need for continuing with regulated attire.

Clothing was still, however, meaningful to the sisters. In fact, the sisters' lack of uniform stood out against the consistent, orderly, and sometimes elaborate attire of the male leadership. Plainly dressed sisters conveyed to onlookers that the Catholic Church is not a corporation but, rather, a church where, in the tradition of Catholic Action advocates, members should "observe, judge, and act" rather than merely follow. Embracing ordinary clothing was as powerful a statement of values as any uniform would be in the context of Catholic culture and symbolism.

After most sisters relinquished their habits, a curious phenomenon occurred. The school uniforms lost their linkage to habited teachers. The connection that habits and uniforms shared became severed, and Catholics loosened their hold on the "trademark" of school uniforms. Perhaps the public school administrators had attended Catholic school, but it seems that the purposes of uniforms could be more readily shared when they did not include a potential future in religious life. These days, Catholic students and public school students, especially in large cities, frequently wear uniforms. Most of the rationale for the public schools is the same as it was for the Catholic schools in the early twentieth century: Uniforms promote discipline, school spirit, and classlessness while reducing competition.[1] Sharing the uniform look with "the publics" took on a unique and perhaps unconscious form of ecumenism.

To some extent, Catholicism's attention to clothing has been one way back to the social leadership the church enjoyed in the post–World War II era, when Catholicism was akin to Americanism. Following the lead of Catholic-affiliated human rights activist Charles Kernaghan, the director of the National Labor Committee Education Fund in Support of Workers and Human Rights in Central America, and the Archdiocese of Newark, New Jersey, the church turned its attention to the people who sewed school uniforms and whether they were paid fairly and worked in acceptable conditions.[2] Along with the Archdiocese of Newark, the Dioceses of Chicago, San Francisco, Albany, and Hamilton, Ontario, and universities such as Notre Dame, Duke, Wisconsin, St. Mary's, Georgetown, Harvard, DePaul, Loyola-Chicago, Loyola–New Orleans, and St. John's adopted "sweat free" purchasing policies for their clothing. State governments and public school districts also climbed aboard the "No Sweat" movement.

Although church leaders were willing to scrutinize labor practices, they did not do the same for gender roles. Oddly enough, even while many religious sisters have made a clear statement, through their own garments, of rejecting the church's gender ideology, they nonetheless do not challenge the traditional uniform on young girls. Uniform dresses, rather than pants, subtly reinforce essentialist gender ideology, and while girls negotiate clothing regulations, as the Hallahan girls pictured in figure 37 did by frolicking in the fountain in John F. Kennedy Plaza to celebrate the end of the school year, the girls continue to be outfitted in traditionally female attire.

Catholic schools are not alone in retaining and emphasizing traditionalism through clothing. A campaign to emphasize distinctive clerical and religious dress originated in the days of Vatican II. Just as renewal experiments were getting under way among the religious, Father Gommar De Pauw, JCD,

Figure 37. John W. Hallahan Catholic Girls' High School students frolicking in the fountain at John F. Kennedy Plaza, 1970. Courtesy of Special Collections Research Center, Temple University Libraries, Philadelphia, Pa.

a Belgian-born priest, issued *The Catholic Traditionalist Manifesto* to "halt . . . any further progress of vernacularism" and to encourage priests to "wear their distinctive black street clothing with Roman collar, while our Sisters introduce only those dress changes that will still allow their uniform to remain indicative of their special position among God's people."[3] Although the primary aim of the Traditionalist movement was and is the continuation of the Tridentine, or Latin Rite, mass, the movement is also aimed at protecting clerical hegemony in the church. Traditionalists employ habits, cassocks, and ornate and ceremonial vestments to distinguish the priesthood with an imperial and powerful display of clothing and sacramental accessories.

Shortly after he became pope, John Paul II reinforced the Traditionalists' position on distinctive garments for religious. In his 1983 pronouncement, "Essential Elements," Pope John Paul II explicitly stated that religious "wear religious garb that distinguishes them as consecrated persons."[4] Catholic women's orders such as the Slaves of the Immaculate Heart of Mary, Sisters of Life, and Carmelite Sisters of the Most Sacred Heart wear traditional habits, and observers of church trends are quick to point out that it is the habit-wearing orders that are winning the few recruits entering orders.

Whether religious pull away from or gravitate toward habits, both groups of Catholics tend to endorse Catholic school uniforms for students; they see wisdom in encouraging orderliness and specific gender roles. This is usually where the common understanding ends, however. Habitless sisters see themselves as educated *ecclesia* who are mature enough to choose their own attire, while habited sisters see value in being an unmistakable symbol of the church for the people. Uniform clothing symbolizes submission, and certain orders, such as members of the Council of Major Superiors, want to be linked to the magisterium. The habit conveys that message for the sisters.

Beyond women religious, students, and clergy, there are other Catholics who employ clothing to assert their beliefs. In 2011 Father Bob Wurm, a Detroit priest, defied Archbishop of Detroit Allen Vigeron by saying a mass for what the church viewed as a heretical organization, the American Catholic Council, with alleged "liturgical abuses."[5] Approximately 1,500 worshippers attended the mass, and everyone in the congregation "wore stoles, usually only worn by clergy, to symbolize equality and the idea that all Catholics, not just the clergy, represent the church. On the stoles, the artist drew a dove with the words: 'Come Holy Spirit. Fill the hearts of your faithful and kindle in them the fire of your love.'" One attendee explained, "I'm disturbed by what's taking place. . . . The Church is going backwards. It's more feudal, more authoritative."[6] The rebel congregants employed a sacramental and cherished symbol, the stole, because Catholics who "take clothing seriously" recognize that the message of their desired inclusion would be clear.

Finally, Catholics not only continue to employ clothing as a material symbol; they utilize it as a metaphoric device because it resonates so powerfully among co-religious. In 1984 Cardinal Joseph Bernardin used the "seamless garment" metaphor to explain what a consistent ethic of life entails. In his choice of a seamless garment, Bernardin demonstrated his Catholic sensibility and skill as a diplomat. The seamless garment symbolically reflects the entirety of the church and its teachings. The warp and weft bind the fibers of the cloth into a durable religious theology for all times. Bernardin reached out to the left with this metaphor of a simple garment. In his own life, Bernardin rejected vestmentary displays often worn by other bishops and, in his "priesthood of believers" approach, introduced himself to Chicago Catholics by saying, "I am Joseph your brother," during his installation mass in Chicago.[7] Bernardin attempted to (and quite successfully) recast the politicized abortion debate as part of a larger ethic of life. To sisters who, like Bernardin, chose not to stress sartorial symbols, the ethic of life and the seamless garment reflected the importance of simplicity, membership, and personalism. This approach did not obligate sisters to emphasize one issue, such as abortion, over other issues pertaining to protecting life or assisting the needy.

To the sisters the garment represented the essence of Catholic teaching. Confronting modernity and recognizing the variety of concerns facing the world—inequality, health care, poverty, discrimination, violence, and education—the agenda had to be bigger than sex and control of women. The "garment" envelops everyone, and all needs should be a concern of the Catholic Church. Co-religious to the right of the sisters also appreciated the symbol of the seamless garment. It is a priest-centered analogy that references Jesus' seamless tunic that the soldiers did not tear. Priests in particular, but not exclusively, distinguish themselves by wearing tuniclike garments, or albs. Cardinal Bernardin's "seamless garment" metaphor found willing listeners on both sides of the Catholic ideology divide.

Almost twenty years later, Pope Francis seems to be echoing Cardinal Bernardin's message and even implying that the sisters' approach might indeed be admirable. Like Bernardin, the simply attired Francis does not appear to be suggesting radical changes, but he does hope to see the church focused more on "healing" than on rules and disheartening criticisms.[8]

Clothing has been a primary mechanism through which Catholics have communicated with one another and those around them for centuries. And as we have observed, Catholic clothing is in no way static and timeless; instead, it is contested and invented. In the United States, distinctive attire played a role in creating a sense of unity and respectability, despite the various origins and economic situations of many Catholic immigrants. Unique clothing and symbols ultimately enabled Catholics to express confidence—a valuable attribute for an outsider faith. Today, Catholic apparel is less unifying than it once was. Nevertheless, Catholics still use their carefully or carefreely, as the case may be, attired bodies to debate who they are, what they believe, and what the priorities of the church should be as it looks to the future.

NOTES

Abbreviations

CGHS	Catholic Girls' High School
CNRA	College of New Rochelle Archive, New Rochelle, N.Y.
JWHCGHS	John W. Hallahan Catholic Girls' High School, Philadelphia, Pa.
MSJAA	Mount St. Joseph Academy Archive, Flourtown, Pa.
MUA	Marquette University Archives, Milwaukee, Wisc.
NCR	*National Catholic Reporter*
PAHRC	Philadelphia Archdiocesan Historical Research Center, Philadelphia, Pa.
SCNY	Sisters of Charity of St. Vincent de Paul of New York Archive, Yonkers, N.Y.
SFC/RFC	Sister Formation Conference/Religious Formation Conference
SFB	*Sister Formation Bulletin*
SSJA	Sisters of St. Joseph Archive, Philadelphia, Pa.
WPCGHS	West Philadelphia Catholic Girls' High School, Philadelphia, Pa.

Introduction

1. Malone, "Clothing Optional?"

2. Thanks to Lynn Eckert, who directed me to Hirschmann's *Subject of Liberty* for an instructive discussion of social construction and the naturalization of language. See Hirschmann, *Subject of Liberty*, 77–95.

3. The 80 percent estimate is based on an interview with Sister Mary Hughes, former president of the Leadership Conference of Women Religious. See National Press Club.

4. Council of Major Superiors of Women Religious.

5. Diocesan schools or central schools drew students from multiple parishes. Establishing central schools lifted the burden of creating individual high schools in each parish from the pastor and placed it with the bishop.

6. Wills, *Bare Ruined Choirs*, 19. Campbell, *Graceful Exits*, 59–60, and Sullivan, *Visual Habits*, 15, also cite Wills's passage.

7. Orsi, "Everyday Miracles," 8.

8. In his examination of the changing prayer habits of Catholics between 1926 and the 1980s, Chinnici refers to the movement away from segmented Catholicism through national organizations such as the Sodality of Mary. See Chinnici, "Catholic Community at Prayer."

9. An excellent monograph that examines the relationships between women religious and college students is Byrne's *O God of Players*. For a study that focuses on children specifically, see Bales, *When I Was a Child*.

10. Orsi, "Close Formation," 32–37.

11. I borrowed the term "visual lexicon" from Vincent's "Camisas Nuevas," 169.

12. See Rubinstein, *Dress Codes*, 3.

13. See Weber's explanation of bureaucracy in *From Max Weber*, 199.

14. Joseph, *Uniforms and Nonuniforms*, 67.

15. See Joseph, *Uniforms and Nonuniforms*, and Keenan, "Clothed with Authority."

16. Orsi identifies the criteria for understanding religious practice. They are

(1) a sense of the range of idiomatic possibilities and limitations in a culture—the limits of what can be desired, fantasized, imagined, and felt; (2) an understanding of the knowledges of the body in the culture, a clear sense of what has been embodied in the corporeality of the people who participate in religious practice . . . ; (3) an understanding of the structures of social experience—marriage and kinship patterns, moral and juridical responsibilities and expectations, the allocation of valued resources . . . ; (4) a sense of what sorts of characteristic tensions erupt with in their particular structures. (Orsi, "Everyday Miracles," 7)

17. See Orsi, "Everyday Miracles."

18. See Arthur, *Religion, Dress and the Body*, 1.

19. Hall, *Lived Religion in America*, viii. See also Hollander, *Sex and the Suit*, 17.

20. In the post-Madonna era, scapulars and rosaries have also been claimed as punk and pop adornment. In this book, however, I will only explore wearing or using sacramentals for religious purposes.

21. Keenan, "Clothed with Authority," 83.

22. Weber, *From Max Weber*, 246–47.

23. Ibid., 262.

24. Ibid., 248.

25. Orsi and Lynch both explore the role of children in Catholicism. Orsi examines the U.S. experience, while Lynch looks at the Irish Industrial Schools run by Catholic orders.

26. Lynch, *Sacred in the Modern World*, 16. Lynch separates the sacred and religion, arguing, "To think of the experience of the sacred as a single phenomenon is to neglect the myriad ways that sacred forms are experienced, reproduced, and shaped through individual subjectivities in modern society." Lynch identifies this approach as a cultural sociology of sacred forms.

27. Keenan, "Clothed with Authority," 85.

28. This punishment was ultimately rejected by the pope, but people had limited recourse if a priest decided to withhold sacraments. During discussions about parents who did not send their children to Catholic schools, Bishop McQuaid suggested that priests use withholding sacraments as a threat. See Zwierlein, *Life and Letters of Bishop McQuaid*, 2:324. See also Tentler, *Seasons of Grace*, 232.

29. See Cummings, *New Women*, for discussions of the careful line Catholic women and the hierarchy walked in support of women's rights.

30. McDannell, *Material Christianity*; Kaufman, *Consuming Visions*, 8.

31. See Arthur, *Religion, Dress and the Body*, for a variety of scholarly essays on the topic.

32. Schreier, *Becoming American Women*, 1.

33. Male religious are men who are members of religious orders, as opposed to diocesan or secular priests.

34. Ewen, *Role of the Nun*; White, *Diocesan Seminary*.

Chapter 1

1. De Tocqueville, *Democracy in America*, 423. Thanks to Katherine Haas, in whose carefully researched work "The Fabric of Religion" I found this citation as well as the old adage "The clothes make the man."

2. A secular priest is a priest who does not belong to a religious order or institute and does not take religious vows. A regular priest or brother is a member of a religious order or institute, makes religious vows, and abides by the *regula*, or rule of the order.

3. See White, *Diocesan Seminary*, 233–34, for comment about "Protestant priests." White is quoting Smith, *Our Seminaries*, 167.

4. Ellis, *American Catholicism*, 32–33.

5. IgnatianSpirituality.com.

6. Pasquier, *Fathers on the Frontier*, 137.

7. Ibid.

8. Duncan, *Citizen or Papist*, 29.

9. Hennesey, *American Catholics*, 52.

10. Zürcher, "Transcultural Imaging." Regarding the Jesuit approach to clothing, Zürcher explained that since they did not live in monasteries, they did not have to wear a specific religious costume and instead could be adaptable.

11. See Society of Jesus in the United States.

12. Pope Clement XIV suppressed the Jesuit order worldwide between 1773 and 1814. Had they worn some distinct habit, they would have likely removed it during those years and worn the dress of a secular priest. Secular priests (those who are not members of a religious order) wore a variety of clothing at this time.

13. Zaplotnik, "Glimpse of the Past," 41.

14. Ibid., 42.

15. Dolan, *American Catholic Experience*, 202. According to an archivist friend, during the 1844 anti-Catholic riots in Philadelphia, Bishop Francis P. Kenrick encouraged his priests to dispense with any garment that might indicate Catholic identity, so as not to put the priests in danger.

16. Tentler, *Seasons of Grace*, 35.

17. Ellis, *American Catholicism*, 49.

18. Cited in Merwick, *Boston Priests*, 42, from Whyte, "Appointment of Catholic Bishops in Nineteenth-Century Ireland," 30. Also in Healy, *Maynooth College*, 285. Maynooth provided seminary education for many priests who came from Ireland.

19. Lefevere to Bishop George Carroll, 20 December 1861, cited in Tentler, *Seasons of Grace*, 35.

20. Cited in Haas, "Fabric of Religion," and consulted by me as well. See Smith, *Notes on the Second Plenary Council*, 123–25.

21. Eventually priests would be encouraged to vacation in groups, and that way they could keep an eye on one another.

22. Ray Allen Billington, while focused on the nineteenth-century western United States, examines American attitudes toward livery, titles, and the appearance of status. He argues that distinction was firmly rejected. See Billington, *America's Frontier Heritage*, 139–57.

23. Merwick, *Boston Priests*, 103, cites correspondence between Williams and Davis in the Boston Chancery Archives, requesting hats. Williams likewise did not endorse separate schools for Catholic children. This stance was none too popular with Rome, although it was not an unusual position for the time.

24. Burtsell, *Diary*, ii.

25. Ibid., 81, 97, 121.

26. Ibid., 315–16.

27. See Curran, "Prelude to 'Americanism.'"

28. Nathan Joseph explains that "enlisted men are issued their uniforms; officers usually procure theirs ready-made, from outside agencies." Clothing independence is significant in that it communicates the level of control over the person wearing the clothing. See Joseph, *Uniforms and Nonuniforms*, 59.

29. Ewen, *Role of the Nun*, 96. A surplice is a generous white garment with yoke-style neckline, but it does not reach the ground. It is often trimmed with lace.

30. Ibid.

31. Tentler, *Seasons of Grace*, 36.

32. Dolan, *American Catholic Experience*, 115.

33. Ellis, *American Catholicism*, 45.

34. O'Toole, *The Faithful*, 58.

35. Ibid., 59.

36. Cited in Ellis, *Catholic Priest*, 37, from de Tocqueville, *Democracy in America*, 283.

37. McAvoy, *Americanist Heresy*, 43. In trying to determine what is dressing "simply" for an archbishop and later cardinal, I am struck by the absence of the biretta. The statue commemorating Gibbons's life has him dressed in a simple cassock with a zucchetta, or skullcap. The biretta is a distinctive European and originally Italian head covering that rises on the head and provides the wearer with distinction. Birettas would become an important part of the American clerical ensemble in both secular and sacred appearances, but the biretta, at least from photographs of Gibbons, seems to be an infrequent choice. See Baltimore Basilica for images of Gibbons and a photograph of his statue. Nainfa offers an intriguing note on Gibbons as well. In his *Costume of Prelates*, he makes the case that American Catholic clergy should dress formally. Nainfa argues that rather than Protestants criticizing Catholics for ostentation, the Protestants instead appreciate and expect an elaborate costume from prelates and would be disappointed if they did not see it. Nainfa uses Gibbons as an example of one who toward the end of his life dressed more formally. The court dress for papal audiences after 1870 was the cassock (academic dress) or *abito piano*, but in America it was not common. According to Nainfa, "In America, the *abito piano* is seldom required in mere social life; but it is decidedly gaining popularity in social circles, and some distinguished hostesses are now evidently grateful to an invited Prelate if he appears, at the dinner hour, as Cardinal Gibbons was wont to do in the last years of his life, in the official dress which he would wear in simi-

lar circumstances in Italy or in France." This leads me to believe that Gibbons was less conspicuous in his earlier years. See Nainfa, *Costume of Prelates*, 234.

38. Ellis, *Life of James Cardinal Gibbons*, 10. Original speech cited by Ellis in *Catholic Sentinel*, 27 January 1890.

39. Finke and Stark, *Churching of America*, 122.

40. Russell, "Catholic Church in the United States," 20.

41. Nolan, *Pastoral Letters*, 60–61.

42. Roger Finke and Rodney Stark put the number of priests in 1830 at 232. They adapted their totals from data compiled by Catherine Ann Curry in "Statistical Study of Religious Women in the United States" (available from George C. Stewart Jr., P.O. Box 7, Fayetteville, NC 29302 [1988]) and Gerald Shaughnessy, *Has the Immigrant Kept the Faith* (New York: Macmillan, 1925). See Finke and Stark, *Churching of America*, 143.

43. Joseph points out that "enlisted men are issued their uniforms; officers usually procure theirs ready-made, from outside agencies. . . . Not only is the mode of distributing clothes important, but also whether it conforms to the prevalent pattern in society. Total institutions like armies or prisons very often rely upon standardized clothing or uniforms to control their member or inmates. Being unable to select their own clothing, inmates are denied a symbol of responsible adulthood" (Joseph, *Uniforms and Nonuniforms*, 59).

44. Haas, "Fabric of Religion," 196.

45. *Ceremonial*, 14.

46. Cited in Zwierlein, *Life and Letters of Bishop McQuaid*, 1:15–16. This would no longer be an issue after the 1829 Provincial Council, as the bishops voted to condemn the trusteeism model and assert temporal and spiritual control over parishes.

47. Kenrick, *Pastoral Address*, 7, cited in Haas, "Fabric of Religion," 195.

48. Ibid.

49. See McCarroll, "Plenary Councils of Baltimore."

50. "Statutes of the Third Synod of the Philadelphia Diocese Held in the Cathedral Church of St. John the Evangelist by the Right Reverend Francis P. Kenrick, Bishop of Philadelphia, October 3rd. 1847," PAHRC.

51. Tentler, *Seasons of Grace*, 36.

52. Ibid., 34–35.

53. Ibid. Despite Borgess's restrictions, Tentler points out that he was "willing to dispense at least some of his priests from the soutane for street wear, but he reminded his clergy in 1882, 'that no priest within our jurisdiction is allowed to wear clothes made after the fashion of the day, and which are not of a strictly black color . . . nor is any priest dispensed from wearing the Roman collar at home or abroad'" (Tentler, *Seasons of Grace*, 36).

54. Nainfa, *Costume of Prelates*, 54.

55. Ibid., 54–55.

56. Ibid., 41.

57. Ibid., 55.

58. "Soutane" is the French term for "cassock."

59. Cited in Smith, *Notes on the Second Plenary Council*, 125.

60. Ibid., vii.

61. Cited in ibid., 123.

62. Ibid., 124.

63. Ibid.

64. Both O'Toole, author of *Militant and Triumphant*, and Morris, author of *American Catholic*, contend that William O'Connell's letters are complete fabrications. However, for my purpose, insight into clerical appearance, I am going to use the source. O'Toole and Morris do not dispute the value O'Connell placed on appearance. See O'Toole, *Militant and Triumphant*, 100, and Morris, *American Catholic*, 123.

65. O'Connell, *Letters of His Eminence*, 86.

66. Ibid., 89.

67. Interestingly, the bishops attending the First Vatican Council in 1869 realized that they did not have the appropriate religious attire for the occasion. According to a 1962 article in *America* magazine,

> Planning for the mass migration to Rome occupied a good deal of episcopal correspondence during 1869. Many bishops were ill-provided with pontifical regalia. Spalding made inquiries about comparative prices for various items of dress in Rome and also at Lyons, France. He then published a notice in the Baltimore *Catholic Mirror* to the effect that the Cardinal Archbishop of Lyons had agreed to lend his *cappa magna* and cope as patterns for robes purchased in his see city. Accommodations were another problem. Eighteen of the bishops made arrangements to live at the American College; the rest were dispersed throughout the city in religious houses and hotels. (Reidy, "First Vatican Council")

68. I am using Byrne's analysis of ultramontanism in America, which distinguishes between the political ultramontanist phenomenon in eighteenth- and nineteenth-century Europe and the cultural expression of ultramontanism that prevailed in the United States from the late nineteenth century through the Second Vatican Council. See Byrne, "American Ultramontanism," 301. For another, more international consideration of ultramontanism, see von Arx, *Varieties of Ultramontanism*.

69. Ellis, *Catholic Priest*, 44.

70. A *vestis talaris* is a gown reaching to the heel. See Nainfa, *Costume of Prelates*, 41.

71. Thurston, "Clerical Costume."

72. White, *Diocesan Seminary*, 232.

73. Ibid., 211.

74. Ibid., 213. The pilgrimage he's referring to is the Way of St. James, which requires pilgrims to walk at least 100 kilometers to achieve a certified indulgence.

75. Maes, "Preparatory Seminaries for Clerical Students," 315–16.

76. Ahern, *Catholic University of America*, 19:40, cited in Ellis, *Catholic Priest*, 89.

77. Smith, *Our Seminaries*, 92–93.

78. Ibid., 16.

79. Burtsell, *Diary*, 167.

80. Timothy Holland to James Driscoll, 6 January 1904, RG 10, box 7, Sulpician Archive, Baltimore, cited in White, *Diocesan Seminary*, 234; Smith, *Our Seminaries*, 97–98.

81. O'Connell, *Letters of His Eminence*, 5.

82. Bederman, *Manliness and Civilization*, 10–42; Murphy, *Political Manhood*, 71.

83. Smith, *Our Seminaries*, 63.

84. Ibid.

85. Stang, *Pastoral Theology*, ix.

86. Broderick, *Catholic Encyclopedia*, 457–58.

87. Stang, *Pastoral Theology*, vii.

88. Ibid.

89. Ibid., 8.

90. Schulze, *Manual of Pastoral Theology*, 5.

91. Ibid.

92. Valuy, *Directorium Sacerdotale*, 76–77.

93. Schulze, *Manual of Pastoral Theology*, 125.

94. Haas, "Fabric of Religion," 196.

95. Zwierlein, *Life and Letters of Bishop McQuaid*, 2:301.

96. Ibid., 2:302.

97. Ibid.

98. See Finke and Stark, *Churching of America*, 123–24, on the challenge of raising donations among immigrant Catholics.

99. Zwierlein, *Letters of Archbishop Corrigan*, 66.

100. Ibid., 117.

101. According to Curran, Burtsell was "deeply respected at home and in Rome for his understanding of Church law and, in a way, this made him a special menace to episcopal authority. Burtsell was continually a goad as a canonist much in demand to defend priests in their contests with ordinaries across the country. His advocacy of priests' rights was making him a threat to episcopal authority" (Curran, "Prelude to 'Americanism,'" 61).

102. Zwierlein, *Letters of Archbishop Corrigan*, 82.

103. Taves argues that Catholic missionaries, particularly Redemptorists, Paulists, Jesuits, and Passionists, capitalized on the available print technology and improved literacy among Catholics and encouraged devotional memberships while conducting "missions" at parishes throughout the United States. Taves contends that until the 1850s, confraternities and sodalities (devotional groups organized by age and sex) were more commonly found at colleges. After the 1850s, however, they became affiliated with parishes, and oversight of the devotions then fell to parish priests. See Taves, *Household of Faith*, 18.

104. Haas, "Fabric of Religion," 194–95.

105. Preston to Archbishop Domenico Jacobini, New York, 2 January 1890, AANY S-1, copy, cited in Curran, "Prelude to 'Americanism,'" 62.

106. Haas, "Fabric of Religion," 194–95.

107. See *Mirae Caritatis*:

Some there are, no doubt, who will express their surprise that for the manifold troubles and grievous afflictions by which our age is harassed We should have determined to seek for remedies and redress in this quarter rather than elsewhere, and in some, perchance, Our words will excite a certain peevish disgust. But this is only the natural result of pride; for when this vice has taken possession of the heart, it is inevitable that Christian faith, which demands a most willing docility, should languish, and that a murky darkness in regard of divine truths should close in upon the mind; so that in the case of many these words should be made good: "Whatever things they know not, they blaspheme" (St. Jude, 10). We, however, so far from being hereby turned aside from the design which We have taken in hand, are on the contrary determined all the more zealously and diligently to hold up the light for the guidance of the well disposed, and, with the help of the united prayers of the faithful, earnestly to implore forgiveness for those who speak evil of holy things.

108. Jacob Schmitt, *Instructions for First Communicants* (New York: Catholic Publication Society, 1881), 116, cited in Haas, "Fabric of Religion," 210.

109. Durand, *Catholic Ceremonies*, 16, personally consulted and cited in Haas, "Fabric of Religion," 210.

110. Haas, "Fabric of Religion," 211.

111. See Joseph, *Uniforms and Nonuniforms*, 50.

112. See "Notification of Deprevation of Ecclesiastical Garb."

113. The stole is a band of fabric draped over the neck and often reaches to the knees.

114. "Offerings Made at Baptism," 1220.

115. "Bicycle Costumes for Clerics."

116. "Priestly Robe."

117. In an 1899 letter to Cardinal Gibbons, Pope Leo XIII wrote, "We cannot approve the opinions which some comprise under the head of Americanism . . . for it raises the suspicion that there are some among you who conceive of and desire a church in America different from that which is in the rest of the world. One in the unity of doctrine as in the unity of government, such is the Catholic Church, and since God has established its center and foundation in the Chair of Peter, one which is rightly called Roman, for where Peter is there is the Church" (Zwierlein, *Letters of Archbishop Corrigan*, 198).

118. Ellis, *Catholic Priest*, 61.

119. For vigilance committees, see ibid., 62.

120. The Americanist controversy refers to "the publication in 1897 of a French translation of a biography of Isaac Hecker." A lengthy preface written by a liberal French priest, Félix Klein, accompanied the volume and glorified Hecker's vision of a church characterized by American ideals such as separation of church and state and a democratic system of government. The popularity of the book threatened the Vatican and its monarchical approach to leadership. As a result of the publication and a culmination of concerns about the liberal factions existing in America and internationally, Pope Leo XIII published *Testem Benevolentiae*, which condemned Americanism and those ideas the pope saw as related to the Americanist position. See Dolan, *American Catholic Experience*, 315.

121. Morris, *American Catholic*, 117. According to D'Agostino, "As the Church's communication and education systems improved, and the Vatican monitored the selection of U.S. bishops, the expectations of the ideology of the Roman Question became internalized, routinized, and reinforced. Deviation diminished among Catholics, at least outside of the unpredictable Italian American community" (*Rome in America*, 67).

122. O'Connell, *Letters of His Eminence*.

123. Ibid., 88.

124. Ibid., 88–89.

125. See Bettoja, "Clerical Dress in the City of Rome in the 19th Century."

126. O'Toole, *Militant and Triumphant*, 40.

127. The poem appears in ibid., 98.

128. Ibid., 31.

129. Kane, *Separatism and Subculture*, 78. On exercising in cassocks, see White, *Diocesan Seminary*, 231.

130. Kauffman, *Tradition and Transformation in Catholic Culture*, 191.

131. Morris, *American Catholic*, 179.

132. Ibid.

133. Kennedy to Farley in Rome, 8 November 1908, *Archive of the Archdiocese of New York*, I-11-K, cited in Ellis, *Catholic Priest*, 68 n. 138.

134. Pecklers, "Liturgical Movement."

135. Mayer-Thurman, *Raiment for the Lord's Service*, 29.

136. In ibid., essay contributor Aidan Kavahagh, OSB, explains that regarding vestments,

> the beauty and symbolic value of the vestment must derive from its material and form rather than from its ornamentation. The vestment is a garment, not a costume. . . . Vestments that are serious according to norms other than those to which the act of worship itself gives rise, not only transgress the authentic sentiments of the community but comment on a shift of Christian sentiment into areas foreign to the basic purposes of Christian worship—areas such as aestheticism, triumphalism, saccharine emotionalism, or cheap tastelessness. The liturgical garment then becomes less than sacred, a mere vehicle for applied "symbolism" chosen at whim; less than a garment, a mere costume overly ornamented and ignoble in form; a billboard whose purpose is to shout ideologies instead of clothing a creature in beauty.

While the weight of ornamentation could have driven wealthy churches to board- and fiddlebacks, a lack of funds could have inspired the same chasuble selection. In the thirteenth century the Church required four to seven colors for a complete set of liturgical vestments. Likewise, the chasubles were to be made of silk. The board chasuble was a dramatically cut-down version of the original conical chasuble, and the seams moved to the shoulders, giving the priest angular rather than more sloping shoulders.

137. Roulins, *Vestments and Vesture*, 9.

138. Ibid.

139. Ibid., 10.

140. Ibid., 40.

141. This seems to be the case as the Liturgical movement pointed to Pope Pius XI looking at a collection of Gothic or ample vestments and blessing them in 1925.

142. Letter, Father Hocter to Father Burgio and enclosure to Cardinal Dougherty, 10 September 1941, Dougherty Collection, Group 80.00+, shelf 1, box 6, item 80.2125, PAHRC.

143. Ibid.

144. Nainfa, *Costume of Prelates*, 222–23.

Chapter 2

1. The term "sister" refers to a Catholic woman who is a member of a congregation and has taken the simple vows of poverty, chastity, and obedience.

2. In this context, by "conservative" I am referring to anti-Americanists, and by "liberal" to Americanists.

3. Even in a monastic order the First Order Regulars are made up of men who take solemn vows; the Second Order includes the women who make solemn vows and who are cloistered; and the Third Order is made up of men and women who commit themselves to the spiritual works of the family order but are not cloistered. See Thomas, *Women Religious History Sources*, xxvii.

4. Not all nuns or sisters were virgins. Originally, widows would enter convents, and the founder of the Sisters of Charity, Mother Elizabeth Ann Seton, was a widow, too. However, most orders eventually adopted an age limit, almost guaranteeing that widows would not enter.

5. Koehlinger, "'Are You the White Sisters or the Black Sisters?,'" 261.

6. Valuy, *Directorium Sacerdotale*, 68.

7. Ibid., 68–69.

8. Ibid., 69.

9. Ibid.

10. Stang, *Pastoral Theology*, 154.

11. Valuy, *Directorium Sacerdotale*, 158.

12. Stang, *Pastoral Theology*, 240.

13. Koehlinger, "'Are You the White Sisters or the Black Sisters?,'" 262.

14. Ibid., 261.

15. Regarding terminology, the glossary of Thomas, *Women Religious History Sources*, xxv–xxvii, provides definitions. A religious institute is an "ecclesiastically authorized society of members living a common life and striving for Christian perfection by following the three vows of poverty, chastity, and obedience. The term embraces orders, congregations, institutes of pontifical or diocesan rank, and clerical and lay institutes." An order is "used popularly to denote any religious community, but strictly, a community professing the religious life with a certain austerity in accordance with a rule approved by the Church and recognized as having the obligation of solemn vows." A congregation has a few definitions: "(1) Uncloistered community of religious with simple vows. (2) Group of monasteries or convents forming a subdivision of an order. (3) Group of orders associated together under a common spiritual ideal." Finally Thomas defines a community as a "body of men or women who are voluntarily under a common rule."

16. "Charism" is another word for "apostolate."

17. Technically, only nuns were religious, and sisters were pious women.

18. Ewen, "Women in the Convent," 24–25. For total numbers (49,620 sisters), I used Finke and Stark, *Churching of America*, 143. Their statistics are adapted from other studies but are adjusted based on their own research.

19. Dominican Nuns of Summit; Thomas, *Women Religious History Sources*, 13.

20. Thomas, *Women Religious History Sources*, xxvii.

21. Kuhns, *The Habit*, 103.

22. Ibid., xxvi.

23. Fitzgerald, *Habits of Compassion*, 38–39.

24. Ewen, *Role of the Nun*, 17–18.

25. Ibid., 253.

26. Ibid., 19; see also McNamara, *Sisters in Arms*, 461–63.

27. An academic explained to me that the "nun dolls" originate from mockups of habits that nuns sent to the Vatican to gain approval for their habit. Rather than evaluating the habit on a real woman, the priests viewed it on the doll.

28. Evangelisti, *Nuns*, 29.

29. Ibid.

30. Ewen, *Role of the Nun*, 19.

31. Madame de Barberey Bailly, *Elizabeth Seton*, trans. from the 6th French ed. and adapted by the Reverend Joseph B. Code (New York: Macmillan, 1927), 303, quoted in Ewen, *Role of the Nun*, 89.

32. True to St. Vincent de Paul's ideals, the Daughters of Charity did not wear a "veil" as cloistered nuns did. In a letter Louise de Marillac wrote, "I should not dare to say anything to you with regard to the suggestions of the little veil except that M. Vincent objects to it strongly and with reasons; I have several times proposed to him that the Sisters should wear, not a veil which would be quite objectionable, but something which would screen the face in great cold, or great heat, and for this the Sisters who had been recently clothed have been allowed to wear a white linen cornette on their heads for protection; but as for black, no, that seems to me out of the question" (quoted in Lovat, *Life of the Venerable Louise de Marillac*, 187). However, it appears that within fifteen years of the deaths of St. Vincent de Paul and the foundress, Louise de Marillac, both in 1660, the Daughters officially added the well-known cornette to the *toquois*. The cornette had only been worn by Daughters of Charity who lived in the country, but it was adopted by the rest of the order in 1685. See *Life of Mademoiselle Le Gras*, 210. Louise de Marillac seems to have worn a wimple and a type of veil, but not the cornette.

33. Lay sisters could be associated with religious women and live in the same convent but still without the rank of "religious." Several orders had choir nuns, or those who recited or chanted the Divine Office or Breviary, and those "lay sisters" who did not join with a dowry or have any education and who did not chant or recite the Divine Office. The status of the lay sisters was distinguished through chores, seating, and attire.

34. Ewen, *Role of the Nun*, 20.

35. Robert Trisco, *The Holy See and the Nascent Church in the Middle Western States* (Rome: Gregorian University, 1962), 308, quoted in Ewen, *Role of the Nun*, 135.

36. Maes, *Life of Rev. Charles Nerinckx*, 508, consulted and quoted in Ewen, *Role of the Nun*, 51.

37. Ewen, *Role of the Nun*, 53.

38. Flaget to Rosati, 11 September 1824, St. Louis Archdiocesan Archive, quoted in ibid., 54.

39. Ibid.

40. Sister Benedicta to Bishop Guy Chabrat, 1 September 1840, University of Notre Dame Archive, quoted in Ewen, *Role of the Nun*, 175.

41. Ewen, *Role of the Nun*, 148.

42. Ibid.

43. Ibid.

44. McNamara, *Sisters in Arms*, 555.

45. McCarthy, *Guide to the Catholic Sisterhoods*, 314.

46. Italian Unification Chronology.

47. For a discussion of the Kulturkampf and nuns, see McNamara, *Sisters in Arms*, 568–69.

48. Ewen, *Role of the Nun*, 119.

49. Ibid., 120.

50. For Sisters of St. Joseph in black bonnets, see Abbé Rivauz, *Life of Mother St. John Fontbonne, Foundress and First Superior-General of the Congregation of the Sisters of St. Joseph in Lyons* (New York: Benziger, 1887), 224, quoted in Ewen, *Role of the Nun*, 120. For the School Sisters of Notre Dame, see Peter M. Abbelen, *Mother M. Caroline Friess* (St. Louis: Herder, 1893), 125, quoted in Ewen, *Role of the Nun*, 120.

51. Coburn and Smith, *Spirited Lives*, 2; "Copy of a Letter from Mother St. John Fournier." This letter is cited in Coburn and Smith, *Spirited Lives*, 241.

52. Dunne, *Congregation of St. Joseph*, 113.

53. Ewen, *Role of the Nun*, 211.

54. Fitzgerald, *Historical Sketch of the Sisters of Mercy*, 55–56. Monsignor Charles Coen (Red Hook, N.Y.), a native of Ireland, indicated that "going McCracken" translates to "in one's own skin."

55. Ibid.

56. Ewen, *Role of the Nun*, 211.

57. Ibid.

58. Sister Mary Hortense Kohler, *Life & Work of Mother Benedicta Bauer* (Milwaukee: Bruce, 1937), 208–9, quoted in Ewen, *Role of the Nun*, 204–5.

59. Alice Worthington Winthrop, "Work of the Sisters in the War with Spain," *Ave Maria* 49 (1899): 429, quoted in Ewen, *Role of the Nun*, 282.

60. Mother M. Clarissa and Sister Olivia, *With the Poverello* (New York: Kenedy, 1948), 23, quoted in Ewen, *Role of the Nun*, 122.

61. Ibid.

62. Sister Mary Borromeo Brown, *The History of the Sisters of Providence of Saint Mary-of-the-Woods*, vol. 1, *1806–1856* (New York: Benziger, 1949), 75, quoted in Ewen, *Role of the Nun*, 122.

63. Anna Blanche McGill, *Sisters of Charity of Nazareth* (New York: Encyclopedia Press, 1917), 68, quoted in Ewen, *Role of the Nun*, 122.

64. See Coon, "Sisters of Charity in Nineteenth-Century America," https://scholarworks.iupui.edu/bitstream/handle/1805/2185/thesis_kathi_coon_final.pdf?sequence=1.

65. Coon, "Sisters of Charity in Nineteenth-Century America," 114, 126–27.

66. Ibid.

67. Mary A. Livermore, *My Story of the War: A Woman's Narrative of Four Years Personal Experience* (Hartford: Worthington, 1889), 219, cited in Coon, "Sisters of Charity in Nineteenth-Century America," 133.

68. "Christmas in the District Hospital," *Cleveland Daily Herald*, 30 December 1862, cited in Coon, "Sisters of Charity in Nineteenth-Century America," 131.

69. "Hospital Scenes—Heartrending Sights," *Advocate*, 23 January 1863, cited in Coon, "Sisters of Charity in Nineteenth-Century America," 132.

70. As quoted in Virginia Walcott Beauchamp, "The Sisters and the Soldiers," *Maryland Historical Magazine* 81, no. 2 (Summer 1986): 118, cited in Coon, "Sisters of Charity in Nineteenth-Century America," 118.

71. Ambrose Kennedy, "Nuns of the Battlefield," in *These Splendid Sisters*, ed. James Joseph Walsh, 179–221 (Freeport, N.Y.: Books for Libraries Press, 1926), 218, cited in Coon, "Sisters of Charity in Nineteenth-Century America," 119.

72. Eleanor C. Donnelly, *Life of Sister Mary Gonzaga Grace of the Daughters of Charity of St. Vincent de Paul, 1812–1897* (Philadelphia: Festival of Sts. Peter and Paul, 1900), 203, cited in Coon, "Sisters of Charity in Nineteenth-Century America," 119.

73. Reilly, *School Controversy*, 76; Connors, "Church-State Relationships," 109–10.

74. Shannon, "Religious Garb Issue," 217. Regarding Indian schools, see Prucha, *Church and the Indian Schools*, 189.

75. In Batavia, New York, the Sisters of Mercy conducted a summer school to prepare their members for the certification exam required for teaching in public school. See Shannon, "Religious Garb Issue," 66.

76. The school board in Suspension Bridge, Niagara County, New York, required St. Raphael's to change its texts when it became "School Number 2." See ibid., 8.

77. Ibid., 34–36; Coburn and Smith, *Spirited Lives*, 133. In the Indian schools, however, the Catholic orders treated the classroom as their own and did not remove religious items until the arrangement was challenged in 1911. See Prucha, *Church and the Indian Schools*, 197.

78. Justice, *War That Wasn't*, 13.

79. Peter Guilday, *A History of the Councils of Baltimore* (New York: Macmillan, 1932), 179, cited in McCarroll, "Plenary Councils of Baltimore," 11.

80. William W. Brickman and Stanley Lehrer, eds., *Religion, Government, and Education* (New York: Society for the Advancement of Education, 1961), 260, cited in McCarroll, "Plenary Councils of Baltimore," 21.

81. Becket Fund for Religious Liberty, "Blaine Amendments." For a debate about whether the Blaine Amendments targeted Catholics specifically, see also U.S. Commission on Civil Rights, "School Choice."

82. The fact that Father Richard Burtsell mentioned "beards" as one of those items that should not be under the legislation of bishops suggests that it was.

83. Thomas S. Preston, *The Catholic View of the Public School Question* (New York: Robert Coddington, 1870), 14, 19, 21, cited in Connors, "Church-State Relationships," 107.

84. *New York Sun*, 13 April 1870, cited in Connors, "Church-State Relationships," 107.

85. *New York Sun*, 30 April 1870, cited in Connors, "Church-State Relationships," 107–8.

86. See Burtsell, *Diary*, iv–vi. Callahan (Burtsell's editor) differentiates between "Americanists" and "Americanizers," but for the purposes of this project the distinction is not significant.

87. Bernard J. McQuaid, "Religion in Schools," *North American Review* 132 (April 1881): 343, cited in Connors, "Church-State Relationships," 126.

88. Bernard J. McQuaid, "Religious Teaching in Schools," *The Forum* 8 (December 1889): 385, cited in Connors, "Church-State Relationships," 117. An early reference iden-

tified Bernard McQuaid writing to the superior of the Sisters of St. Joseph and noting that the Marcelline Sisters attended classes without their habits. McQuaid's interest was in the sisters attaining higher education, which he knew would be important if Catholic schools were going to be able to compete with public schools. In referring to dress he was also likely pointing out that the sisters could be flexible. Both Americanists and anti-Americanists wanted women religious to listen to them, and that was their idea of flexibility.

89. Americanists seem to be critical of "religious" in general. Burtsell accused them of being "outmoded, stifled by their traditions and dominated by small minded men whose vision was fixed to the past" (Curran, "Prelude to 'Americanism,'" 53).

90. Burtsell, *Diary*, v–283. Burtsell discusses a conversation he had with Father Nilan in which Nilan said "that the Catholic religion is like the human race, adaptable to every climate and form of government whilst the sects are like the brute creature, only fit for a limited number of climates and forms of government" (ibid., 100). In this case Nilan was referring to the Jesuits, and Burtsell was in agreement. Burtsell seems to put certain orders of women religious in the same category as the Jesuits. For instance, Burtsell complains in his diary that "Sisters of the Sacred Heart are haughty in their ways: and too cool towards common priests to be popular among the secular clergy. They only think Jesuits worthy of their esteem. . . . The Children of Mary are a sodality under charge of the Sacred Heart. . . . They only admit the 'aristocracy' of this city" (ibid., 283).

91. Ibid., 100 (11 July 1866).

92. Ibid. Based on the context of the entry, by "sect" he is referring to religious orders.

93. Ewen, *Role of the Nun*, 93.

94. The Divine Office refers to prayers recited throughout the day and evening. They were originally published in Latin, and only the ordained and those who took solemn vows were required to recite them throughout the hours of the day and evening. However, in the twentieth century the church increasingly encouraged lay Catholics to read the Breviary where the Divine Office is found. See Broderick, *Catholic Encyclopedia*, 80.

95. Constitutions of the Institute of the Ursulines (1905), 38–39, CNRA. See also Ewen, *Role of the Nun*, 278–79, on the distinctions made between the habits of lay and choir sisters.

96. Ewen, *Role of the Nun*, 278–79.

97. Nainfa, *Costume of Prelates*, 37–38.

98. Constitutions of the Institute of the Ursulines (1905), 38–39, CNRA.

99. Connors, "Church-State Relationships," 117.

100. Thomas E. Finegan, ed., *Special Statutes and Provisions of Charters Regulating School Systems in the Several Cities of New York State* (Albany: University of the State of New York, 1915), 538, cited in Connors, "Church-State Relationships," 118.

101. Shannon, "Religious Garb Issue," 36.

102. Ibid., 38.

103. Ibid., 39.

104. Ibid., 49.

105. Fr. J. Nilan to Rev. Mother, 30 May 1898, SCNY.

106. It was a common rule for women religious with active apostolates to travel in pairs outside the convent. In this case, Sister Alphonse had worked without a fellow sis-

ter, which Nilan is pointing out was an adjustment to the rule. Sisters in "pairs" became standard practice in 1900 when Pope Leo XIII issued his bull, *Conditae a Christo*, which recognized women who took simple vows as "religious" women. See Ewen, *Role of the Nun*, 253–56.

107. Fr. J. Nilan to Reverend Mother, 6 June 1898, SCNY.

108. See Figure 7, showing Father Nilan without distinctive clerical dress.

109. Thomas, *Women Religious History Sources*, xxvi.

110. Fr. J. Nilan to Reverend Mother, 30 May 1898, SCNY.

111. Sister M. Edmund Crogan, *Sisters of Mercy in Nebraska, 1864–1910* (Washington, D.C.: Catholic University of America Press, 1942), 41, cited in Ewen, *Role of the Nun*, 281.

112. See Ewen, *Role of the Nun*, 255–56, for a discussion of *Conditae a Christo* and the *Normae*.

113. Ewen, "Women in the Convent," 20. Ewen in this case is referring to the constitution, but before there is a constitution, there is usually a rule regarding dress.

114. See Russo, *History of the Eastern Province*.

115. Ibid., 10.

116. "Rules and Constitutions of the Roman Union of the Order of St. Ursula" (Catholic Record Press, 1937), 6–7, Ursuline Collection, CNRA. For a translation of the Rule of St. Augustine, see Halsall, "Rule of St. Augustine." Ironically, the Rule of St. Augustine requires that the clothing should not attract attention, but since most habits were based on century-old styles, they certainly attracted attention.

117. McCarthy, *Guide to the Catholic Sisterhoods*, 314. According to the online *Catholic Encyclopedia*, the guimpe was added later. See Congregation of the Sisters of St. Joseph.

118. McCarthy, *Guide to the Catholic Sisterhoods*, 236.

119. Fialka, *Sisters*, 28.

120. Fr. Vincent de Paul had not wanted the Daughters of Charity to be obvious either and required them to wear the secular dress of mid-seventeenth-century France. See Coburn and Smith, *Spirited Lives*, 20.

121. *Modifications in the Text of the Constitutions of the Ursuline Institute, Proposed by the General Chapter of 1910 and Ratified by the Sacred Congregation of Regulars*. This is a pamphlet included in the Constitutions of the Institute of the Ursulines (1905), 168, CNRA.

122. Shannon, "Religious Garb Issue," 57.

123. Correspondence and copies of notes donated by Louis Zuccarello, Catholic Studies Collection, Marist College Archive, Poughkeepsie, N.Y.

124. Poughkeepsie School Board Minutes, 194, cited in Shannon, "Religious Garb Issue," 86.

125. McNamara, *Century of Grace*, 125.

126. Ibid.

127. Sr. M. Bertille to Reverend Mother, n.d., SCNY.

128. Ewen, *Role of the Nun*, 256.

129. Both Massa and Keenan see this as the crux of the problem with the Immaculate Heart of Mary sisters and the Marist brothers, respectively. Bureaucratization overwhelmed charism.

130. Ewen, *Role of the Nun*, 281.

131. Peters, *The 1917 Pio-Benedictine Code of Canon Law*, 190.

Chapter 3

1. Digital Archive of the Catholic University of America, clippings #8, n.d., *Boston Recorder*, 1837.

2. Uniformity required industrialization.

3. Zwierlein, *Life and Letters of Bishop McQuaid*, 1:137.

4. Oates, *Catholic Philanthropic Tradition*, 146.

5. Tager, *Boston Riots*, 111. See also "History of the Archdiocese of Boston." The magnificence of the school made an impression on former student Louise Whitney, who wrote about the convent's "broad halls, long galleries, and massive walls." She mused that "the whole establishment was as foreign to the soil whereon it stood as if, like Aladdin's Palace, it had been wafted from Europe by the power of a magician." For Boston, the presence of a European-style private academy run by mysterious and rumored-to-be-deviant religious women, job-draining Irish immigrants, and collaborative Boston Brahmins was ultimately too much to bear for the working-class Yankees. Local rioters burned the Ursuline convent to the ground in 1834 after stories circulated about a sister who had to escape to get away from alleged abusers. The Ursulines attempted to continue their educational apostolate in Boston, educating wealthy Catholics and Protestants alike, as the article noted. But hostility proved too damaging to their enrollments, and the Ursulines left for Canada in 1838.

6. In 1837 it would be on its last legs but still operating.

7. Holloran, *Boston's Wayward Children*. Holloran explained that girls who were thought to have too much interest or experience with boys were denied admittance. They feared that a girl with any sexual experience would be a bad influence on the other student residents.

8. Ibid., 67.

9. Ibid.

10. In 1871 the United States stopped making treaties with tribes. The 1887 Dawes Severalty Act offered Indian men 160 acres with the possibility of citizenship. The government's goal was to undo the reservation system and enforce assimilation.

11. The Catholic Church taught, at this time, that there was no salvation outside the church and, therefore, baptism in the Catholic Church was absolutely irreplaceable. Additionally, Protestants were active in the field of Native American education, and Catholics had to participate in order to compete. See Holloran, *Boston's Wayward Children*, 69, for the kind of traits expected of "graduates."

12. Ketcham, "An Appeal," 33.

13. Oates, *Catholic Philanthropic Tradition*, 147.

14. Zwierlein, *Life and Letters of Bishop McQuaid*, 1:137.

15. Ibid., 1:138.

16. Religious women were so concerned about how attention to clothing could promote sin they gave careful consideration to who would wash it. Washing one's own clothes, for instance, might encourage vanity.

17. Valuy, *Directorium Sacerdotale*, 69.

18. The church thought girls were more likely to sin in fashion-related ways and thus needed more controls. See O'Toole, "From Advent to Easter." Regarding the sermons of

an early-nineteenth-century Catholic priest, O'Toole wrote, "Kohlman seems occasionally to have thought that women were particularly susceptible to some of these failings. They were too often 'vain and worldly,' he said, spending 'whole hours before a looking glass' in pursuit of 'an animal and sensual life so repeatedly anathematized by the gospel.' They were more likely than men to become absorbed in 'reading romances,' thereby failing in their responsibilities 'to instruct' their children in religion or 'get them instructed'" (ibid., 372).

19. Nuns, bound by enclosure regulations, could not operate a school on an ungated property without violating enclosure.

20. Regarding clothing, the Roman Union of the Order of St. Ursula, or the Ursulines, followed the Rule of St. Augustine for their order's clothing directives. The Ursuline constitution instructed them to

> keep your clothes in common. . . . As your food is given out to you all from one and the same place, so let it be with your clothing. As far as possible you will not concern yourselves with the choice of what you are to wear according to the different seasons, whether one receives the garments she had before or those worn by another. . . . If disputes and murmurs arise among you on this subject . . . judge thereby how greatly you lack the interior clothing of holiness in your hearts, since you dispute on the subject of clothing for the body. . . . Your progress many be measured therefore, by the preference you give to what is in common over your personal advantage, so that with regard to all things of passing utility, charity, which never passes away, may be preeminent. (Halsall, "Rule of St. Augustine")

Of course the sisters did not expect the girls to wear a habit or take clothing the school handed out. However, the nuns did expect clothing to inculcate a sense of living in common and prioritizing holiness and charity over "personal advantage."

21. Burns and Kohlbrenner, History of Catholic Education, 241.

22. Brewer, Nuns and the Education of American Catholic Women, 65.

23. "Mt. St. Joseph Academy Centenary Booklet, 1858–1958," SSJA.

24. Holloran, Boston's Wayward Children, 69. In our world of ready-made inexpensive clothing, it is easy to forget that clothing was hard to come by before it became part of the global economy. Letters to Eleanor Roosevelt during the Depression asking for clothes for school indicate that families would not send their children to school if they did not have presentable clothing. See Cohen, Dear Mrs. Roosevelt.

25. Escapees are mentioned in Holloran's Boston's Wayward Children, 89, 111.

26. The same was done at the Carlisle School, which also required a uniform, but for Catholics, the uniform became a more common practice.

27. "Little Indian Life," 19.

28. Lindauer, "Archaeology of the Phoenix Indian School."

29. Cited in ibid.

30. Banner, American Beauty, 31.

31. Ibid., 32.

32. Morgan, Laboring Women. This work assisted my thinking about how class and race operate as tropes for morality and civility.

33. Holloran, Boston's Wayward Children, 77.

34. Lindauer, "Archaeology of the Phoenix Indian School."

35. Smocks rather than uniforms were often required in European schools. See the History of Clothing website. This site is not scholarly but is certainly exhaustive on the topic of the history of clothing.

36. "Souvenir of the Centenary of the Ursuline Convent," 47, CNRA. The alumnae providing the "Reminiscences" did not indicate their year, but these former students likely attended in the twentieth century rather than the nineteenth, since they were alive to remember and write down their memories.

37. See Pastoureau, *Devil's Cloth*, xii. See also Zakin, *Ready-Made Democracy*, for an examination of how ready-made usurps the artisanal polity, rendering everyman well dressed in America; hence "ready-made democracy."

38. Dwyer-McNulty, "Hems to Hairdos."

39. See Kirtley and Kirtley, "City of Spindles," 69.

40. Morris, *American Catholic*, 74.

41. Tentler, *Seasons of Grace*, 230.

42. Gabert, *In Hoc Signo?*, 54.

43. Tentler, *Seasons of Grace*, 232.

44. Sisters always hoped to recruit girls for religious life from their convent schools. Parochial schools could also provide postulants, but girls in the convent were exposed to "living the rule" in a way commuting students were not.

45. Zwierlein, *Life and Letters of Bishop McQuaid*, 1:138–39.

46. Brewer, *Nuns and the Education of American Catholic Women*, 15. The numbers bounce up again to 662 in 1900 and then 692 in 1905, but the drop at just the time when the parish schools were required appears to be significant.

47. Peril, *College Girls*, 41–42.

48. Zwierlein, *Life and Letters of Bishop McQuaid*, 1:137.

49. Peril, *College Girls*, 39.

50. Ruth (Elbright) Finley, *The Lady of Godey's, Sarah Josepha Hale* (Philadelphia: Lippincott, 1931), 216, cited in Peril, *College Girls*, 39.

51. Men's fashion expectations can be found in Joselit, *Perfect Fit*, 79.

52. Warner, *When the Girls Came Out to Play*, 164.

53. Ibid., 191.

54. Letter to *American Ecclesiastical Review*.

55. Ibid.

56. Tentler, *Seasons of Grace*, 233.

57. See Cummings, *New Women*, 59, for a discussion of how Catholic sisters pitched college education for Catholic women as a unique experience, different from Progressive women's education experiences, yet also liberating.

58. Ibid., 61. Cummings points out that Trinity College was unique among the Catholic colleges for women, due in great part to the fact that there was not a preexisting academy. According to Cummings, "In 1895, the School Sisters of Notre Dame turned their Baltimore Institute into the College of Notre Dame. . . . At St. Mary's in Notre Dame, Indiana, the Sisters of the Holy Cross paid scant attention to either the implementation of a college course in 1903 or the official separation between the academy and college three years later. The Ursuline Sisters greeted the conversion of their board-

ing school in New Rochelle, New York, into the College of St. Angela (later the College of New Rochelle) with similar nonchalance" (ibid., 61–62).

59. Banner, *American Beauty*, 31.

60. Cunningham, *Reforming Women's Fashion*, 207–8.

61. Brewer, *Nuns and the Education of American Catholic Women*, 65.

62. "Academy of Mount St. Vincent On-the-Hudson Handbook," 8, SCNY.

63. Ibid.

64. "Mt. St. Joseph Academy Centenary Booklet, 1858–1958," SSJA.

65. Mt. St. Joseph Academy, "Regulations for Wardrobe," SSJA.

66. Initially the school's title was Mount St. Joseph on-the-Wissahickon, but as time went on the name was shortened to Mount St. Joseph.

67. Brewer, *Nuns and the Education of American Catholic Women*, 65; quote from Dominican Sisters, *Rule of St. Augustine*, 93.

68. Carroll, "Equalizing of Parishioners," 299.

69. "Parish That Came Back," 33.

70. Ibid.

71. Ibid.

72. Ibid., 27–28.

73. Ibid., 36.

74. La Follette, "Progress in Dress."

75. "Punahou Mothers Taking Steps toward School Dress Simplicity."

76. In 1924, Norman Rockwell memorialized the uniformed Girl Scout on the cover of *Life* magazine.

77. "Cardinal Hayes Urges Modesty."

78. *St. Peter's Parish Monthly Calendar*, July 1927, 20, PAHRC.

79. *St. Peter's Parish Monthly Calendar*, August 1927, 7, PAHRC.

80. *St. Edward's Parish Monthly Calendar*, August 1927, 7, PAHRC.

81. *St. Peter's Parish Monthly Calendar*, September 1927, 5, PAHRC.

82. Donaghy, *Philadelphia's Finest*, 238.

83. Bendinger interview.

84. Ryan, "Monsignor John Bonner and Progressive Education," 2.

85. There is a delightful video on the Chicago Historical Society's website on Catholic schools in Chicago. There are lots of uniforms. See http://www.chicagohs.org/did-you-see-this/video.

86. McMahon, *What Parish Are You From?*, 92.

87. Spiers, *Central Catholic High School*, 162.

88. Ibid., 36.

89. In a questionnaire circulated among all diocesan superintendents of schools across the United States, almost one-half (45 percent) stated that they had a policy of establishing central schools whenever possible. In the schools where this policy existed, more than two-thirds (69 percent) of the schools instituted this policy after 1925. See ibid., 43.

90. See Warren, "Character, Public Schooling, and Religious Education," 66.

91. The Catholic Church did not build Catholic high schools at the same pace as they did the grade schools. Contributing to this delay was the religious orders' various clus-

tering of grades within an institution. Boys, for instance, often received secondary education from colleges. Girls' schools, however, often mixed elementary education with secondary studies. See Burns and Kohlbrenner, *History of Catholic Education*, 242–46.

92. Catholic high schools existed in the late eighteenth century in the United States, but these were private, tuition-driven schools under the auspices of individual religious orders. Diocesan schools departed from the elite Catholic academies and preparatory schools by opening their doors to academically, rather than economically, qualified students. For information on entrance qualifications, see Donaghy, *Philadelphia's Finest*, 153.

93. Ibid., 162.

94. A center (centre) was the name given to a parish school where girls could continue their education one to two years beyond eighth grade. The teaching sisters at the parish school held separate classes for interested and qualified girls.

95. Burns and Kohlbrenner, *History of Catholic Education*, 248.

96. Before opening CGHS, the teaching staff met to study the curriculums of three public school programs for girls (West Philadelphia Girls' High School, William Penn High School, and Philadelphia Girls' High School) as well as the Pennsylvania School Code. See Donaghy, *Philadelphia's Finest*, 164.

97. Ryan, "Monsignor John Bonner and Progressive Education," 250.

98. This was a significant issue for Catholics. It was not until the class of 1917 that students from CGHS were eligible for acceptance into Normal School in Philadelphia or the much-sought-after scholarships offered by the University of Pennsylvania. See *Annual of C.G.H.S.*, 1917, 12, JWHCGHS.

99. Fass, *The Damned and the Beautiful*, 5. Warren, "Character, Public Schooling, and Religious Education," discusses how religious educators attempted to address this new age of youthful independence and agency through character education. Warren looks only at Protestants, but Catholics had similar, though arguably more overtly religious remedies, including uniforms.

100. See Fass, *The Damned and the Beautiful*, and Walkowitz, "Making of a Feminine Professional Identity," for more extensive discussions of female youth and negotiating culture in the early twentieth century.

101. *Ave Maria*, 22 July 1922, 121.

102. *St. Edward's Parish Monthly Calendar*, July 1920, PAHRC.

103. The need to fill this parenting void was not unlike the rationale for uniforms in asylums.

104. Kelly, "New Woman."

105. Ibid.

106. Anna McArdle, "Catholic Woman in the Business World," in *Annual of C.G.H.S.*, 1917, 19, JWHCGHS.

107. Luck, "Trouble in Eden, Trouble with Eve."

108. See Cummings, *New Women*, for a Catholic alternative to secular feminism.

109. *Annual of C.G.H.S.*, 1924, 63, JWHCGHS.

110. Joseph, *Uniforms and Nonuniforms*, 16.

111. This argument was substantiated by Sister Paul's experience. As a high school student, she felt she was offered a job by a Jewish store owner because she was a Catholic school student and the owner believed her training made her trustworthy. (It also might

show how minority religious groups worked off one another to expand their clientele.) See P. M. questionnaire.

112. Fass, *The Damned and the Beautiful*, 6.

113. Joseph, *Uniforms and Nonuniforms*, 59.

114. "Signed Pledge for Modesty in Dress."

115. "Lady Armstrong for Modest Dress."

116. *The Marion* (1929), 80.

117. O'Hara interview.

118. Burns-Eisenberg interview and questionnaire.

119. O'Hara interview.

120. Ibid.

121. Oates, *Catholic Philanthropic Tradition*, 150.

122. "Pastor and the Education of Girls and Young Women."

123. Ibid.

124. Academy of Mount St. Vincent On-the-Hudson, brochure, c. 1915–1925, 7, SCNY.

125. Ursuline Academy catalog, 1923–24, CNRA.

126. Mount St. Joseph Academy High School Brochure, 1917, 25–27, MSJAA.

127. *Annual of C.G.H.S.*, 1924, 76, JWHCGHS. In the "Fashion Notes," yearbook staff writers make comments, jokes, and predictions for and about their classmates.

128. *Annual of C.G.H.S.*, 1925, JWHCGHS. The original "Believe me, if all those endearing young charms" is one of a collection of Irish melodies written by Thomas Moore between 1808 and 1834. Moore's troubadour contends that even if beauty fades, "the heart that has truly loved never forgets." The student writer has replaced the young girl with a uniform and the troubadour with a student. Unlike the lover in the original, the student is encouraging change by either fading or dyeing—anything that might alter the appearance of the uniform. For the original lyrics, see http://ingeb.org/songs/believem.html.

129. *Annual of C.G.H.S.*, 1924, 87, JWHCGHS.

130. Ibid., 91.

131. Ibid., 93.

132. Ibid., 110.

133. P. M. questionnaire.

134. *Annual of W.P.C.G.H.S.*, 1929, 157, WPCGHS.

135. P. M. and A. E. questionnaires discuss school rules. Pictures, however, indicate variety.

136. *Annual of W.P.C.G.H.S.*, 1928, 34, WPCGHS.

137. *Annual of C.G.H.S.*, 1924, 113, JWHCGHS.

138. Ibid., 116.

139. *Annual of W.P.C.G.H.S.*, 1929, WPCGHS.

140. P. M. and A. E. questionnaires.

141. *Annual of W.P.C.G.H.S.*, 1929, 82, WPCGHS.

Chapter 4

1. Fialka, *Sisters*, 172.

2. Daly, "Immaculata Joins 'Citizens' Parade."

3. On Coughlin, see Morris, *American Catholic*, 147, and on Sheen, see Massa, *Catholics and American Culture*, 89.

4. Mazzenga, "Difference a Century Makes."

5. Pope Pius XII, however, denounced evolution in the 1950s as a tool used by communists to undermine papal authority and as a "weapon for defending and popularizing their system of dialectical materialism." See Perry and Echeverría, *Under the Heel of Mary*, 243.

6. "What the Star Students Are Like."

7. The other contributing influence was the Catholic worker movement. It was led by Canon Joseph Cardijn of Belgium, who encouraged young people to form vocational groups or cells that would provide a Catholic-inspired platform for labor organizing without resorting to communism. Pope Pius XI issued his encyclical *Quadragisimo Anno* in 1931 calling for vocational groups to aid "the helpless working man" and provide for "the common good." These worker movements expanded to the United States and inspired lay activism in the workplace as well as in other areas of Catholic life. See Peihl, *Breaking Bread*, 113, and Dwyer-McNulty, "Moving Beyond the Home."

8. Massa, *Catholics and American Culture*, 33.

9. Pius XII, *Mystici Corporis Christi*.

10. Ibid.

11. Caterine, *Conservative Catholicism and the Carmelites*, 5, rightly argues that using analogies of the body equates the "church with the Body of Christ . . . sanctifying ecclesiastical hierarchy." While I agree with Caterine, I also see *Mystici Corporis Christi* endorsing a greater role for the laity through Catholic Action. As historian Mark Massa has described, this pronouncement allowed Catholics to "abandon the fortress of the immigrant Church subculture for the fair and broad plains of mainstream American culture" (*Catholics and American Culture*, 36). See also O'Brien, *Public Catholicism*, and Herberg, *Protestant, Catholic, Jew*.

12. Chinnici, "Catholic Community at Prayer," 50.

13. Morris, *American Catholic*, 202; Kane, "Marian Devotion since 1940," 100.

14. See "We Beg to Announce."

15. "Prize Pictures of the Month."

16. "No Money for Indecency."

17. Ibid.

18. Southard, "Cover Girls of 1950," 16.

19. Notre Dame Academy in Cleveland, Ohio, read about the sodalists at Seton High School in the *Catholic Universe Bulletin*. See Southard, "Cover Girls of 1950," 16.

20. "S.D.S. Booms Along."

21. Kane, "Marian Devotion since 1940," 105.

22. Southard, "Cover Girls of 1950," 17.

23. Catholic girls participated in non-Catholic pageants but ran the risk of hearing from an annoyed sister, priest, or bishop if they brought unwanted publicity to a Catholic school. Pageants usually identified the winning contestant's school name, and if there was a bathing suit competition, the Catholic school administrators were not too pleased.

24. See "Answers to Questions," 169–71.

25. Lord, "What's Modest." See also Drolet, "SDS Follow-up," which identifies the number of attendees.

26. See images of fashion show models in *Queen's Work*, April 1953, 18; June 1953, 28; and June 1954, 16–17.

27. Rooney, "Modesty, Chastity, and Purity."

28. *Queen's Work*, January 1955, 28 (Pittsburgh), and November 1955 (Syracuse), and Rooney, "Here's Looking at You."

29. "Blessing for Your Clothes."

30. Jay, "'In Vogue with Mary.'"

31. "Sodality Pageant," 27.

32. "Sign of Your Faith."

33. Ibid., 21.

34. Perry and Echeverría, *Under the Heel of Mary*, 252.

35. Ibid.

36. Ibid.

37. Gesu School Sodality Record Book, Gesu School SJWIS or Gesu, series 3, box 3, MUA.

38. Windeatt, "The Medal," 20.

39. Ibid., 21.

40. *The Grail*, April 1950, 17.

41. Ibid.

42. *The Grail*, July 1950, 16.

43. Gesu School Sodality Record Book, Gesu School SJWIS or Gesu, series 3, box 3, MUA.

44. Ibid.

45. Kane, "Marian Devotion since 1940," 100.

46. O'Hara interview.

47. Virtuous purchases as identified by May, *Homeward Bound*, are different from Christian retailing, defined by McDannell, *Material Christianity*.

48. "History and Tradition."

49. *The Signet*, 1945–50, SSJA.

50. O'Hara interview.

51. Burns-Eisenberg interview and questionnaire.

52. "Senior Girls at Alvernia Revise Uniform Styling."

53. Ibid.

54. Cobert interview.

55. "Address of Right Reverend Monsignor Bonner to the Sisters of Notre Dame de Namur, Moylan, PA," 6 December 1944, PAHRC.

56. Minutes of the Mount St. Joseph Student Council, 1942–47, MSJAA.

57. Ibid.

58. Author Mary Gordon likewise participated in determining punishments for girls at her school who were seen entering a boy's car while in uniform. See Gordon, *Seeing through Places*, 243.

59. Plaids are attributed to George Bendinger of Bendinger Brothers Philadelphia. See O'Hara interview.

60. Corrigan, *Leave Me Alone, I'm Reading*, 135.

61. Barry, "Green Grass, Cape Cods, and Suburban Catholicism."

62. Parish Histories, Record Group 102, box 2, St. Agatha–St. James, PAHRC.

63. *The News Leaf: St. Agatha's School Paper*, 13 October 1967, 1; Parish Histories, Record Group 102, box 2, St. Agatha–St. James, PAHRC.

64. Barry, "Green Grass, Cape Cods, and Suburban Catholicism."

65. "Fr. Y," "I Love My Cassock," 889.

66. Smith, "America's Favorite Priest," 121.

67. Ibid., 122.

68. Donovan, "Answers to Questions," 59.

69. The smoking, drinking, casually dressed priest is a character in a short story by Walker, "The Principal's Ganymedes." The story was about a principal who wanted to give a hot and sweaty visiting pastor a cold drink. In the tale, the pastor thought to himself while smoking a cigarette, "I could be at the rectory in a half hour . . . and change into more comfortable clothes. The thought of being showered and relaxing on the side porch, with a cooling Tom Collins, brightened him a little."

70. Secular institutes were not new, just newly recognized in the twentieth century.

71. Twomey, "Caritas Builds Dignity in the Slums."

72. Wakin and Scheuer, "American Nun," 40.

73. SFB 3, no. 1 (Autumn 1956): 1.

74. Kuhns, *The Habit*, 140.

75. See Sullivan, *Visual Habits*.

76. For the Home Visitors, see Sommer, "Detroit Sodalists Found New Religious Order," and for the Divine Spirit, see "Nuns Will Wear Modern Clothes."

77. "Nuns Will Wear Modern Clothes."

78. Briggs, *Double Crossed*, 48.

79. "Minutes of the Meeting of the Sisters Formation Conference, 1956," SFC/RFC Collection, MUA.

80. "Columbia Expects 13,000 Enrollment"; Briggs, *Double Crossed*, 49.

81. Walters and Bradley, "Renewal and Its Counterfeits," 2, SFC/RFC Collection, MUA.

82. Briggs, *Double Crossed*, 48–49. Briggs identifies Sister Bertrand Meyers's 1941 dissertation, "The Education of Sisters," as advancing the idea that the training and education of sisters was in need of reform. Sister Madeleva Wolff, CSC, president of St. Mary's College in South Bend, Indiana, formed the Teacher-Education Section of the National Catholic Educational Association in 1948 and, as Briggs mentions, gave her paper "The Education of Sister Lucy" at the 1949 National Catholic Educational Association Conference, using a hypothetical character to illustrate the necessity of providing sisters with the proper education.

83. See Sullivan, *Visual Habits*, 124.

84. Sister Judith, "Report on the Sister Formation Conferences' Vocation Survey," 1.

85. Ibid., 2–3.

86. Ibid., 3.

87. Ibid., 4.

88. Ibid., 5.

89. Ibid.

90. Walters and Bradley, "Renewal and Its Counterfeits," xiv, SFC/RFC Collection, MUA.

91. Francis, "Special Problems in the Spiritual Formation of Sisters," 11.

92. Giuliani, "Role of the Sister in the Church," 4.

93. Lord, *Letters to a Nun*, 132.

94. Ibid., 133.

95. "Minutes of the Meeting of the Sisters Formation Conference, 1956," SFC/RFC Collection, MUA.

96. Sullivan, *Visual Habits*, 18–19.

Chapter 5

1. Sullivan, *Visual Habits*, 36–37. The information I found in the SFC/RFC papers suggests that while Suenens may have been applauding the work of American sisters, as Sullivan notes, not all sisters were activists, and sisters also felt challenged by Suenens's critique.

2. Ewen, "Women in the Convent," 38.

3. Suenens, *Nun in the World*, 9.

4. Ibid.

5. Ibid., 18.

6. Ibid., 25–26.

7. Ibid., 34.

8. Ibid.

9. Koehlinger, "'Are You the White Sisters or the Black Sisters?,'" 262.

10. Suenens, *Nun in the World*, 38.

11. Ibid., 39.

12. "Preliminary Discussion Questions," 1, SFC/RFC Collection, MUA.

13. Ibid., 3.

14. Ibid., 4.

15. Ibid.

16. In the summer of 1963, 400 Franciscan Sisters of Perpetual Adoration in La Crosse, Wisconsin, discussed Suenens's book. See SFB 10, no. 1 (Autumn 1963): 21. In Dubuque, Iowa, the Presentation Sisters used Suenens's book "as a springboard for the discussion of the religious, professional, communal, and apostolic facts of their lives" during the summer of 1963. See ibid., 22. He was invited to speak to the "Sisters of the Boston Area" by Cardinal Cushing in 1964. See announcement in SFB 10, no. 4 (Summer 1964): 20.

17. "Archbishop Alter Urges Nuns to Adopt Customs When Needed to Meet Needs of Modern World," SFC/RFC Collection, MUA.

18. Ibid.

19. SFB 10, no. 1 (Autumn 1963): 20.

20. Ibid.

21. Ibid.

22. Steinfels, "Robert G. Hoyt."

23. "New Deal for Nuns."

24. Walters and Bradley, "God's Geese," 2.

25. Ibid., 7.

26. "Nuns, Parents, Pupils Pleased by New Habits."

27. "New Habit Arrives for Sisters of Sion."

28. "Kickbacks on Kicking the Habit."

29. See NCR, 6 October 1965, and "A Lay Vote for 'Forum,'" NCR, 1 December 1965, 10.

30. "No Habit Can Be More Than the Person Wearing It."

31. "Not a Crying Towel."

32. Ibid.

33. Ibid.

34. "Habit Is to Hide Behind."

35. "Down with Habits and Cassocks."

36. Steinfels, "Robert G. Hoyt." The inventory description on the University of Notre Dame Archive website (archives.nd.edu/findaids/ead/html/ncr.htm) has the circulation number for NCR at 90,000 in 1968.

37. "Antoniutti on Proper Attire for Sisters."

38. Ibid.

39. Fialka, *Sisters*, 195.

40. Ibid.

41. Ibid. See also McGreevy, *Parish Boundaries*, 142–43.

42. "Are Sisters Getting in the Fashion Dilemma?"

43. Koehlinger, "'Are You the White Sisters or the Black Sisters?'"

44. "What's Fitting, Sister?"

45. Hubbard, "Criteria for New Garb."

46. Joseph, *Uniforms and Nonuniforms*, 67.

47. "Nuns—Marchers out of Place."

48. Koehlinger, "'Are You the White Sisters or the Black Sisters?,'" 257.

49. Walters and Bradley, "Renewal and Its Counterfeits," 18, SFC/RFC Collection, MUA.

50. McAllister, "Self Image and Self Acceptance."

51. Ibid.

52. Thanks to John Ritschdorff of Marist College, who explained to me the wardrobe options available to male religious.

53. Address by Mother Mary Consolatrice, BVM, Mother General of the Sisters of Charity, Dubuque, "Formation for the Urban Apostolate," reprinted in SFB 11, no. 3 (Spring 1966): 7.

54. Ibid., 12.

55. *Perfectae Caritatis*.

56. Thrapp, "Nuns Seek to Reinforce Earlier Ruling by Pope."

57. *Ecclesia Sanctae*.

58. Haring, "Asceticism in Religious Life."

59. Haring, "Religious Witness in the World."

60. Philippe, "New Orientations of the Sacred Congregation."

61. "Final Motion" regarding the Meeting of the International Union of Superiors General in Rome, SFB 13, no. 3 (Spring 1967): 21.

62. Walters and Bradley, "Renewal and Its Counterfeits," 5, SFC/RFC Collection, MUA.

63. Ibid.

64. Suenens, "Open to the World."

65. Sister Mary Emil Penet, IHM, "Is There a Future for Sisters in Education inside Our Own Institutions?," reprint of address to Sister Formation Section, College and University Department, National Catholic Educational Association Convention, Atlantic City, 29 March 1967. Reprinted in SFB 13, no. 3 (Spring 1967): 5.

66. Ibid., 6.

67. Ibid.

68. See Sullivan, *Visual Habits*, for a thoughtful analysis of *The Flying Nun*.

69. Thrapp, "Immaculate Heart Sisters," SG1.

70. Ibid., SG12.

71. Massa, *Catholics and American Culture*, 173.

72. Ibid., 174.

73. Ibid., 175.

74. Ibid., 188.

75. "13 Jesuits Praise L.A. Nuns' Renewal," NCR, 31 January 1968, 10. Cited in Massa, *Catholics and American Culture*, 187 n. 29.

76. Massa, *Catholics and American Culture*, 176.

77. "Religion: You've Come a Long Way Baby."

78. Townsend, "Habit Called Segregation."

79. "3 Nuns Withdrawn in Pastoral Dispute."

80. Henold, *Catholic and Feminist*, 74.

81. Ibid., 77.

82. "Religion: You've Come a Long Way Baby."

83. "Religion: The New Nuns."

84. Ibid.

85. "Silks Abolished."

86. Ibid.

87. Broucher, *Suenens Dossier*, 15. The quote is from an interview with Suenens.

88. Townsend, "Priest's Message."

89. Phibrick, "Some Priests to Trade Cassocks for Suits."

90. Thrapp, "Wants Reverse Collar Junked."

91. Phibrick, "Some Priests to Trade Cassocks for Suits."

92. Meconis, *With Clumsy Grace*, 72.

93. Unger, "Judge Robson Gags All."

94. Ibid.

95. Littrell, "Liturgical Vestments and the Priest Role," 156.

96. Ibid., 153.

97. Ibid., 154.

98. "'Shave!' Priests Ordered."

99. "Overview of Authority Patterns in General," 12.

100. Ibid., 8.

Epilogue

1. Counihan interview.

2. Kernaghan's brother was a Jesuit priest, and Kernaghan was concerned with the killing of peasants and union workers as well as the corporations, such as the Gap, Walmart, and Disney, that bought sweatshop-produced clothing. The Archdiocese of Newark took the wider concern over the pay and conditions of garment workers and applied it to Catholic apparel.

3. De Pauw, *Catholic Traditionalist Manifesto.*

4. "Essential Elements on the Church's Teaching on Religious Life."

5. Warikoo, "Archbishop Blasts Mich. Priest's Leading of Liberal Mass."

6. Ibid.

7. Archdiocese of Chicago.

8. Spadaro, "Big Heart Open to God," 4–6.

REFERENCES

Archival Sources

Flourtown, Pennsylvania
    Mount St. Joseph Academy Archive
        Annals
        Minutes of the Mount St. Joseph Student Council, 1942–47
        Mount St. Joseph Academy High School Brochure
Milwaukee, Wisconsin
    Marquette University Archives
        CmSw-Sister Formation Conference Relations
        Gesu Series
        The Raynor Memorial Library Digital Archive
        Sister Formation Conference/Religious Formation Conference Collection
            "Archbishop Alter Urges Nuns to Adopt Customs When Needed To Meet
                Needs of Modern World." Series 3, box 5, SMSW-SFC Relations,
                Archbishop Philippe—NCNW News Service Article.
            "Minutes of the Meeting of the Sisters Formation Conference, 1956."
                Series 1, box 1, folder 3.
            "Preliminary Discussion Questions." Series 3, box 5, CMSW-SFC Relations—
                Suenens Meeting, Chicago, 17 May 1963.
            Walters, Sister Annette, and Sister Ritamary Bradley. "Renewal and Its
                Counterfeits: A Squabble among Nuns." 1969. Unpublished manuscript.
                Series 9, box 8.
New Rochelle, New York
    College of New Rochelle Archive
        Constitutions of the Institute of the Ursulines
        "Souvenir of the Centenary of the Ursuline Convent, 1847–1947"
        Ursuline Academy Catalogues
        Ursuline Collection
Philadelphia, Pennsylvania
    John W. Hallahan Catholic Girls' High School
        Annuals of the Catholic Girls' High School
    Philadelphia Archdiocesan Historical Research Center
        Dougherty Collection
        Monsignor Bonner Papers
        Parish Histories
        Statutes of Diocesan Synods
    Sisters of St. Joseph Archive
        Cecilian Academy Yearbooks, *The Signet*

"Mt. St. Joseph Academy Centenary Booklet, 1858–1958"
Mt. St. Joseph Academy on-the-Wissahickon. "Regulations for Wardrobe."
    1890
St. Mary's Academy Yearbooks, *The Marion*
Temple University Urban Archive
    Bulletin Collection
    Clippings Files
West Philadelphia Catholic Girls' High School
    Annuals of the West Philadelphia Catholic Girls' High School
Poughkeepsie, New York
    Dutchess County Historical Society
        Dutchess County Historical Society Yearbook Collection
    Marist College Archive
        Catholic Studies Collection
Yonkers, New York
    Sisters of Charity of St. Vincent de Paul of New York Archive
        "Academy of Mount St. Vincent On-the-Hudson Handbook, c. 1890–1900"
        "Sisters teaching in public school: The Poughkeepsie Plan"

Digital Archives

Digital Archive of the Catholic University of America
    Catalog #b01f20-a04-001
        Boston Recorder, 1837, http://dspace.wrlc.org/view/ImgViewer?url=http://dspace
            .wrlc.org/doc/manifest/2041/2500
Illinois Digital Archives
    University of St. Mary of the Lake Collection
Wabash Valley Visions & Voices Digital Memories Project
    Partner Projects: Sisters of Providence of St. Mary-of-the-Woods, Indiana

Questionnaires and Interviews

A. E. Questionnaire. Flourtown, Pa., 18 February 1999.
Bendinger, George. Interview with author. Philadelphia, Pa., January 2005.
Burns-Eisenberg, Catharine. Telephone interview with author and questionnaire.
    15 January 2005.
Cobert, Pat. Interview with author. Poughkeepsie, N.Y., 3 September 2009.
Counihan, Martha, an Ursuline sister of the Roman Union. Telephone interview with
    author, 11 February 2013.
Crosby, Father Vincent de Paul, OSB, liturgical artist. Telephone interview with author,
    30 October 2012.
O'Hara, Ned. Telephone interview with author, 20 July 2009.
P. M. Questionnaire. Flourtown, Pa., 18 February 1999.

Books, Articles, Essays, Dissertations, and Websites

"3 Nuns Withdrawn in Pastoral Dispute." *Chicago Tribune*, 30 January 1969.

Ahern, Patrick H. *The Catholic University of America, 1887–1896: The Rectorship of John J. Keane*. Washington, D.C.: Catholic University of America Press, 1948.

"Antoniutti on Proper Attire for Sisters." *National Catholic Reporter*, 1 June 1966, 10.

"Answers to Questions." *Homiletic and Pastoral Review* 30, no. 2 (November 1929): 169–72.

Archdiocese of Chicago. http://archives.archchicago.org/jcbselecteddocs.htm. 1 February 2012.

"Are Sisters Getting in the Fashion Dilemma?" *National Catholic Reporter*, 13 January 1965, 4.

Arminio, P. "History of the Birettum." *American Ecclesiatical Review* 8 (March 1893): 201–5.

Arthur, Linda B., ed. *Religion, Dress and the Body*. Oxford: Berg, 1999.

———. *Undressing Religion: Commitment and Conversion from a Cross-Cultural Perspective*. Oxford: Berg, 2000.

Bales, Susan Ridgely. *When I Was a Child: Children's Interpretations of First Communion*. Chapel Hill: University of North Carolina Press, 2005.

The Baltimore Basilica. http://www.baltimorebasilica.org/index.php?page=james -cardinal-gibbons. 14 June 2013.

Banner, Lois W. *American Beauty*. New York: Knopf, 1983.

Barry, Dan. "Green Grass, Cape Cods, and Suburban Catholicism." In *Catholics in New York: Society, Culture, and Politics, 1808–1946*, ed. Terry Golway, 189. New York: Fordham University Press, 2008.

Becket Fund for Religious Liberty. "Blaine Amendments." http://www.blaineamendments .org/Intro/whatis.html. 7 June 2012.

Bederman, Gail. *Manliness and Civilization: A Cultural History of Gender and Race in the United States, 1880–1917*. Chicago: University of Chicago Press, 1995.

Bettoja, Maurizio. "Clerical Dress in the City of Rome in the 19th Century." Pt. 1 of 2. www.newliturgicalmovement.org/2010/09/clerica-dress-in-city-of-rome-in-19th .html#.UkHCbRDO-So. 24 September 2013.

"Bicycle Costumes for Clerics." *American Ecclesiastical Review* 7, no. 3 (September 1897): 319–20.

Billington, Ray Allen. *America's Frontier Heritage*. New York: Holt, Rinehart and Winston, 1967.

"A Blessing for Your Clothes." *Queen's Work*, October 1956, 15.

Brewer, Eileen Mary. *Nuns and the Education of American Catholic Women, 1860–1920*. Chicago: Loyola University Press, 1987.

Briggs, Kenneth. *Double Crossed: Uncovering the Catholic Church's Betrayal of Nuns*. New York: Doubleday, 2006.

Broderick, Robert C., ed. *The Catholic Encyclopedia*. Rev. and updated. Nashville: Thomas Nelson, 1987.

Broucher, José de. *The Suenens Dossier: A Case for Collegiality*. Notre Dame: Fides Publishers, 1970.

Burns, J. A., and Bernard J. Kohlbrenner. *A History of Catholic Education in the United States: A Textbook for Normal Schools and Teachers' Colleges*. New York: Benziger Brothers, 1937.

Burtsell, Richard Lalor. *The Diary of Richard L. Burtsell, Priest of New York*. Edited by Nelson J. Callahan. New York: Arno Press, 1978.

Byrne, Julie. *O God of Players: The Story of the Immaculata Mighty Macs*. New York: Columbia University Press, 2003.

Byrne, Patricia. "American Ultramontanism." *Theological Studies* 56, no. 2 (June 1995): 301–38.

Campbell, Debra. *Graceful Exits: Catholic Women and the Art of Departure*. Bloomington: Indiana University Press, 2003.

"Cardinal Hayes Urges Modesty." *New York Times*, 10 October 1927, 26.

Carroll, P. J., CSC. "Equalizing of Parishioners." *Ecclesiastical Review* 10, no. 3 (March 1919): 296–99.

Caterine, Darryl V. *Conservative Catholicism and the Carmelites: Identity, Ethnicity, and Tradition in the Modern Church*. Bloomington: Indiana University Press, 2001.

Ceremonial: For the Use of the Catholic Churches in the United States of America: Published by order of the First Council of Baltimore. Baltimore: J. Murphy & Co., 1852.

Chinnici, Joseph P., OFM. "The Catholic Community at Prayer, 1926–1976." In *Habits of Devotion: Catholic Religious Practice in Twentieth-Century America*, ed. James M. O'Toole, 9–88. Ithaca: Cornell University Press, 2004.

Coburn, Carol K., and Martha Smith. *Spirited Lives: How Nuns Shaped Catholic Culture and American Life, 1836–1920*. Chapel Hill: University of North Carolina Press, 1999.

Cohen, Lizabeth. *A Consumers' Republic: The Politics of Mass Consumption in Postwar America*. New York: Knopf, 2003.

Cohen, Robert, ed. *Dear Mrs. Roosevelt: Letters from Children of the Great Depression*. Chapel Hill: University of North Carolina Press, 2002.

"Columbia Expects 13,000 Enrollment." *New York Times*, 7 July 1925, 4.

Congar, Yves, OP. *Power and Poverty in the Church*. Baltimore: Helicon Press, 1964.

Congregation of the Sisters of St. Joseph. www.newadvent.org/cathen/08511a.htm. 3 July 2012.

Connors, Reverend Edward M. "Church-State Relationships in Education in the State of New York." Ph.D. diss., Catholic University of America, 1951.

Coon, Katherine E. "The Sisters of Charity in Nineteenth-Century America." https:// scholarworks.iupui.edu/bitstream/handle/1805/2185/thesis_kathi_coon_final .pdf?sequence=1. 6 June 2012.

———. "The Sisters of Charity in Nineteenth-Century America: Civil War Nurses and Philanthropic Pioneers." Partial fulfillment of the requirements for an M.A., University of Indiana, May 2010.

"Copy of a Letter from Mother St. John Fournier to the Superior General of the Sisters of St. Joseph in Lyons." In *Sisters of St. Joseph of Philadelphia: A Century of Growth and Development, 1847–1947*, by Maria Kostas Logue, 327–52. Westminster, Md.: Newman Press, 1950.

Corrigan, Maureen. *Leave Me Alone, I'm Reading: Finding and Losing Myself in Books*. New York: Random House, 2005.

Council of Major Superiors of Women Religious. http://www.cmswr.org/about /aboutus.html. 27 June 2013.

Cummings, Kathleen Sprows. *New Women of the Old Faith: Gender and American Catholicism in the Progressive Era*. Chapel Hill: University of North Carolina Press, 2009.

Cunningham, Patricia A. *Reforming Women's Fashion, 1850–1920: Politics, Health, and Art*. Kent, Ohio: Kent State University Press, 2003.

Curran, Robert Emmett. "Prelude to 'Americanism': The New York Accademia and Clerical Radicalism in the Late Nineteenth Century." *Church History* 47, no. 1 (March 1978): 48–65.

D'Agostino, Peter R. *Rome in America: Transnational Catholic Ideology from the Risorgimento to Fascism*. Chapel Hill: University of North Carolina Press, 2004.

Daly, Juanita. "Immaculata Joins 'Citizens' Parade." *Chicago Daily Tribune*, 19 January 1941, N1.

De Pauw, Father Gommar, JCD. *The Catholic Traditionalist Manifesto* (1964). http://www.latinmass-ctm.org/. 13 June 2013.

de Tocqueville, Alexis. *Democracy in America*. Translated, edited, and with an introduction by Harvey C. Mansfield and Delba Winthrop. Chicago: University of Chicago Press, 2000.

Dolan, Jay P. *The American Catholic Experience: A History from Colonial Times to the Present*. Notre Dame: University of Notre Dame Press, 1992.

Dominican Nuns of Summit, New Jersey. http://nunsopsummit.org/history. 5 June 2012.

Dominican Sisters. *The Rule of St. Augustine, and, the Constitutions of the Sisters of Penance of the Third Order of St. Dominic*. Racine, Wisc.: The Sisters, 1987.

Donaghy, Thomas J., FSC., *Philadelphia's Finest: A History of Education in the Catholic Archdiocese, 1692–1970*. Philadelphia: American Catholic Historical Society, 1972.

Donovan, Joseph P., CM, JCD. "Answers to Questions." *Homiletic and Pastoral Review* 45, no. 1 (October 1944): 58–59.

"Down with Habits and Cassocks." *National Catholic Reporter*, 6 January 1965, 4.

Drolet, Francis K. "SDS Follow-up." *Queen's Work*, October 1952, 26.

Duncan, Jason K. *Citizen or Papist: The Politics of Anti-Catholicism in New York, 1685–1821*. New York: Fordham University Press, 2005.

Dunne, Sister Mary of the Sacred Heart, MA. *The Congregation of St. Joseph of the Diocese of Buffalo, 1854–1933: A Brief Account of Its Origin and Work*. Buffalo, N.Y.: Holling Press, 1934.

Durand, Alfred. *Catholic Ceremonies and Explanations of the Ecclesiastical Year*. New York: Benziger Brothers, 1896.

Dwyer-McNulty, Sara. "Hems to Hairdos: Cultural Discourse and Philadelphia Catholic High Schools in the 1920s, a Case Study." *Journal of American Studies* 37, no. 2 (2003): 179–200.

———. "Moving Beyond the Home: Women and Catholic Action in Post-War America." *U.S. Catholic Historian* 20, no. 1 (Winter 2002): 83–97.

Ecclesia Sanctae. http://www.papalencyclicals.net/Pau106/p6ecclss.htm.13 March 2013.

Ellard, Gerald, SJ. "Will the Mass go Vernacular?" *Queen's Work*, January 1953, 12–13.

Ellis, John Tracy. *American Catholicism*. 2nd ed. Chicago: University of Chicago Press, 1969.

————. *The Life of James Cardinal Gibbons, Archbishop of Baltimore, 1834–1921.* Vol. 2. Milwaukee: Bruce Publishing Co., 1952.

————, ed. *The Catholic Priest in the United States.* Collegeville, Minn.: Saint John's University Press, 1971.

"Essential Elements on the Church's Teaching on Religious Life." 31 May 1983. http://vatican.va/roman curia#34.

Evangelisti, Silvia. *Nuns: A History of Convent Life.* New York: Oxford University Press, 2008.

Ewen, Mary. *The Role of the Nun in Nineteenth-Century America.* New York: Arno Press, 1978.

————. "Women in the Convent." In *American Catholic Women: A Historical Exploration,* ed. Karen Kennelly, 17–47. New York: Macmillan, 1989.

Fass, Paula S. *The Damned and the Beautiful: American Youth in the 1920s.* New York: Oxford University Press, 1977.

Fialka, John J. *Sisters: Catholic Nuns and the Making of America.* New York: St. Martin's Press, 2003.

Finke, Roger, and Rodney Stark. *The Churching of America, 1776–2005: Winners and Losers in our Religious Economy.* Piscataway, N.J.: Rutgers University Press, 2005.

Fitzgerald, Mary Innocentia. *A Historical Sketch of the Sisters of Mercy in the Diocese of Buffalo, 1857–1942.* Buffalo, N.Y.: Mount Mercy Academy, 1942.

Fitzgerald, Maureen. *Habits of Compassion: Irish Catholic Nuns and the Origins of New York's Welfare System, 1830–1920.* Urbana: University of Illinois Press, 2006.

"Fr. Y." "I Love My Cassock." *Homiletic and Pastoral Review* 56, no. 10 (July 1954): 888–93.

Francis, Sister Victoria, OP. "Special Problems in the Spiritual Formation of Sisters Engaged in Professional Social Work." *Sister Formation Bulletin* 3, no. 4 (Summer 1957): 8–15.

Gabert, Glen. *In Hoc Signo? A Brief History of Catholic Parochial Education in America.* Port Washington, N.Y.: Kennikat Press, 1973.

Giuliani, Reverend Maurice, SJ. "The Role of the Sister in the Church." *Sister Formation Bulletin* 4, no. 1 (Autumn 1957): 1–5. Reprinted from *Etudes* (Paris), June 1957, 386–99.

Gordon, Mary. *Seeing through Places: Reflections on Geography and Identity.* New York: Scribner, 2000.

Grenhouse, Steven. "A Crusader Makes Celebrities Tremble." *New York Times,* 18 June 1996, B4.

Haas, Katherine. "The Fabric of Religion: Vestments and Devotional Catholicism in Nineteenth-Century America." *Material Religion* 3, no. 2 (July 2007): 190–217.

"A Habit Is to Hide Behind." *National Catholic Reporter,* 3 February 1965, 4.

Hall, David D., ed. *Lived Religion in America: Toward a History of Practice* Princeton: Princeton University Press, 1997.

Halsall, Paul, ed. "Rule of St. Augustine." Internet History Sourcebooks Project. http://www.fordham.edu/halsall/source/ruleaug.html. 8 June 2012.

Haring, Bernard, CSSR. "Asceticism in Religious Life." Translated by Sr. M. Hilga Gunther, OSF. *Sister Formation Bulletin* 12, no. 3 (Spring 1966): 1–2.

————. "Religious Witness in the World." *Sister Formation Bulletin* 14, no. 2 (Winter 1968): 6.

Healy, John. *Maynooth College: Its Centenary History, 1795–1895*. Dublin: Browne & Nolan, 1895.

Hennesey, James, SJ. *American Catholics: A History of the Roman Catholic Community in the United States*. New York: Oxford University Press, 1981.

Henold, Mary J. *Catholic and Feminist: The Surprising History of the American Catholic Feminist Movement*. Chapel Hill: University of North Carolina Press, 2008.

Herberg, Will. *Protestant, Catholic, Jew: An Essay in American Religious Sociology*. Garden City, N.Y.: Anchor Books, 1960.

Hirschmann, Nancy J. *The Subject of Liberty: Toward a Feminist Theory of Freedom*. Princeton: Princeton University Press, 2002.

"History and Tradition: A Brief History of Cathedral High School." http://www.cathedralhigh.org/history.htm. 5 July 2011.

History of Clothing. http://histclo.com/style/skirted/Smock/schsmock.html. 14 June 2012.

"History of the Archdiocese of Boston." www.bostoncatholic.org. 27 May 2011.

Hollander, Anne. *Sex and the Suit: The Evolution of Modern Dress*. New York: Kodansha International, 1995.

Holloran, Peter C. *Boston's Wayward Children: Social Services for Homeless Children, 1830–1930*. Rutherford, N.J.: Fairleigh Dickinson University Press, 1989.

Hubbard, Celia. "Criteria for New Garb Suggested by Designer." *National Catholic Reporter*, 1 September 1965, 11.

IgnatianSpirituality.com. http://ignatianspirituality.com/ignatian-voices/16th-and-17th-century-ignatian-voices/matteo-ricci-sj. 1 June 2012.

Italian Unification Chronology. www.sas.penn.edu/~mercerb/chitunif.html. 3 July 2013.

Jay, Kathryn. "'In Vogue with Mary': How Catholic Girls Created an Urban Market for Modesty." In *Faith in the Market: Religion and the Rise of Urban Commercial Culture*, ed. John M. Giggie and Diane Winston, 178. New Brunswick, N.J.: Rutgers University Press, 2002.

Joselit, Jenna Weissman. *A Perfect Fit: Clothes, Character, and the Promise of America*. New York: Metropolitan Books, 2001.

Joseph, Nathan. *Uniforms and Nonuniforms: Communication through Clothing*. New York: Greenwood Press, 1986.

Justice, Benjamin. *The War That Wasn't: Religious Conflict and Compromise in Common Schools of New York State, 1865–1900*. Albany: Albany State University Press, 2005.

Kane, Paula M. "Marian Devotion since 1940: Continuity or Casualty?" In *Habits of Devotion: Catholic Religious Practice in Twentieth-Century America*, ed. James M. O'Toole, 98–130. Ithaca: Cornell University Press, 2004.

———. *Separatism and Subculture: Boston Catholicism, 1900–1920*. Chapel Hill: University of North Carolina Press, 1994.

Kauffman, Christopher J. *Tradition and Transformation in Catholic Culture: The Priests of Saint Sulpice in the United States from 1791 to the Present*. New York: Macmillan, 1988.

Kaufman, Susanne K. *Consuming Visions: Mass Culture and the Lourdes Shrine*. Ithaca: Cornell University Press, 2005.

Keenan, William J. F. "Clothed with Authority: The Rationalization of Marist Dress

Culture." In *Undressing Religion: Commitment and Conversion from a Cross-Cultural Perspective*, ed. Linda B. Arthur, 83–100. Oxford: Berg, 2000.

Kelly, Blanche Mary. "New Woman." *Catholic Mind*, 22 August 1920, 321.

Kennelly, Karen. *American Catholic Women: A Historical Exploration*. New York: Macmillan, 1989.

Kenrick, Bishop Francis Patrick. *Pastoral Address of the Rt. Reverend Dr. Kenrick, to the Clergy of the Diocese of Philadelphia, On the Occasion of the Promulgation of the Decrees of the Provincial Council*. Philadelphia: Eugene Cumminskey, 1831.

Ketcham, William H. "An Appeal in Behalf of Catholic Indian Mission Schools." *Indian Sentinel*, 1902–1903, 28–33.

"Kickbacks on Kicking the Habit." *National Catholic Reporter*, 23 December 1994, 1–2.

Kirtley, Bill, and Pat Kirtley. "City of Spindles: The Lessons of Lowell, Massachusetts." http://www.nssa.us/journals/pdf/NSS_Journal_37_1.pdf. 14 July 2013.

Koehlinger, Amy. "'Are You the White Sisters or the Black Sisters?': Women Confounding Categories of Race and Gender." In *The Religious History of American Women: Reimagining the Past*, ed. Catherine A. Brekus, 253–78. Chapel Hill: University of North Carolina Press, 2007.

Kuhns, Elizabeth. *The Habit: A History of the Clothing of Catholic Nuns*. New York: Doubleday, 2003.

"Lady Armstrong for Modest Dress." *New York Times*, 6 December 1925, 28.

La Follette, Mrs. Robert. "Progress in Dress." *Pittsburg Press*, 18 October 1911, 14. http://news.google.com/newspapers?id=bCwbAAAAIBAJ&sjid=6EgEAAAAIBAJ&pg=5959,4663536&dq=peter-thompson-suit&hl=en. 17 December 1912.

Larkin, Emmet. "Cardinal Paul Cullen." In *Varieties of Ultramontanism*, ed. Jeffrey von Arx, SJ, 61–84. Washington D.C.: Catholic University of America Press, 1998.

Letter to *American Ecclesiastical Review*, 3rd ser., 3, no. 4 (October 1900): 407.

Life of Mademoiselle Le Gras (Louise de Marillac), Foundress of the Sisters of Charity. New York: Benziger Brothers, 1884, 1917.

Lindauer, Owen. "Archaeology of the Phoenix Indian School." *Archaeology*, 27 March 1998. http://www.archaeology.org/online/features/phoenix/index.html. 4 January 2012.

"A Little Indian Life." *Indian Sentinel*, 1893.

Littrell, Mary Ann. "Liturgical Vestments and the Priest Role." *Home Economics Research Journal* 14, no. 1 (September 1985): 152–62.

Lord, Daniel A. *Letters to a Nun*. St. Louis: Queen's Work, 1947.

———. *Queen's Work Booklets*. St. Louis: Queen's Work, 1925.

———. "What's Modest." *Queen's Work*, April 1951, 8–9.

Lovat, Alice Mary Weld-Blundell Fraser. *Life of the Venerable Louise de Marillac (Mademoiselle Le Gras), Foundress of the Company of Sisters of Charity of St. Vincent de Paul*. New York: Longmans, Green, 1917.

Luck, Kate. "Trouble in Eden, Trouble with Eve: Women, Trousers & Utopian Socialism in Nineteenth-Century America." In *Chic Thrills: A Fashion Reader*, ed. Juliet and Elizabeth Wilson, 202. Berkeley: University of California Press, 1992.

Lynch, Gordon. *The Sacred in the Modern World: A Cultural Sociological Approach*. New York: Oxford University Press, 2012.

Maes, Camillus P. *Life of Rev. Charles Nerinckx*. Cincinnati: Robert Clark and Co., 1880.

———. "Preparatory Seminaries for Clerical Students." *American Ecclesiastical Review* 4 (April 1896): 312–19.

Malone, Matt. "Clothing Optional?" http://americamagazine.org/content/all-things /clothing-optional (3/15/13). 24 May 2013.

Massa, Mark Stephen. *Catholics and American Culture: Fulton Sheen, Dorothy Day, and the Notre Dame Football Team*. New York: Crossroad, 1999.

May, Elaine Tyler. *Homeward Bound: American Families in the Cold War Era*. New York: Basic Books, 1988.

Mayer-Thurman, Christa C. *Raiment for the Lord's Service: A Thousand Years of Western Vestments*. Chicago: Art Institute, 1975.

Mazzenga, Maria. "The Difference a Century Makes: A Tale of Two Ryans." Religion & Politics. http://religionandpolitics.org/2012/08/14/the-difference-a-century-makes -a-tale-of-two-ryans/. 10 March 2013.

McAllister, Robert J. "Self Image and Self Acceptance." *Sister Formation Bulletin* 7, no. 2 (Winter 1966): 16–17.

McAvoy, Thomas T., CSC. *The Americanist Heresy in Roman Catholicism, 1895–1900*. Notre Dame: University of Notre Dame Press, 1963.

McCarroll, Sean. "The Plenary Councils of Baltimore (1852–1884): The Formation of America's Catholic School System amidst Anti-Catholicism in the United States." http://www.umich.edu/~historyj/docs/2011-fall/mccarroll.pdf. 3 June 2013.

McCarthy, Thomas P. *Guide to the Catholic Sisterhoods in the United States*. Washington, D.C.: Catholic University of America Press, 1964.

McDannell, Colleen. *Material Christianity: Religion and Popular Culture in America*. New Haven: Yale University Press, 1995.

McGreevy, John T. *Parish Boundaries: The Catholic Encounter with Race in the Twentieth-Century Urban North*. Chicago: University of Chicago Press, 1996.

McMahon, Eileen M. *What Parish Are You From? A Chicago Irish Community and Race Relations*. Lexington: University Press of Kentucky, 1995.

McNamara, Jo Ann. *Sisters in Arms: Catholic Nuns through Two Millennia*. Cambridge, Mass.: Harvard University Press, 1996.

McNamara, Robert F. *A Century of Grace: The History of St. Mary's Roman Catholic Parish, Corning, N.Y., 1848–1948*. Corning, N.Y.: St. Mary's Church, 1948.

Meconis, Charles A. *With Clumsy Grace: The American Catholic Left, 1961–1975*. New York: Seabury Press, 1979.

Merwick, Donna. *Boston Priests, 1848–1910: A Study of the Social and Intellectual Change*. Cambridge, Mass.: Harvard University Press, 1973.

Meyers, Bertrand. *The Education of Sisters: A Plan for Integrating the Religious, Social, Cultural and Professional Training of Sisters*. New York: Sheed and Ward, 1941.

Mirae Caritatis. http://www.vatican.va/holy_father/leo_xiii/encyclicals/documents/hf_1 -xiii_enc_28051902_mirae-caritatis_en.html. 6 December 2012.

Morgan, Jennifer L. *Laboring Women: Reproduction and Gender in New World Slavery*. Philadelphia: University of Pennsylvania Press, 2004.

Morris, Charles. *American Catholic: The Saints and Sinners Who Built America's Most Powerful Church*. New York: Vintage, 1997.

Murphy, Kevin. *Political Manhood: Red Bloods, Mollycoddles, and the Politics of Progressive Era Reform*. New York: Columbia University Press, 2008.

Nainfa, John Abel, SS, DCL. *Costume of Prelates of the Catholic Church, According to Roman Etiquette*. Baltimore: John Murphy Co., 1926.

National Press Club. http://press.org/news-multimedia/news/catholic-nuns%E2%80%99-leader-defends-group%E2%80%99s-work-tries-work-vatican. 1 October 2013.

"New Deal for Nuns Urged as Council Discusses Orders." *National Catholic Reporter*, 18 November 1964, 1.

"A New Habit Arrives for Sisters of Sion." *National Catholic Reporter*, 24 February 1965, 11.

"No Habit Can Be More Than the Person Wearing It." *National Catholic Reporter*, 24 February 1965, 11.

Nolan, Hugh J., ed. *Pastoral Letters of the United States Catholic Bishops*. Vol. 1, 1792–1940. Washington, D.C.: United States Catholic Conference, 1983.

"No Money for Indecency, Demand Controls Supply." *Queen's Work*, February 1947, 9.

"Not a Crying Towel, but a Chance to Think Aloud." *National Catholic Reporter*, 4 August 1965, 11.

"Notification of Deprevation of Ecclesiastical Garb." *Homiletic and Pastoral Review* 28, no. 1 (October 1927): 85.

"Nuns, Parents, Pupils Pleased by New Habits." *National Catholic Reporter*, 16 December 1964, 1.

"Nuns Making Change to Habits by Dior." *Los Angeles Times*, 31 August 1964, 2.

"Nuns—Marchers out of Place—Card. Cushing." *National Catholic Reporter*, 19 May 1965, 5.

"Nuns Will Wear Modern Clothes." *New York Times*, 3 October 1954, 38.

Oates, Mary J. *The Catholic Philanthropic Tradition in America*. Bloomington: Indiana University Press, 1995.

O'Brien, David J. *Public Catholicism*. New York: Macmillan, 1989.

O'Connell, William H. *The Letters of His Eminence William Cardinal O'Connell, Archbishop of Boston*. Vol. 1, *From College Days 1876 to Bishop of Portland 1901*. Cambridge, Mass.: Riverside Press, 1915.

"Offerings Made at Baptism." *Homiletic and Pastoral Review* 27, no. 11 (August 1927): 1220–21.

Orsi, Robert A. "Close Formation." *Boston College Magazine*, Winter 2004, 32–37.

———. "Everyday Miracles: The Study of Lived Religion." In *Lived Religions in America: Toward a History of Practice*, ed. David D. Hall, 3–21. Princeton: Princeton University Press, 1997.

O'Toole, James M. *The Faithful: A History of Catholicism in America*. Cambridge, Mass.: Harvard University Press, 2008.

———. "From Advent to Easter: Catholic Preaching in New York City, 1808–1809." *Church History* 63, no. 3 (September 1994): 365–77.

———. *Habits of Devotion: Catholic Religious Practice in Twentieth-Century America*. Ithaca: Cornell University Press, 2004.

———. *Militant and Triumphant: William Henry O'Connell and the Catholic Church in Boston, 1859–1944*. Notre Dame: University of Notre Dame Press, 1993.

"Overview of Authority Patterns in General." Pt. 1. *Sister Formation Bulletin* 13, no. 4 (Summer 1967): 6–16.

"The Parish That Came Back." *American Ecclesiastical Review* 1, no. 1 (July 1919): 27–36.

Parkin, Wendy, ed. *Fashioning the Body Politic: Dress, Gender, Citizenship*. New York: Berg, 2002.

Pasquier, Michael. *The Fathers on the Frontier: French Missionaries and the Roman Catholic Priesthood in the United States, 1789–1870*. New York: Oxford University Press, 2010.

"Pastor and the Education of Girls and Young Women." *American Ecclesiastical Review* 4, no. 1 (January 1921): 74.

Pastoureau, Michel. *The Devil's Cloth: A History of Stripes and Striped Fabric*. Translated by Jody Gladding. New York: Columbia University Press, 2001.

Pecklers, K. F. "Liturgical Movement. I: Catholic." In *New Catholic Encyclopedia*, 2nd ed., 8:670–77. Detroit: Gale, 2003.

Peihl, Mel. *Breaking Bread: The Catholic Worker and the Origin of Catholic Radicalism in America*. Philadelphia: Temple University Press, 1982.

Perfectae Caritatis. www.vatican.va/archive/hist_councils/ii_vatican_council/documents /vat-ii_decree_19651028_perfectae-caritatis_en.html. 13 July 2013.

Peril, Lynn. *College Girls: Bluestockings, Sex Kittens, and Coeds, Then and Now*. New York: Norton, 2006.

Perry, Nicholas, and Loreto Echeverría. *Under the Heel of Mary*. London: Routledge, 1988.

Peters, Edward N. *The 1917 Pio-Benedictine Code of Canon Law: In English Translation with Extensive Scholarly Apparatus*. San Francisco: Ignatius Press, 2001.

Phibrick, Richard. "Some Priests to Trade Cassocks for Suits." *Chicago Tribune*, 4 May 1969, A6.

Philippe, Paul, OP. "New Orientations of the Sacred Congregation of Religious for the 'Aggiornamento' of the Postulancy and Novitiate." *Sister Formation Bulletin* 13, no. 3 (Spring 1967): 18.

Pius XII. *Mystici Corporis Christi* (On the Mystical Body of Christ). *Eternal Word Television Network* (1999). http://www.ewtn.com/library/ENCYC/P12MYSTI.HTM. 21 October 2009.

"The Priestly Robe." *American Ecclesiastical Review* 8, no. 1 (January 1898): 87–89.

"The Prize Pictures of the Month." *Queen's Work*, February 1926, 39.

Prucha, Francis Paul. *The Church and the Indian Schools, 1888–1912*. Lincoln: University of Nebraska Press, 1980.

"Punahou Mothers Taking Steps toward School Dress Simplicity." *Honolulu Star-Bulletin*, 13 May 1915.

Reidy, Maurice Timothy. "The First Vatican Council." Conciliaria.com/2012/09/the-first -vatican-council/. 5 December 2012.

Reilly, Daniel F., OP. *The School Controversy, 1891–1893*. Washington, D.C.: Catholic University of America Press, 1943.

"Religion: The New Nuns." *Time*, 20 March 1972. http://www.time.com/time/printout /0,8816,942531,00.html. 17 July 2011.

"Religion: You've Come a Long Way Baby." *Time*, 23 February 1970. http://time.com /time/printout/0,8816,876640,00.html. 18 July 2011.

Rogers, Carole Garibaldi. *Habits of Change: An Oral History of American Nuns.* New York: Oxford University Press, 2011.

Rooney, Richard L., SJ. "A Discussion on the Younger Generation." *Queen's Work,* January 1952, 8–9.

———. "Here's Looking at You." *Queen's Work,* February 1956, 14–15.

———. "Modesty, Chastity, and Purity Are Not Synonymous." *Queen's Work,* February 1954, 14–15.

Roulins, E. A., OSB. *Vestments and Vesture: A Manual of Liturgical Art.* Translated by Justin McCann. St. Louis: B. Herder Book Co.; London: Sands & Co., 1931.

Rubinstein, Ruth P. *Dress Codes: Meanings and Messages in American Culture.* Boulder, Colo.: Westview Press, 1995.

Russell, John A. "The Catholic Church in the United States." In *The Memorial Volume: A History of the Third Plenary Council of Baltimore, November 9–December 7, 1884,* ed. John Murphy, 9–28. Baltimore: Baltimore Publishing Co., 1885.

Russo, Mary, OSU. *A History of the Eastern Province of the United States of the Roman Union of the Order of St. Ursula, 1535–1989.* New Rochelle, N.Y.: Ursuline Community of St. Teresa, 1989.

Ryan, Francis J. "Monsignor John Bonner and Progressive Education in the Archdiocese of Philadelphia, 1925–1945." *Record of the American Catholic Historical Society of Philadelphia,* Spring 1991, 27.

Schreier, Barbara. *Becoming American Women: Clothing and the Jewish Immigration Experience, 1880–1920.* Chicago: Chicago Historical Society, 1994.

Schulze, Reverend Frederick. *A Manual of Pastoral Theology: A Practical Guide for Ecclesiastical Students and Newly Ordained Priests.* 8th ed. St. Louis: B. Herder Book Co., 1935.

"S.D.S. Booms Along." *Queen's Work,* October 1948, 29.

"Senior Girls at Alvernia Revise Uniform Styling." *Chicago Tribune,* 22 June 1941, H4.

Shannon, William. "The Religious Garb Issue as Related to the School Question in New York State." Ph.D. diss., University of Ottawa, 1952.

"'Shave!' Priests Ordered." *Chicago Tribune,* 1 November 1975, B11.

"Signed Pledge for Modesty in Dress Asked from 700,000 Catholic Women." *New York Times,* 21 July 1924, 1.

"Sign of Your Faith." *Queen's Work,* November 1952, 20–21.

"Silks Abolished." *Chicago Tribune,* 3 February 1965, 9.

Sister Judith, FCSP. "Report on the Sister Formation Conferences' Vocation Survey." *Sister Formation Bulletin* 3, no. 1 (Autumn 1956): 1–7.

Smith, Anthony Burke. "America's Favorite Priest: *Going My Way* (1944)." In *Catholics in the Movies,* ed. Colleen McDannell, 107–26. Oxford: Oxford University Press, 2008.

———. *The Look of Catholics: Portrayals in Popular Culture from the Great Depression to the Cold War.* Lawrence: University Press of Kansas, 2010.

Smith, Reverend John Talbot. *Our Seminaries: An Essay on Clerical Training.* New York: William H. Young & Co., 1896.

Smith, Sebastian Bach. *Notes on the Second Plenary Council of Baltimore.* New York: P. O'Shea, 1874.

Society of Jesus in the United States. http://www.jesuit.org/index.php/main/about-us /faqs/. 14 July 2013.

"Sodality Pageant." *Queen's Work*, February 1949, 27.

Sommer, Joseph A., SJ. "Detroit Sodalists Found New Religious Order." *Queen's Work*, November 1954, 28–29.

Southard, Robert E. "Cover Girls of 1950." *Queen's Work*, February 1950, 16–17.

Spadaro, Antonio, SJ. "A Big Heart Open to God." http://www.americamagazine.org /print/156341. 1 October 2013.

Spiers, Edward Francis. *The Central Catholic High School: A Survey of Their History and Status in the United States*. Washington, D.C.: Catholic University of America Press, 1951.

Stang, Reverend William. *Pastoral Theology*. New York: Benziger Brothers, 1897.

Steele, Valeri, ed. *Encyclopedia of Clothing and Fashion*. Vol. 1, *Academic Dress to Eyeglasses*. Detroit: Thomson Gale, 2005.

———. *Encyclopedia of Clothing and Fashion*. Vol. 2, *Fads to Nylon*. Detroit: Thomson Gale, 2005.

———. *Encyclopedia of Clothing and Fashion*. Vol. 3, *Occult Dress to Zoran*. Detroit: Thomson Gale, 2005.

Steinfels, Peter. "Robert G. Hoyt, 81, Founder of *National Catholic Reporter*." *New York Times*, 12 April 2003. http://www.nytimes.com/2003/04/12/nyregion/robert-g-hoyt -81-founder-of-national-catholic-reporter.html?scp=1&sq=Robert+G+Hoyt%2C +81%2C+Founder+of+National+Catholic+Reporter&st=nyt. 18 July 2011.

Suenens, Cardinal Leon Joseph. *The Nun in the World: Religious and the Apostolate*. Westminster, Md.: Newman Press, 1963.

———. "Open to the World." *Sister Formation Bulletin* 15, no. 4 (Summer 1969): 3–4.

———. "The Religious, Inspiration of the Adult Laity." Translated by Sister Mary of the Visitation, SND de Namur. *Sister Formation Bulletin* 3, no. 1 (Autumn 1961): 7–10.

Sullivan, Rebecca. *Visual Habits: Nuns, Feminism, and American Postwar Popular Culture*. Toronto: University of Toronto Press, 2005.

Tager, Jack. *Boston Riots: Three Centuries of Social Violence*. Boston: Northeastern University Press, 2001.

Taves, Ann. *The Household of Faith: Roman Catholic Devotions in Mid-Nineteenth Century America*. Notre Dame: University of Notre Dame Press, 1986.

Tentler, Leslie Woodcock. *Seasons of Grace: A History of the Catholic Archdiocese of Detroit*. Detroit: Wayne State University Press, 1990.

Thomas, Evangeline, CSJ, ed. *Women Religious History Sources: A Guide to Repositories in the United States*. New York: R. R. Bowker Co., 1983.

Thrapp, Dan L. "Immaculate Heart Sisters: Order of Nuns Here Plans to Modernize Dress and Ideas." *Los Angeles Times*, 18 October 1967, SG1, SG12.

———. "Nuns Seek to Reinforce Earlier Ruling by Pope." *Los Angeles Times*, 17 March 1968, 9.

———. "Wants Reverse Collar Junked, Dress for U.S. Priests Should Be Modernized, Editor Thinks." *Los Angeles Times*, 23 October 1967, A6.

Thurston, Herbert. "Clerical Costume." *The Catholic Encyclopedia*. Vol. 4. New York: Robert Appleton Co., 1908. http://www.newadvent.org/cathen/04419b.htm. 30 July 2010.

Townsend, Dorothy. "Habit Called Segregation: Nuns Explain New Conduct as Need for Basic Change." *Los Angeles Times*, 7 April 1968, G1.

———. "Priest's Message: Not Conversion, but Unity." *Los Angeles Times*, 11 June 1966, B6.

Twomey, Louis J., SJ. "Caritas Builds Dignity in the Slums." *Queen's Work*, June 1957, 12–13.

Unger, Rudolph. "Judge Robson Gags All for Trial on Draft." *Chicago Tribune*, 25 February 1970.

U.S. Commission on Civil Rights. "School Choice: The Blaine Amendments & Anti-Catholicism." http://www.usccr.gov/pubs/BlaineReport.pdf. 3 July 2013.

Valuy, F. Benedict, SJ. *Directorium Sacerdotale: A Guide for Priests in Their Public and Private Life*. Dublin: M. H. Gill and Son, 1898.

Vincent, Mary. "Camisas Nuevas: Style and Uniformity in Falange Espanola 1933–43." In *Fashioning the Body Politic: Dress, Gender, Citizenship*, ed. Wendy Parkin, 167–87. New York: Berg, 2002.

von Arx, Jeffrey, SJ, ed. *Varieties of Ultramontanism*. Washington, D.C.: Catholic University of America, 1998.

Wakin, Edward, and Father Joseph F. Scheuer. "The American Nun: Poor, Chaste, and Restive." *Harper's Magazine*, August 1965, 35–40.

Walker, Rev. Herbert O'H., SJ. "The Principal's Ganymedes." *Queen's Work*, June 1950, 6–7.

Walkowitz, Daniel J. "The Making of a Feminine Professional Identity." *American Historical Review* 95, no. 4 (1 October 1990): 1051–75.

Walters, Sister Annette, and Sister Ritamary Bradley. "God's Geese," *Los Angeles Times*, 31 August 1964, 2, 7.

Warikoo, Niraj. "Archbishop Blasts Mich. Priest's Leading of Liberal Mass." *Detroit Free Press*, 12 June 2011. http://www.lexisnexis.com.online. 15 June 2013.

Warner, Patricia Campbell. *When the Girls Came Out to Play: The Birth of American Sportswear*. Amherst: University of Massachusetts Press, 2006.

Warren, Heather A. "Character, Public Schooling, and Religious Education, 1920–1934." *Religion and American Culture: A Journal of Interpretation* 7, no. 1 (Winter 1997): 61–80.

"We Beg to Announce." *Queen's Work*, December 1925, 1.

Weber, Max. *From Max Weber: Essays in Sociology*. Translated and with an introduction by H. H. Gerth and C. Wright Mills. New York: Oxford University Press, 1958.

"What's Fitting, Sister?" *National Catholic Reporter*, 19 May 1965, 6.

"What the Star Students Are Like." *Chicago Daily Tribune*, 15 June 1941, S1.

White, Joseph M. *The Diocesan Seminary in the United States: A History from the 1780s to the Present*. Notre Dame: University of Notre Dame Press, 1989.

Whyte, John H. "The Appointment of Catholic Bishops in Nineteenth-Century Ireland." *Catholic Historical Review* 48 (April 1962):12–32.

Wills, Gary. *Bare Ruined Choirs: Doubt, Prophecy, and Radical Religion*. New York: Doubleday, 1972.

Windeatt, Mary Fabyan. "The Medal." *The Grail*, February 1950, 20–21.

Wolff, M. Madeleva. *The Education of Sister Lucy: A Symposium on Teacher Education and Teacher Training*. Holy Cross, Ind.: Saint Mary's College, Notre Dame, 1949.

Zakin, Michael. *Ready-Made Democracy: A History of Men's Dress in the American Republic, 1760–1860*. Chicago: University of Chicago Press, 2003.

Zaplotnik, Msgr. John. "Glimpse of the Past: Father George Reš (Roesch)." Translated by Joann Birsa. In *Slovenian Heritage*, vol. 1, ed. Gedward Gobetz. Willoughby Hills, Ohio: Slovenian Research Center of America, 1981. Reprinted in *Dutchess County Historical Society Year Book* 71 (1986): 41–42.

Zürcher, Erik. "Transcultural Imaging: The Jesuits and China." *Ching Feng* 5, no. 2 (2004): 145–61. http://search.proquest.com/docview/927046813?accountid=28549. 14 June 2013.

Zwierlein, Frederick J. *Letters of Archbishop Corrigan to Bishop McQuaid and Allied Documents*. Rochester, N.Y.: Art Print Shop, 1946.

———. *The Life and Letters of Bishop McQuaid Prefaced with the History of Catholic Rochester before His Episcopate*. Vol. 1. Rochester, N.Y.: Art Print Shop, 1925.

———. *The Life and Letters of Bishop McQuaid Prefaced with the History of Catholic Rochester before His Episcopate*. Vol. 2. Rochester, N.Y.: Art Print Shop, 1926.

———. *The Life and Letters of Bishop McQuaid Prefaced with the History of Catholic Rochester before His Episcopate*. Vol. 3. Rochester, N.Y.: Art Print Shop, 1927.

INDEX